I0819301
BREAD
CRUMBS

BROTH
BROTH

Maxi's Kitchen

Photographs by ***Amy Neunsinger***
Illustrations by ***Elizabeth Hart***
Storytelling in collaboration with ***Sanaë Lemoine***

Clarkson Potter/Publishers
New York

EASY GO-TO RECIPES

to make again and again

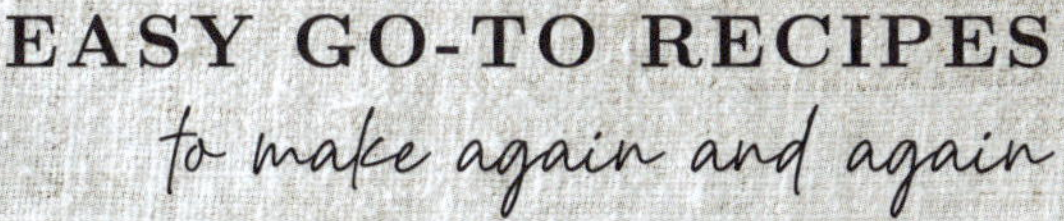

Maxi's Kitchen

MAXINE SHARF

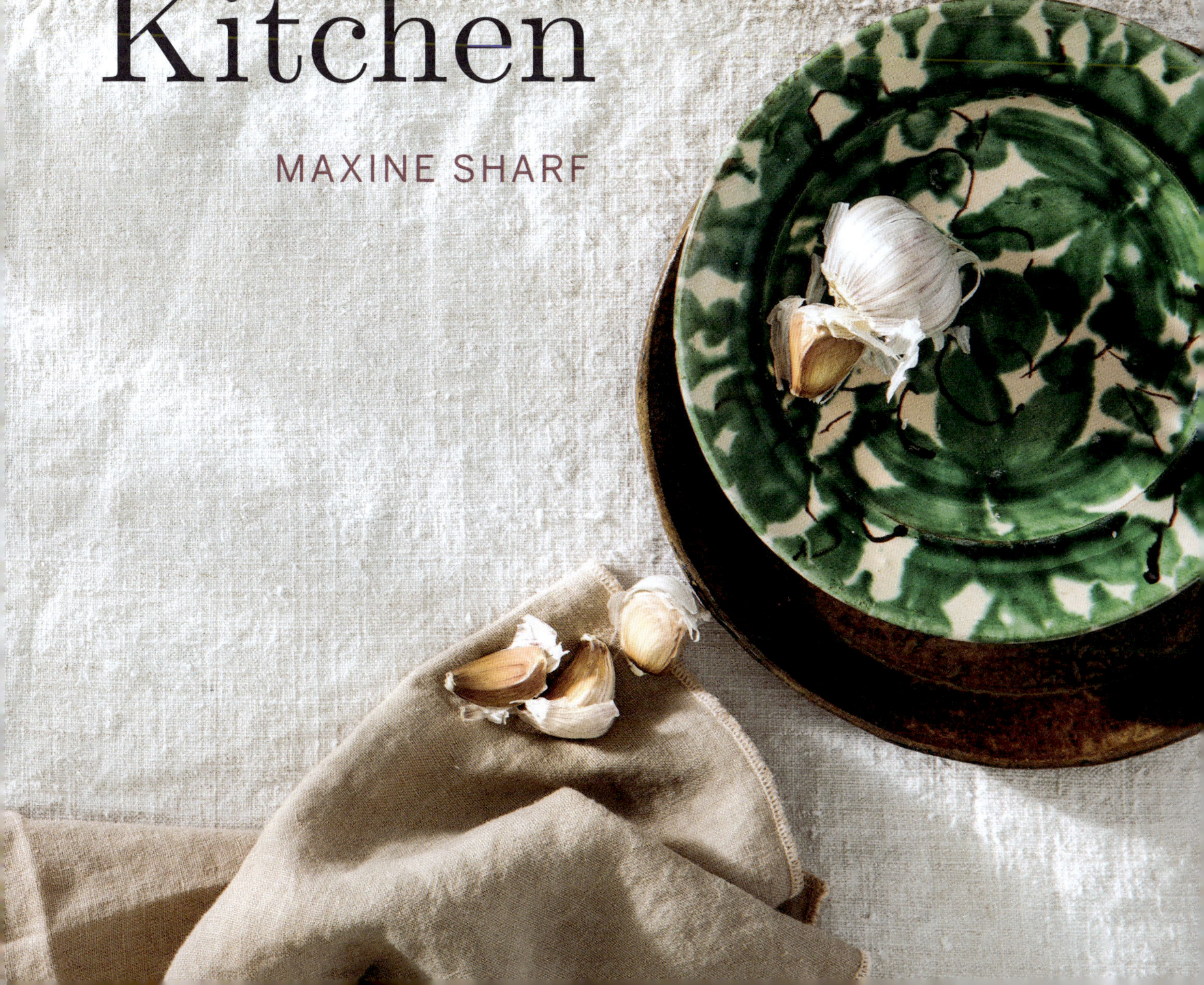

This book is dedicated to my parents. Mom, for being my best friend and making the kitchen my happy place. Dad, for teaching me countless life lessons and making me the woman I am today. Both, for your unconditional love and support.

My dream for this book is that it becomes covered in stains from repeated use, with hand-scribbled notes in the margins and lots of dog-eared pages bookmarking your favorite recipes the old-school way. I hope you use it often and return to these recipes again and again.

CONTENTS

Friday

LET'S COME TOGETHER

Saturday

LET'S ADVENTURE

Sunday

LET'S BRUNCH

Simple Sides

FOR EVERY DAY OF THE WEEK

INTRODUCTION

Welcome to my *first-ever* cookbook! I'm honored and excited that you're here reading this, and I appreciate your support so much. It's honestly surreal. If we're just meeting for the first time: Hi, I'm Maxine! I've always loved to cook (since I was a little girl—more on that below), and in 2018 I started a cooking blog called *Maxi's Kitchen* while working a full-time corporate job. When I was laid off in 2022, I decided to take the leap and dedicate myself to the art and science of recipe development. Thanks for joining me in this next chapter of my journey!

During the early creative process of writing this book, I reflected on the many cookbooks in my home. My collection essentially falls into two categories: books I turn to all the time (few), and those that look nice on my bookshelf but sit gathering dust (most). My dream for this book is that it falls into the former category in *your* collection. I hope that in the coming weeks, months, and years, *Maxi's Kitchen* will become covered in stains from repeated use, with hand-scribbled notes in the margins and lots of dog-eared pages bookmarking your favorite recipes the old-school way.

My mission in everything I do is to inspire people to cook more. Don't get me wrong, I love a good restaurant (understatement), so it's not about staying home instead of dining out. Rather, what I've come to realize is that many people view cooking as a chore, and some even find it stressful. However, I am here to tell you that cooking can be a calm, meditative experience that you can enjoy and look forward to.

That's what this cookbook is all about: discovering your weekly go-to recipes that help you build confidence and have fun in the kitchen. I've organized the chapters by day of the week, along with a chapter at the end for simple sides, because I've found that the natural rhythm of a week influences what I'm in the mood to cook and eat. On busier, more stressful days, I need something simple and quick. Later in the week, I tend to have more time, so I might be inspired to cook a recipe that requires a bit more energy and love. And no matter what day it is, I'm always trying to keep it nourishing and delicious.

On **Monday,** you'll start the week with quick and easy recipes like Creamy Mushroom Chicken (page 34). **Tuesday** is centered on one-pot meals like Shrimp and Broccoli Stir-Fry (page 53), where the entire dish is cooked in one skillet, pan, or wok. **Wednesday** is for having some fun to get through the midweek slump: sandwiches, tacos, and wraps, along with colorful and vibrant bowls. **Thursday,** as we near the end of the week, is about indulging in restaurant-grade date-night meals, such as Spicy Creamy Shrimp Spaghetti (page 114). **Friday** is an opportunity to host a group of friends or family with tapas-style recipes, like French Onion Crostini (page 160) and Grandpa's Korean Vegetable Pancakes (page 157). **Saturday** is for experimentation and fun projects, without time restrictions, like Mom's Red and White Lasagna (page 167) or Chinese Hand-Pulled Noodles with Chili Oil and Scallions (page 165). And **Sunday** is all about brunch, rest, and relaxation, with lots of eggs and the fluffiest pancakes you'll ever taste (page 208). My hope is that by breaking down the week with these different intentions and providing a wide variety of flavors, ingredients, and cuisines, you can find something that matches what you're in the mood for, no matter the day.

I can't wait to hear which recipes become part of your weekly rotation, and let me tell you a secret: My real dream is for these dishes to really become yours, for my mom's spaghetti and meatballs to become *your* family recipe. My brothers and I would constantly ask my mom to make the dishes we craved, and I'd love for the same to happen in your household—for the recipes in this book to become the ones you return to over and over again, until you know them as well as I know my grandma's wontons.

And speaking of those wontons, you could say that's where much of my journey into cooking began.

Although I was too young to remember, baby Maxine really loved food. It was actually a running joke in my family (and still is to this day). My mom and grandma always tell the story of when they fed me a banana, then another, and another, and another, until my grandma finally turned to my mom and said that was probably enough. I could not stop eating!

It makes sense, given that there was no shortage of amazing food at home when I was growing up. My mom, Ann, is an incredible cook. Her parents were both first-generation immigrants (my grandma is Chinese, and my grandpa was Korean) and taught her recipes from their countries of origin. Because my mom is the eldest of three sisters and her parents worked late as pharmacists, she often cooked dinner for the family. When she met my dad in San Francisco in her early twenties, she wooed him with her cooking, surprising him with fried rice and chocolate chip cookies at the end of a workday. My dad, on the other hand, grew up in a Jewish family on Long Island. His parents were of Romanian, Polish, and Russian descent. As you cook through my book, you'll see that many of the dishes are inspired by my family's rich and diverse culinary traditions—often recipes that were passed down from my grandparents to my parents, from their home countries to their kitchens in Illinois and New York, and finally to my home in Los Angeles.

My mom and I have always been close, so when I went through a lonely year in middle school after a falling-out with my friends, she took me under her wing and taught me all our family recipes. That year, she really became my best friend. Since I had a lot more time at home and no invitations to hang out with the girls at school, my mom said: "Every time I cook something, let's do it together." Over the course of many, many hours spent together in the kitchen, learning to make dishes like my grandma's wontons and my nana's broccoli and cheese–stuffed chicken, something sparked inside me, and I started to really enjoy the process and ritual of cooking. That year with my mom lit a fire in me that still burns to this day. We joke that I learned to fold wontons before I ever held hands with a boy. (It's true!) Though my culinary education began from a painful adolescent experience, it showed me how food can be comforting—I'll forever associate cooking with the feeling of being home and cared for.

In 2017, I was in my twenties, living alone in New York City in a tiny studio apartment, when I started to miss cooking at home with my mom. If you've lived in New York before, you're familiar with the infamously cramped apartments and comically small kitchens. That, plus the world-class dining scene, is why it's so tempting to eat every meal out. However, right there in the mecca of the restaurant world, I found myself starting to rekindle some of the magic of home-cooked food.

I had also recently gotten into a serious relationship, and I was consciously (or subconsciously) trying to reel in my boyfriend (now husband), Doug, with my cooking—folding wontons in a flash and making him veggie scrambles and smoothies before work (sound familiar?). Writing that last sentence makes me giggle—it's a little embarrassing, but it's true: My love language is food.

One day, Doug and I were talking, and I shared a "crazy idea" I had about starting a cooking blog on Instagram. We both laughed and then thought about it for a minute. *Why not? Who cares if no one sees it!* This would be a fun creative outlet on evenings and weekends, when

I wasn't working my day job in sales at a tech company. At first it was terrifying; it took me a whole year to muster the courage to film and post a video of my go-to spaghetti sauce. But once I got going, working on my cooking blog quickly became my passion. I loved building a community around my recipes and felt so fulfilled inspiring people to cook.

Four years later, in December 2022, I had built a modest following on Instagram. That's when I got the news that I had lost my job. Embarrassed and dejected, I spent most of the day crying. I was a model employee, took pride in my work, and had a great relationship with my colleagues. Although it was a gut punch at that moment, I woke up the next day and decided to consider it a blessing in disguise. I was going to bet on myself and find a way to make cooking my full-time job.

What has followed has been the craziest chapter of my life (in a good way!). Ever since then, I've been chasing my dream at full speed, filming hundreds of recipes and sharing them with you all! When I develop a recipe, I'm always thinking about how to make it easy, doable, and exciting for you, whether you're a student on a tight budget, someone completely new to the kitchen feeling nervous about getting started, a busy parent feeding their family, or an experienced cook who's stuck in a dinner rut.

Writing this cookbook and fine-tuning every recipe so it's just right for you allowed me to slow down, trust my instincts more, and remember what I love the most about cooking: the pure joy of being in the kitchen and unwinding as I prep dinner. Although it sounds cheesy, I honestly feel that *this* is what I was put on earth to do, and there's nothing else I'd rather be doing.

Thank you so much for your support ♡ It means the world to me. I hope you enjoy the book and am sending lots of love your way.

Love,
Mary

HOW TO USE THIS BOOK

There are eight chapters in this book: one for each day of the week (Monday through Sunday), plus a bonus chapter for simple sides (veggies, salads, and grains).

Each day follows a different intention, which I describe at the beginning of the chapter. Earlier in the week, you'll find simple and quick recipes, while more elaborate dishes fall later in the week.

With that said, the only rule is that . . . **there are no rules**! This is not a meal plan. Think of the chapters as a tool to help guide you. My hope is that you choose recipes based on the occasion and how you're feeling.

This is how I like to cook—I follow the inspiration. It's so much more fun to make things I actually *want* to cook (and eat) rather than forcing myself to make a meal according to a set schedule. I hope this cookbook can inspire you to do the same and find the dishes you are genuinely excited for.

pantry staples

I've organized my pantry staples into flavor categories to help you think about how different elements come together to create balance in a dish. At the end, you'll find my go-to dry goods, like rice, pasta, and flour.

SALTY

KOSHER SALT

Diamond Crystal is my go-to workhorse salt. Keep it in a salt cellar or bowl for easy pinching. Salt varies a lot from one brand to another—some are much saltier than others—so if you're following the amounts in this book, use Diamond Crystal! Otherwise, I recommend seasoning to taste.

MALDON SEA SALT

My favorite finishing salt for both savory and sweet dishes. The flakes are big and crunchy, with a pyramid-like structure.

SOY SAUCE

Made from fermented soybeans, this is an essential condiment for seasoning Asian dishes. You'll find it in so many of my recipes. I love Kikkoman soy sauce.

FISH SAUCE

Another fermented condiment, essential to Southeast Asian cuisine. It smells pungent right out of the bottle, but when added to a dish, it adds a savory, salty depth of flavor. I recommend Red Boat brand.

OYSTER SAUCE

Made from oyster extract, this thick, dark sauce lends a complex umami flavor to Chinese dishes. You'll find it in my stir-fries. I like the one from Lee Kum Kee.

MISO PASTE

A fermented soybean paste, and a staple of Japanese cooking. It has a complex, salty, umami flavor and a touch of sweetness. I usually use white miso paste.

ANCHOVIES

Look for anchovy fillets packed in oil. I use them in chimichurri-style sauces and Italian preparations. They add a great saltiness and often just melt into the other ingredients, so you don't notice their "fishiness."

CAPERS

Little salt bombs! I especially love pairing them with fish.

SPICY & SPICES

FRESHLY GROUND BLACK PEPPER

Because, duh! I always recommend freshly ground versus preground for the best flavor. If you don't have them already, buy some whole black peppercorns and a pepper mill.

WHITE PEPPER

It has such a different aroma from black pepper. I buy it finely ground and use it in some of my Asian dishes, like hot and sour soup.

CRUSHED RED PEPPER FLAKES

My go-to for adding heat with a clean flavor in both Italian and Asian cuisines.

CAYENNE PEPPER

My mom taught me to put a dash of cayenne in white sauces for depth of flavor and a subtle, lingering heat. It's spicy, so go easy!

CHILI GARLIC SAUCE

Great for spicing up stir-fries and other Asian dishes. I recommend the one in the red bottle with the green top from Huy Fong Foods.

CRUSHED CALABRIAN CHILI PEPPERS IN OIL

Super spicy and delicious—this is one of my favorite spicy condiments. I love it in pasta sauces, on pizza and eggs . . . honestly, on almost everything.

GOCHUJANG

A spicy and sweet Korean red chili paste. It's sticky and thick, and is a go-to for Korean dishes like jjigae. Look for the one in a little red tub with a gold lid from O Foods.

SRIRACHA

Made with chili peppers, this Thai condiment adds heat and subtle sweetness to Asian-inspired dishes. I recommend the one in the red bottle with the green top from Huy Fong Foods.

CHILI CRISP

Delicious over hand-pulled noodles, eggs, rice, and more. It adds amazing texture and spice. I love the "chili crunch" from Momofuku.

JALAPEÑOS

I use these fresh peppers for adding heat to both Asian and Mexican dishes. For less spice, remove the ribs and seeds.

THAI RED CHILIES

VERY spicy, so use with caution, depending on your preference. (I love spicy ingredients!)

THAI CURRY PASTE

I like to have both red and green curry pastes on hand. Curry pastes vary greatly from brand to brand; my favorite is Mae Ploy.

GROUND SPICES

Paprika, cumin (ground and seeds), ground coriander, chili powder, garlic powder, and ground cinnamon—I keep all these in my spice drawer.

SWEET

GRANULATED SUGAR

It adds sweetness without any flavor, and the granules dissolve easily. Sometimes I'll add a teaspoon to savory preparations like tomato sauce to balance the dish.

HONEY

I love that it's a natural sweetener, but it does have a distinct flavor, so only use it when it complements the dish.

MAPLE SYRUP

Another great natural sweetener. In my opinion, it has a slightly milder flavor than honey. Look for 100% pure maple syrup.

LIGHT BROWN SUGAR

It adds a slight molasses flavor, especially when cooked. I often use light brown sugar in Vietnamese-inspired marinades, as it helps brown and caramelize the protein.

SOUR

FRESH LEMON JUICE

Adds a bright pop of acidity to dishes. I love squeezing it on at the end, especially for fish and Mediterranean dishes. (The zest is great, too, and adds a floral lemony flavor without the acidity of the juice.) One 4- to 6-ounce lemon should yield about 2 to 3 tablespoons juice and 1 teaspoon grated zest.

FRESH LIME JUICE

My go-to acid for Mexican- and Vietnamese-inspired dishes. One lime will yield about 2 tablespoons juice.

DISTILLED WHITE VINEGAR

Adds a really nice tang and has a mild flavor. It's my go-to for pickling and finishing a dish. I usually buy the one from Heinz.

RICE VINEGAR

An essential vinegar for Asian dishes. It's a little less tart than distilled white vinegar.

BALSAMIC VINEGAR

I often use it for salad dressings or when I need a touch of acidity with some sweetness. Look for balsamic vinegar imported from Italy.

RED WINE VINEGAR

A versatile vinegar for salad dressings and Mediterranean-inspired dishes.

DIJON MUSTARD

Wonderful for salad dressings and cooking when you need a creamy tang. Look for Grey Poupon or Maille (stronger). They vary in heat, so make sure to taste it first!

RICH

BUTTER

I really love Kerrygold—it has such a rich flavor—and I almost always buy salted butter, as I use that for toast. The recipes in this book were developed with unsalted butter (unless salted is specified), but feel free to use your favorite kind. You may just need to slightly adjust the seasoning.

AVOCADO OIL

This is my favorite neutral oil for cooking at high heat, like for a good sear or shallow-frying. It has a high smoke point and won't burn easily. I usually buy the one from Chosen Foods.

AVOCADO OIL SPRAY

For spritzing wire racks and getting a perfectly crispy exterior on foods baked in the oven, like breaded chicken cutlets. I recommend the one from Chosen Foods.

EXTRA-VIRGIN OLIVE OIL

My everyday oil for salad dressings and lower-smoke-point cooking. I like Kirkland 100% Italian extra-virgin olive oil from Costco. For a finishing oil with a more robust flavor, I love Graza Drizzle. It comes in a squeeze bottle that makes it easy to drizzle on at the end.

PEANUT OIL

My go-to oil for deep-frying. It's less expensive than avocado oil and has a nice, subtle nutty flavor.

TOASTED SESAME OIL

An essential ingredient for Asian dishes. It adds a rich, toasty aroma. Because it loses its flavor as it cooks, I usually add it at the very end of a dish. Store it in a cool, dark place or in the refrigerator. Look for the Japanese brand Kadoya.

MAYONNAISE

Mayo adds creaminess and a bit of richness to slaws and dipping sauces. Sometimes I even add a tablespoon to a yogurt sauce to make it a little more indulgent. Hellmann's (also known as Best Foods) is my favorite brand!

PARMESAN CHEESE

This Italian cheese adds saltiness and richness. I often use pregrated Parmesan to save time, but I recommend keeping a block of Parm on hand for grating fresh over pasta (or other dishes) right before serving. And I highly recommend splurging on Parmigiano Reggiano.

CREAM CHEESE

I often use it in appetizers and for creamy pan sauces. I love Philadelphia brand.

WHOLE MILK

My go-to for white sauces like béchamel! I use milk instead of heavy cream whenever I can.

GREEK YOGURT

I love Fage full-fat or 2% Greek yogurt. It adds a tangy freshness while also being lusciously creamy.

SOUR CREAM

I'll use both full-fat and light. Doug is obsessed with sour cream, so I cook with it a lot. We love the one from Daisy.

COCONUT MILK

Adds a delicious richness to Thai curries. Look for full-fat.

PEANUT BUTTER

A favorite for Asian dishes, such as stir-fries, sauces, and dressings. My go-to for cooking is creamy natural peanut butter (just peanuts and salt—no added sugar!).

EGGS

All the recipes in this book were developed with large eggs. I love the ones from Vital Farms—they have such gorgeous orange yolks! If you have whites or yolks left over from a dish, they will keep in an airtight container in the refrigerator for up to 2 days.

AROMATICS & HERBS

ONIONS (YELLOW, RED, AND SWEET)

I use onions in so many recipes—raw and cooked—for sweetness, crunch, softness, and freshness! They vary greatly in size, so make sure to follow the weight measurements I've included throughout (small = 6 ounces, medium = 10 ounces, large = 12 ounces).

GARLIC

One of my top aromatics, regardless of the type of cuisine. I've specified the size of the clove when necessary. Otherwise, look for medium cloves, or use two small cloves for one medium.

FRESH GINGER

Adds bright, bold flavor to Asian dishes. No need to peel it! Just give it a good wash and trim off any tough or knobby spots.

SCALLIONS

A core ingredient in Chinese and Korean cooking, along with ginger and garlic. I also love to add it at the end for color and freshness.

PARSLEY

It looks so pretty sprinkled on top and elevates any dish. Look for flat-leaf (Italian), not curly parsley.

CHIVES

These add a yummy, subtle oniony flavor and a nice green pop of color.

DILL

This is probably my favorite herb for pairing with fish. It goes so well with lemon and really any Mediterranean dish.

DRY GOODS

ALL-PURPOSE FLOUR

For baking, breading, and thickening. I recommend using a scale to weigh the precise amount for baking recipes and doughs.

CORNSTARCH

For thickening Asian sauces, like in a stir-fry, and helping things crisp up!

JASMINE RICE

My go-to rice for Asian meals.

LONG-GRAIN WHITE RICE

And my preferred rice for non-Asian meals.

PASTA

I always keep several shapes and sizes in my pantry for quick and easy meals. My favorites are spaghetti and rotini from Barilla.

QUINOA

A fairly quick-cooking and nutritious, protein-rich whole grain. Quinoa is a nice alternative to rice when I want something filling and healthy.

COUSCOUS

Perfect for Mediterranean grain bowls and soaking up sauces.

CANNED WHOLE PEELED SAN MARZANO TOMATOES

A base for soups, sauces, and stews. Look for certified DOP San Marzano tomatoes imported from Italy. When you add them to a dish, break them up with your hands, pressing your thumbs into the tomatoes to crush them. Careful, as the juice and seeds can squirt!

CANNED BEANS

I always keep a few cans in my pantry. My favorites are cannellini beans, chickpeas, and black beans. They add protein and heartiness to a dish.

CHICKEN STOCK

I prefer stock over broth, as I find it adds an amazing depth of flavor to soups and stews. Kirkland brand from Costco and Kitchen Basics are both great options. I also love Better Than Bouillon when I need a small amount of stock and don't want to open a big carton.

PANKO BREADCRUMBS

Large, airy, crunchy flakes. These are ideal for super-crispy breading or a toasted topping.

These crumbs are finer than panko and are flavored with Italian seasonings.

INSTANT YEAST AND ACTIVE DRY YEAST

For breads and doughs. Make sure to check the expiration date before using! Active dry yeast needs to be dissolved in warm liquid prior to use, whereas instant yeast can be used right out of the packet.

I always keep some in my pantry for a rice paper egg wrap (the easiest lunch!) and other Asian recipes.

DRIED SHIITAKE MUSHROOMS

They have a chewier texture and more pronounced flavor than fresh shiitakes. I love using them in Asian dishes! Just set aside some time to soak them in hot water so they can rehydrate before using.

These add flavor and texture to Asian dishes. You can easily find them at Asian supermarkets or traditional grocery stores in the Asian foods section. Buy a big jar or container, as you'll use them throughout the book!

season to taste

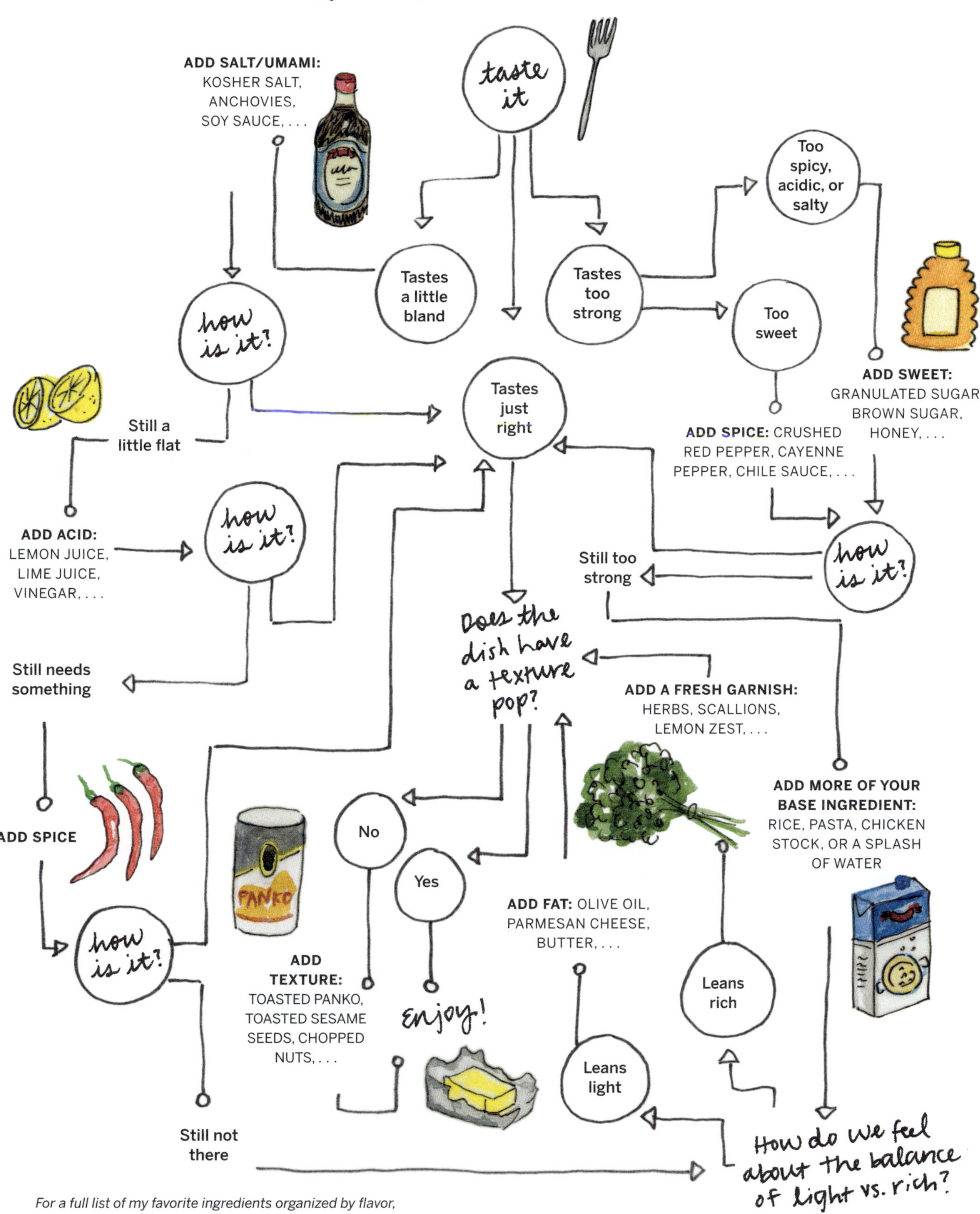

For a full list of my favorite ingredients organized by flavor, check out my pantry staples on pages 13 to 16.

MAXI'S
Kitchen Tools

These are my go-to kitchen essentials that I use all the time. It's not an exhaustive list, but it's a great guide to help you equip your kitchen with the tools you'll need to cook through this book.

10- OR 11-INCH HEAVY SKILLET WITH HIGH SIDES

For searing, frying, and one-pot meals. I recommend an enameled cast-iron skillet from Le Creuset or Staub. They're durable and retain heat evenly.

DUTCH OVEN

For soups, stews, pastas, and homemade bread. Le Creuset and Staub are both fabulous! I've also heard good things about Lodge for a lower-cost option. I recommend a 5½-quart or a 7-quart Dutch oven (depending on the size of your family). It's an investment that will last you a lifetime.

12-INCH STAINLESS-STEEL SKILLET

Also great for searing and sautéing. Look for 5-ply construction for even heat distribution.

12-INCH NONSTICK SKILLET WITH A LID

For cooking more delicate items that can easily stick to a skillet, like dumplings and fish fillets.

WOK

My go-to for stir-fries, although you can also use a large nonstick skillet instead.

LARGE POT WITH A LID

For boiling pasta, or when you simply need a second large pot alongside a Dutch oven.

MEDIUM POT WITH A LID

For smaller quantities, such as sauces.

HALF- AND QUARTER-SHEET PANS

For prepping ingredients and baking. I recommend having at least one half-sheet (13 by 18-inch) pan and two quarter-sheet (9 by 13-inch) pans for the recipes in this book.

WIRE RACK

Set it over a sheet pan for baked chicken cutlets and other crispy oven preparations to allow the hot air to circulate around the food for even crisping!

9 BY 13-INCH BAKING DISH

For one-pan meals, such as lasagna, mac and cheese, frittatas, and many more.

STAINLESS-STEEL PREP BOWLS (OF ALL SIZES)

Lightweight and easy to clean—they are essential for mixing ingredients and prepping the components of a recipe, like for a stir-fry.

STAND MIXER

I love my KitchenAid stand mixer. Yes, it's a splurge, but it will last for years and years and is so useful for making dough (think pizza, hand-pulled noodles, and potstickers). It takes all the hard work out of kneading and makes the process so much faster.

CUTTING BOARD

I recommend a large wooden cutting board so you have plenty of room to chop and organize your ingredients. No spilling onto your counter!

CHEF'S KNIFE

I use my 8-inch Global chef's knife for almost everything. It's lightweight, sturdy, and razor-sharp.

SERRATED KNIFE

For slicing all kinds of bread.

PARING KNIFE

For small jobs, such as peeling citrus and deveining shrimp.

BENCH SCRAPER

I love the one from OXO. This might be my most-used item in the kitchen, after my chef's knife. It's so helpful for transferring chopped veggies to a prep bowl or skillet.

MICROPLANE (RASP GRATER)

A must-have for grating garlic and Parmesan cheese, and for zesting lemons.

JULIENNE PEELER

For quickly and easily making veggie matchsticks, like carrots or cucumbers. I recommend the one from OXO.

SPIDER STRAINER

This is one of my most-used tools. It's perfect for tasks like transferring pasta straight from the pot to a skillet to finish cooking in a sauce, fishing wontons out of boiling water, and lifting fried foods from hot oil.

CITRUS SQUEEZER

It's so much easier than squeezing by hand and keeps the seeds from falling into the dish.

TONGS

For flipping ingredients in a skillet and mixing or tossing salads and pastas. Opt for long tongs to keep your hands and arms safe from oil splatters.

THIN METAL SPATULA

For flipping and releasing items from a skillet and transferring them to a plate.

WHISKS

A big whisk for evenly incorporating milk into white sauces (no lumps!), and a small one for emulsifying dressings or whisking cornstarch with water.

DIGITAL KITCHEN SCALE

I highly recommend a scale for weighing flour for doughs, as it's hard to get a precise and accurate measurement with measuring cups. I also use my scale for weighing produce and other ingredients. It's an affordable tool that you'll use all the time.

GLASS MEASURING CUPS FOR LIQUIDS

For measuring and mixing sauces (like for stir-fries) and making dressings. I love my set from Anchor Hocking.

DRY MEASURING CUPS AND SPOONS

Essential for ensuring correct amounts.

COOKIE SCOOPS (IN DIFFERENT SIZES)

I love these for quickly shaping meatballs and adding fillings to wontons and potstickers. I recommend getting three sizes (1, 2, and 3 table-spoons) for the recipes in this book.

INSTANT-READ DIGITAL THERMOMETER

I use this to check internal temperatures whenever I'm cooking poultry or red meat. (I'll never forget the time I accidentally served raw chicken to my guests!)

WOODEN ROLLING PINS

A big one for rolling out dough for pie crusts, and a small one for rolling out small rounds of dough for dumplings and buns. (Trust me, it'll make it much easier!)

PASTRY BRUSH

For brushing egg wash and melted butter onto doughs before baking.

chopping 101

I use my **8-inch Global chef's knife** 95 percent of the time! It's *almost* the only knife you'll need. Make sure to keep it sharp, as it's actually more dangerous to use a dull knife—it can slip against the ingredient (since you're using more force), and that's how you get hurt.

I also recommend having a **serrated knife** for slicing bread and a **paring knife** for small jobs, such as trimming fruits and vegetables.

Make sure your **cutting board** is the right size for whatever you're chopping (meaning, make sure it's big enough to hold the ingredient). If your cutting board is sliding around on the counter, place a damp dish towel (or paper towel) beneath it between the board and the counter. That will secure it in place.

Think of **dicing** as the art of cutting things into neat little cubes. If the ingredients are cut the same size, they'll cook more evenly. Dicing also gives you a more polished presentation in the finished dish. In this book, you'll find three sizes for dicing:

SMALL DICE: ~¼-INCH CUBES

MEDIUM DICE: ~½-INCH CUBES

LARGE DICE: ~¾-INCH CUBES

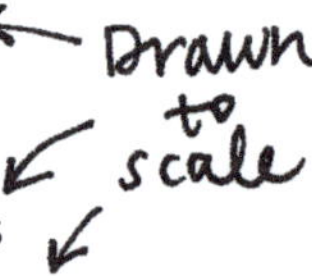

To dice, slice the ingredient into uniform slices of the thickness you need. Stack a few of the slices and cut them lengthwise into strips. Then cut the strips crosswise to form evenly sized cubes.

HOW TO DICE AN ONION

Chopping is the quick and easy way to cut ingredients when precision isn't super important. Just aim for similarly sized pieces and you're good to go!

Finely chopping (or mincing) is for when you need a fine texture, like for garlic, ginger, herbs, or any other ingredient where you want tiny pieces to evenly flavor the recipe. To finely chop, first coarsely chop the ingredient. Then hold one hand down on the nose of the knife and rock the blade back and forth in a smooth motion, keeping the tip in contact with the cutting board while guiding the knife with your other hand.

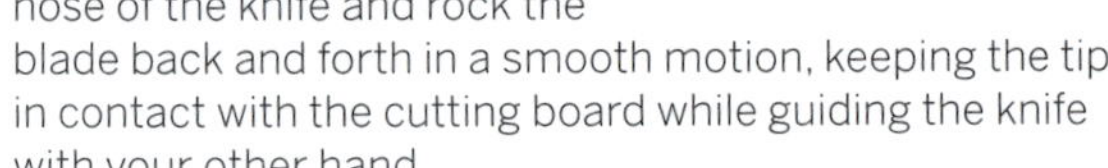

Julienne is a fancy-sounding technique for cutting your veggies into thin strips, like matchsticks. This is great for stir-fries, slaws, or anything that calls for a crisp bite. Julienne works best with firmer veggies like carrots and cucumbers. For most veggies, you can use a julienne peeler instead of cutting by hand (see Maxi's Kitchen Tools, page 18).

To julienne, cut the ingredient into thin slices, then stack a few of the slices and carefully cut them into thin, uniform strips resembling matchsticks.

WOLF

Monday

let's keep it simple

Quick and Easy Recipes *with Minimal Chopping and Maximum Flavor*

I totally get it—making dinner on a Monday isn't usually a top priority. That's why the recipes in this chapter are super simple: They feature short ingredient lists, quick prep and cooking times (most are ready in 30 minutes or less), and minimal chopping (think a whole piece of protein coated in a flavor-packed sauce). Most important, these meals are incredibly delicious. You'll discover how dishes that look complex and elegant—like Honey-Mustard Salmon with Pistachio and Dill (page 49) or Creamy Mushroom Chicken (page 34)—are actually so easy to pull off. These recipes will nourish you and set you up to take on the week ahead.

Sticky Sweet and Sour Ginger Tofu

SERVES 2 ◆ PREP TIME: 15 MINUTES ◆ TOTAL TIME: 30 MINUTES

SAUCE

½ cup water

2 tablespoons light brown sugar

1 tablespoon plus 1 teaspoon soy sauce

1 teaspoon cornstarch

TOFU

1 (14-ounce) package firm or extra-firm tofu, drained

Kosher salt and freshly ground black pepper

2 tablespoons cornstarch

2 tablespoons avocado oil or other neutral oil, such as grapeseed

1 tablespoon finely chopped fresh ginger

3 garlic cloves, finely chopped

1 tablespoon distilled white vinegar

FOR SERVING

1 scallion, thinly sliced

Toasted sesame seeds

The crust on this tofu reminds me of agedashi tofu, a Japanese dish I love to order at restaurants, where the tofu is deep-fried and served in a dashi broth. Here there's no frying; instead, the tofu is coated in cornstarch and seared in a skillet to create a sticky, golden crust. The heat makes the tofu incredibly soft and tender inside. It's the kind of meal that tastes like it requires skill but is surprisingly quick and easy to make. And don't worry—this tofu is *anything* but bland. It's glazed with an insanely delicious, sweet, and tangy sauce that you'll be licking off the plate. A sprinkle of fresh scallions adds bursts of color to complete the dish.

I love serving this with freshly cooked Jasmine Rice (page 231) or Sesame Quinoa and Kale (page 228).

1. **Make the sauce:** In a small bowl, mix together the water, brown sugar, soy sauce, and cornstarch. Set aside.
2. **Make the tofu:** Using a sharp knife, slice the tofu in half to create two rectangular slabs, each about 1 inch thick. (See illustration.) Cut each slab into four pieces to make eight equal pieces. Using paper towels, press on the tofu all over to blot excess moisture, getting it as dry as possible. (This will yield the best crust.) Season the tofu all over with salt and pepper.
3. Place the cornstarch in a shallow bowl or large plate and spread it in an even layer. Working with one piece at a time, add the tofu to the cornstarch and press to coat. Flip and press to coat on the other side (no need to coat the edges). Transfer to a plate and set aside.
4. In a large nonstick skillet, heat the oil over medium-high heat. Add the tofu and cook until golden brown, about 5 minutes per side. Transfer to a plate.
5. Reduce the heat to low. Add the ginger and cook, stirring, until golden brown, about 1 minute. Add the garlic and cook, stirring, until fragrant, about 1 minute.
6. Stir the sauce (the cornstarch will have settled) and pour it into the skillet. Increase the heat to medium-high and cook, stirring, until the sauce bubbles and thickens, 2 to 3 minutes. Remove from the heat and stir in the vinegar. Return the tofu to the skillet and toss each piece in the sauce to coat.
7. **To serve:** Spoon extra sauce over the tofu, sprinkle with the scallion and some sesame seeds, and enjoy!

Vietnamese Caramel Chicken Thighs

SERVES 3 ◆ PREP TIME: 10 MINUTES ◆ TOTAL TIME: 30 MINUTES

4 boneless, skinless chicken thighs (about 1½ pounds total)

Kosher salt and freshly ground black pepper

2 tablespoons avocado oil or other neutral oil, such as grapeseed, divided

¼ cup water

3 tablespoons light brown sugar

2 tablespoons fish sauce

1 tablespoon soy sauce

3 tablespoons finely chopped fresh ginger

4 garlic cloves, finely chopped

1 tablespoon unsalted butter

1 tablespoon rice vinegar

Fresh cilantro leaves, for serving

1 Thai chili (very spicy) or Fresno chili (less spicy), sliced into thin rounds, for serving (optional)

Doug and I visited Vietnam a few years ago, and I'm still dreaming about all the incredible street food. Vietnamese cuisine has this magical way of packing in bold flavors while still feeling light and fresh. One thing I can't get enough of is this sweet and savory caramel sauce called nước màu. It's used in Vietnamese cooking to braise proteins like pork, fish, and shrimp. Here, it coats chicken with a rich and sticky glaze. Top it with a handful of fresh cilantro and some fiery chilies (if you love heat like I do), and you've got a sensational dinner on the table in just 30 minutes.

I love serving this with freshly cooked Jasmine Rice (page 231) and sautéed bok choy.

1. Season the chicken on both sides with salt and pepper. In a large skillet, heat 1 tablespoon of the avocado oil over medium-high heat. Add the chicken thighs in one layer and cook until golden brown and the internal temperature registers 165°F on an instant-read thermometer, 5 to 7 minutes per side.
2. Meanwhile, in a small bowl, mix together the water, brown sugar, fish sauce, and soy sauce. Set the sauce aside.
3. Once the chicken is cooked, transfer it to a large plate. Reduce the heat to low and add the remaining 1 tablespoon oil to the skillet. Add the ginger and garlic and cook, stirring, until fragrant, 30 seconds to 1 minute.
4. Pour the sauce into the skillet and increase the heat to medium. Cook, stirring, until the sauce begins to bubble and thicken, 1 to 2 minutes. Add the butter and vinegar and stir until the butter has melted.
5. Return the chicken to the skillet and turn each piece to coat in the sauce. Cook until the sauce is thick and glossy and clings to the chicken, 1 to 2 minutes more.
6. To serve, divide the chicken among three plates and spoon the sauce on top. Garnish with cilantro and the chilies, if desired, and enjoy!

Aunt Susan's Pan-Seared Fish *with Tomatoes and Capers*

SERVES 2 ◆ PREP TIME: 10 MINUTES ◆ TOTAL TIME: 25 MINUTES

¼ cup all-purpose flour

2 (6-ounce) skinless snapper or striped bass fillets

Kosher salt and freshly ground black pepper

2 tablespoons extra-virgin olive oil, divided

2 tablespoons unsalted butter, divided

⅓ cup finely chopped yellow onion

2 garlic cloves, finely chopped

½ cup halved cherry tomatoes

3 tablespoons drained capers

½ cup dry white wine

1 tablespoon finely chopped fresh parsley

Doug and I spent the first few months of the pandemic quarantining in Florida with my aunt Susan; my cousin, Abby; and her husband, Drew. In between endless hours of crocheting blankets while watching the guys play *Call of Duty* Battle Royale (don't worry, they won three times, and we were all screaming), we did *a lot* of cooking, and I learned so much from my aunt. She's an incredible cook, and this is one of her signature dishes. It's light and elegant with thin fillets of fish, sweetness from cherry tomatoes, brininess from capers, and richness from butter to round it all out. Dusting the fish with flour before pan-searing creates a slightly crisp exterior and helps the sauce stick to the fish, so don't skip that step!

1. Place the flour in a large shallow bowl or quarter-sheet pan. Season each fish fillet with salt and pepper on both sides. Working with one fillet at a time, dredge the fish in the flour, turning to coat. Shake off any excess flour and transfer the fish to a large plate.
2. In a large skillet, heat 1 tablespoon of the olive oil with 1 tablespoon of the butter over medium-high heat. When the butter has melted, add the fish and cook until golden brown and cooked through, 2 to 3 minutes per side. Transfer to a large serving plate and cover with foil to keep warm.
3. Reduce the heat to medium (or medium-low, if the skillet is super hot) and add the remaining 1 tablespoon olive oil. Add the onion and garlic and cook, stirring, until starting to soften, about 2 minutes. Add the tomatoes, capers, and wine. Bring to a simmer and cook, stirring, until the wine has reduced by about half, 2 to 3 minutes. Add the remaining 1 tablespoon butter and stir until melted.
4. Spoon the sauce over the fish and sprinkle with the parsley. Serve immediately and enjoy!

Asian Marinated Skirt Steak

SERVES 4 ◆ PREP TIME: 5 MINUTES
◆ TOTAL TIME: 30 MINUTES, PLUS 15 MINUTES FOR MARINATING

¼ cup soy sauce

2 tablespoons light brown sugar

1 tablespoon toasted sesame oil

3 garlic cloves, finely chopped

1 teaspoon finely chopped fresh ginger

¼ teaspoon freshly ground black pepper

1 pound skirt steak

1 tablespoon avocado oil or other neutral oil, such as grapeseed

1 scallion, thinly sliced at an angle, for serving

Toasted sesame seeds (optional), for sprinkling

This steak marinade, inspired by Korean BBQ, turns a simple cut of meat into something truly special. With just a few ingredients, it's incredibly easy to make and infuses the meat with delicious sweet and savory flavor. Sprinkle on some scallions at the end for a fresh finish. Doug and I love steak, but we don't have it often, so making this dish always feels like a treat. I hope it does for you, too!

I love serving this steak with freshly cooked Jasmine Rice (page 231) or a Simple Korean Salad (page 236). You can make the rice or salad while the steak is marinating.

1. In a large bowl, mix together the soy sauce, brown sugar, sesame oil, garlic, ginger, and pepper.
2. Cut the steak into large pieces that will fit in a skillet. Add the steak to the marinade and toss to coat evenly. Marinate at room temperature for 15 minutes or in the refrigerator for up to 1 hour (bring the steak to room temperature before cooking).
3. Heat a large cast-iron or other heavy skillet over high heat until smoking, 3 to 5 minutes. Add the avocado oil and tilt the pan to evenly coat.
4. Working with one piece at a time, lift the skirt steak from the bowl, allowing the excess marinade to drip back into the bowl, and add it to the skillet, making sure not to overcrowd the skillet (you may need to cook it in two batches). Cook until browned and cooked through (130°F on an instant-read thermometer for medium-rare), 2 to 3 minutes per side. Transfer the skirt steak to a cutting board, cover with foil, and let rest for 5 minutes.
5. To serve, slice the steak against the grain and transfer to a serving plate. Drizzle any accumulated juices over the steak and garnish with the scallion and sesame seeds, if desired. Enjoy!

Cheesy Beans and Greens *with Olive Oil–Fried Bread*

SERVES 4 ◆ PREP TIME: 15 MINUTES ◆ TOTAL TIME: 30 MINUTES

BEANS AND GREENS

2 tablespoons extra-virgin olive oil

6 garlic cloves, finely chopped

1 large head escarole, kale, or Swiss chard (about 11 ounces; see Tip), sliced into 1-inch strips

1½ cups chicken stock or vegetable stock

1 teaspoon kosher salt

½ teaspoon crushed red pepper flakes

½ teaspoon freshly ground black pepper

½ teaspoon Italian seasoning

2 (15-ounce) cans cannellini beans, drained and rinsed

½ cup (2 ounces) grated Parmesan cheese

1 teaspoon balsamic vinegar

TOASTED BREAD

Extra-virgin olive oil

4 slices sourdough bread or other crusty bread

FOR SERVING

Extra-virgin olive oil

Freshly grated Parmesan cheese

Crushed red pepper flakes

Flaky sea salt, such as Maldon

I was shocked when I took my first bite of this dish—who knew beans and a few other simple ingredients could be so good?! The broth is infused with garlic and there's a creaminess from the grated Parmesan, which gets stirred in at the very end. I love the contrast of textures as the broth soaks into the center of the bread and softens it, while the crust and thicker escarole leaves retain a nice crunch. (Feel free to swap in whatever leafy greens you have on hand.) This is an elegant and comforting meal that feels light yet filling, and I can't wait for you to make it!

1. **Make the beans and greens:** In a large skillet, heat the olive oil over medium heat. Add the garlic and cook, stirring, until fragrant, about 1 minute. Add the escarole and cook, stirring, until beginning to wilt, 1 to 2 minutes.
2. Add the stock, kosher salt, red pepper flakes, black pepper, and Italian seasoning. Increase the heat to medium-high, stir, and bring to a simmer.
3. Add the beans and cook, stirring, until heated through, about 3 minutes. Remove from the heat and stir in the Parmesan and vinegar. Cover to keep warm while you toast the bread.
4. **Toast the bread:** Coat the bottom of a large skillet with a thin layer of olive oil and heat over medium heat. When the oil is shimmering, add the bread in a single layer (you may have to do this in batches) to coat the bottom of each slice with oil, then immediately flip the bread and cook, pressing down with a spatula, until deeply golden brown on the bottom, 1 to 2 minutes. Flip the bread and cook until deeply golden brown on the other side, 1 to 2 minutes more.
5. **To serve:** Divide the toasted bread among serving plates. Spoon the beans and greens over the bread, allowing them to spill over the edges of the bread. Garnish with a drizzle of olive oil, some Parmesan, a pinch of red pepper flakes, and some flaky salt. Enjoy!

TIP

If you're using kale or Swiss chard instead of escarole, make sure to remove the thick stems before slicing the leaves.

Creamy Mushroom Chicken

SERVES 3 OR 4 (DEPENDING ON YOUR APPETITE AND SIDES)
◆ PREP TIME: 20 MINUTES ◆ TOTAL TIME: 40 MINUTES

2 boneless, skinless chicken breasts (about 1¼ pounds total)

Kosher salt and freshly ground black pepper

¼ cup all-purpose flour

2 tablespoons avocado oil or other neutral oil, such as grapeseed

2 tablespoons unsalted butter

8 ounces cremini mushrooms or white button mushrooms, sliced ⅛ inch thick

1 shallot (3 ounces), chopped

3 garlic cloves, finely chopped

¾ cup chicken stock

¼ cup (2 ounces) cream cheese, cut into small pieces

2 teaspoons balsamic vinegar

1 teaspoon fresh thyme leaves, finely chopped, plus more for serving

The secret to making this sauce creamy and luscious—without it feeling too heavy—is cream cheese. Just a small amount creates a velvety texture that clings to the chicken breasts. The other star ingredient is balsamic vinegar. It brings a subtle depth with a hint of sweet, caramel-like flavor that pairs perfectly with the earthy mushrooms.

I love serving this with Creamy Mashed Potatoes with Chives (page 232), as they're ideal for soaking up all that sauce.

1. Slice the chicken breasts horizontally (similar to a butterfly cut) all the way through to create two thinner, even pieces. To do this, place your hand flat on top of one chicken breast to keep it steady and use a sharp knife to carefully cut through the middle from one side to the other. Place the chicken pieces side by side on a cutting board and cover with plastic wrap. Gently pound with the smooth side of a meat mallet until the pieces are an even thickness. Season both sides of the chicken with salt and pepper.
2. Place the flour on a large plate. Working with one at a time, coat both sides of each piece of chicken in the flour and transfer to a sheet pan or large plate.
3. In a large skillet, heat the avocado oil over medium-high heat. When the oil is shimmering, add the chicken pieces in one layer, being careful not to overcrowd the skillet. (You may have to do this in two batches.) Cook, undisturbed, until golden brown, about 3 minutes per side. Remove from the heat and transfer the chicken to a large plate.
4. In the same skillet, melt the butter over medium heat. Add the mushrooms and ¼ teaspoon each of salt and pepper. Cook, stirring, until the mushrooms are golden brown and almost tender, 3 to 5 minutes. Add the shallot and cook, stirring, for 1 minute. Add the garlic and cook, stirring, for 1 minute more.
5. Add the stock and cream cheese and stir, scraping up any bits stuck to the skillet. Bring to a simmer and cook, stirring, until the cream cheese has melted and the sauce has reduced by half, 3 to 4 minutes.
6. Stir in the vinegar and thyme. Season with more salt and/or pepper, if desired.
7. Return the chicken to the skillet, nestling it into the sauce. Simmer until the sauce has thickened slightly, 1 to 2 minutes.
8. Transfer the chicken to a serving dish or large plate and spoon the sauce over the top. Sprinkle with some additional thyme and enjoy!

Chinese Steamed Fish *with Sizzling Scallion Oil*

SERVES 2 ◆ PREP TIME: 10 MINUTES ◆ TOTAL TIME: 30 MINUTES

SIZZLING SCALLION OIL

3 scallions, very thinly sliced

2 tablespoons finely chopped fresh ginger

¼ teaspoon kosher salt, plus more if needed

¼ cup peanut oil

2 teaspoons toasted sesame oil

STEAMED FISH

Avocado oil spray or avocado oil, for the plate

2 (5- to 6-ounce) skin-on black cod, striped bass, or sea bass fillets

Kosher salt and freshly ground black pepper

FOR SERVING

2 teaspoons soy sauce

Handful of fresh cilantro (tender stems and leaves)

My grandma used to make the most delicious Chinese steamed fish, topped with scallions, ginger, and a drizzle of sizzling hot oil. Her recipe has always been a favorite, and it inspired me to create this version: a mild, buttery fish paired with a vibrant scallion-ginger oil. The oil is similar to the one served with Hainanese chicken—a simple yet flavorful accompaniment to delicately cooked proteins. Here it's enhanced with a splash of soy sauce and a handful of cilantro for an aromatic finish.

For this dish, I recommend using a slightly fatty white fish like black cod, which becomes melt-in-your-mouth tender. It's the ideal base for the bold, punchy scallion-ginger oil.

I love serving this with freshly cooked Jasmine Rice (page 231). For extra richness, add a little butter to the rice and stir it in until melted.

1. **Make the sizzling scallion oil:** In a heatproof medium bowl, combine the scallions, ginger, and salt.
2. In a small pot, heat the peanut oil until it just starts smoking and reaches 400°F on an instant-read thermometer, then carefully pour the hot oil over the scallions and ginger. Stir in the sesame oil. Set aside to cool, then taste and season with more salt, if desired. (The sauce should have a nice salty zing.)
3. **Steam the fish:** Fill a large pot (with a lid) with about 1 inch of water. Place a steamer rack inside the pot and set a large heatproof plate on top of the rack (or use three crumpled-up balls of foil to elevate the plate above the water line), ensuring the lid can close properly with the plate inside. Lightly spray or coat the plate with a little avocado oil. Bring the water to a boil over high heat.
4. Season the fish fillets with salt and pepper and place on the plate, skin-side down. Cover the pot and reduce the heat to medium-low. Steam until the fish is cooked through and flakes easily, about 8 minutes.
5. **To serve:** Using a spatula, transfer the fish to two plates. Drizzle each fillet with 1 teaspoon of the soy sauce and spoon some of the sizzling scallion oil on top (see Tip for storing leftovers). Top with the cilantro and enjoy!

TIP

The scallion oil can be stored in an airtight container in the refrigerator for up to 4 days. It's delicious over eggs, noodles, chicken, tofu, or rice.

Dad's Pork Chops *with* *Soy Sauce and Onions*

SERVES 4 ◆ PREP TIME: 5 MINUTES ◆ TOTAL TIME: 25 MINUTES

4 (1-inch-thick) boneless pork chops (about 1¾ pounds total)

Kosher salt and freshly ground black pepper

1 tablespoon avocado oil or other neutral oil, such as grapeseed

2 large red onions (about 1¼ pounds), halved and sliced ½ inch thick

¼ cup balsamic vinegar

¼ cup soy sauce

Chopped fresh parsley, for serving

This recipe is a tribute to my dad, who's a huge fan of pork chops. When I was a kid, he made this dish often, and it's still one of my go-tos. It's incredibly simple and has just a handful of ingredients, but is packed with flavor. The magic is all in the sauce: a sweet, tangy, and salty blend of equal parts balsamic vinegar and soy sauce that infuses the red onions, turning them into the juiciest little flavor bombs. The key is to cook the onions until they're just softened on the outside but still have a bit of crunch in the center. Piled on top of the pork, they're both delicious and beautiful. To me, it's just the right blend of comfort and elegance.

I love serving this with Creamy Mashed Potatoes with Chives (page 232) or Mom and Dad's Spinach Salad with Eggs and Mushrooms (page 235).

1. Season both sides of the pork chops with salt and pepper.
2. In a large skillet, heat the avocado oil over medium-high heat. Add the pork chops and cook, undisturbed, until a golden brown crust has formed on the bottom, 4 to 6 minutes. Flip and cook for 2 minutes more.
3. Add the onions, vinegar, and soy sauce. (The onions will sit on top of the pork chops at first, but push them onto the skillet as they cook down.) Cook, stirring the onions occasionally, until they are tender but still have a slight crunch and the pork chops register 145°F on an instant-read thermometer, 4 to 6 minutes. (If the pork is cooked through but the onions still need a little longer, transfer the pork to a plate and continue cooking the onions until they are done.) Remove the skillet from the heat and sprinkle with parsley.
4. Divide the pork chops among four plates and top each with a generous mound of onions. Enjoy!

Quick and Saucy Korean Silken Tofu

SERVES 2 ◆ PREP TIME: 5 MINUTES ◆ TOTAL TIME: 15 MINUTES

1 garlic clove, grated

2 scallions, thinly sliced, plus more for serving

2 tablespoons soy sauce

1 tablespoon toasted sesame seeds, plus more for serving

1 tablespoon rice vinegar

1 tablespoon toasted sesame oil

1 teaspoon gochujang

½ teaspoon sugar

1 (16-ounce) block silken tofu (see Tips)

This is the recipe for those days when you're so tired that even the thought of cooking feels like too much, and you're on the verge of giving in to takeout—until you remember you can make this instead. It's ridiculously simple (almost no cooking required) yet packed with bold flavor. The star of the show is silken tofu: creamy, soft, and delicate, with a texture like egg custard or flan. Its mild flavor makes it the perfect canvas for a bright Asian sauce. If you think you're not a tofu person, I dare you to give silken tofu a try, as it might just win you over!

I love serving this with freshly cooked Jasmine Rice (page 231); to keep things even easier, use ready-made microwavable or frozen rice.

1. In a small bowl, combine the garlic, scallions, soy sauce, sesame seeds, vinegar, sesame oil, gochujang, and sugar. Whisk or stir together until the sugar has dissolved.
2. Run a knife along the inner edge of the silken tofu package. Drain off any liquid and place the tofu block in a large shallow microwave-safe dish. (Turn the package upside down on top of the dish and squeeze the outside to release the tofu.)
3. Microwave the tofu for 2 minutes, then microwave in 30-second increments until warmed all the way through, about 2 minutes more (touch the center of the tofu block with your finger to ensure it's warm). If you don't have a microwave, see Tips.
4. Drain off any excess liquid from the dish or spoon it out (a little moisture is fine) and pour the soy-sesame sauce on top of the tofu block.
5. Sprinkle with some sesame seeds and the reserved scallions. Enjoy!

TIPS

If you don't have a microwave, you can steam the tofu: Fill a large pot (with a lid) with about 1 inch of water. Place a steamer rack inside the pot and place the dish with the tofu on the steamer rack (or place three crumpled-up balls of foil in the pot to elevate the dish above the water line). Bring the water to a boil over high heat, then reduce the heat to low to maintain a simmer, cover, and steam until the tofu is heated through, about 10 minutes. Carefully remove the dish from the pot.

I wouldn't recommend swapping in soft, medium, or firm tofu; they won't work the same here.

Miso-Butter Salmon

SERVES 4 ◆ PREP TIME: 10 MINUTES ◆ TOTAL TIME: 30 MINUTES

¾ cup water

1 tablespoon white miso paste or your favorite type of miso

1½ teaspoons cornstarch

¼ teaspoon freshly ground black pepper, plus more as needed

4 (6-ounce) skin-on salmon fillets

Kosher salt

1 tablespoon avocado oil or other neutral oil, such as grapeseed

2 tablespoons unsalted butter, divided

3 garlic cloves, thinly sliced

3 scallions, thinly sliced

Toasted sesame seeds, for serving

A few years ago, I discovered this method for cooking salmon, and it quickly became one of my go-to ways to prepare fish. You start by searing it in a very hot skillet for that restaurant-quality crust, then finish it in the oven for perfectly tender flesh. What really elevates this dish, though, is the rich, savory miso-scallion-butter sauce. My obsession with miso began when I first tried a miso-butter pasta dish—it completely blew me away. I couldn't believe how such a simple combination could be so good. Miso is a powerhouse ingredient—a single tablespoon adds incredible depth, balancing saltiness with a subtle sweetness.

I love serving this with freshly cooked Jasmine Rice (page 231), Sesame Quinoa and Kale (page 228), or a Simple Korean Salad (page 236).

1. Preheat the oven to 450°F.
2. In a small bowl, whisk together the water, miso, cornstarch, and pepper. Set aside.
3. Generously season the salmon fillets all over with salt and pepper.
4. Heat a large cast-iron skillet (or other heavy ovenproof skillet) over medium-high heat for 5 minutes. Add a droplet of water—if it sizzles and beads off, then the skillet is hot enough. Otherwise, heat it for a few more minutes. Pour the avocado oil into the skillet and tilt to evenly coat.
5. Place the salmon in the skillet, flesh-side down (or skin-side down, if you want crispy skin) and cook, undisturbed, for 2 minutes. Transfer the skillet to the oven and cook until the internal temperature registers 125°F on an instant-read thermometer for super-tender, medium-cooked salmon, or 145°F for more well-done salmon, 6 to 8 minutes.
6. Meanwhile, in a small skillet, melt 1 tablespoon of the butter over medium heat. Add the garlic and cook, stirring, until fragrant and golden, about 1 minute.
7. Stir the miso mixture (the cornstarch will have settled) and pour it into the skillet. Cook, stirring, until the sauce thickens and has reduced by about half, 4 to 5 minutes. Remove from the heat and stir in the scallions and remaining 1 tablespoon butter.
8. Transfer the salmon to a serving dish or four individual plates, then spoon the sauce over the fillets. Sprinkle with sesame seeds and enjoy!

Fennel and Orange Braised Chicken Thighs

SERVES 2 TO 4 (DEPENDING ON YOUR APPETITE)
◆ PREP TIME: 15 MINUTES ◆ TOTAL TIME: 50 MINUTES

4 bone-in, skin-on chicken thighs (about 1½ pounds total)

Kosher salt and freshly ground black pepper

1 tablespoon avocado oil or other neutral oil, such as grapeseed

2 small or 1 large fennel bulb(s) (about 1 pound), bulb(s) thinly sliced, fronds reserved

1 teaspoon dried thyme

2 garlic cloves, finely chopped

1 cup fresh-squeezed orange juice

2 tablespoons Dijon mustard

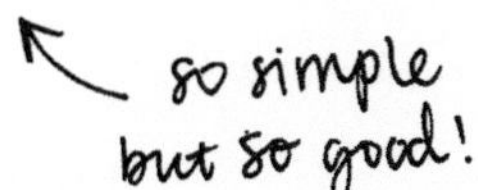

This recipe is proof that just a few ingredients can come together to create something truly special. Fresh orange juice adds a touch of sweetness, Dijon mustard brings tangy creaminess, and fragrant thyme ties it all together. The fennel softens while still keeping a bite (because texture is everything for me!), and the chicken turns out unbelievably tender, soaking up the sauce as it cooks. Speaking of the sauce, it's so good, you'll be tempted to scrape up every last drop!

1. Generously season both sides of the chicken thighs with salt and pepper.
2. In a large deep skillet (or pot) with a lid, heat the avocado oil over medium-high heat. Add the chicken skin-side down and cook, undisturbed, until the skin is deep golden brown and easily releases from the skillet, 5 to 6 minutes. Flip and cook until deep golden brown on the other side, 5 to 6 minutes more. Transfer the chicken to a plate.
3. Place the fennel, ½ teaspoon salt, and the thyme in the skillet and cook, stirring occasionally, until the fennel starts to brown and becomes tender, 3 to 5 minutes.
4. Stir in the garlic, orange juice, and mustard. Bring to a simmer and cook until the liquid reduces a bit, about 2 minutes. Reduce the heat to low, place the chicken skin-side up on top of the fennel, and cover. Cook until the chicken is cooked through and registers 165°F on an instant-read thermometer and the fennel is tender with a slight al dente bite, about 10 minutes.
5. Meanwhile, coarsely chop 1 tablespoon of the reserved fennel fronds.
6. Remove the skillet from the heat, uncover, and sprinkle the fennel fronds on top. Enjoy!

Chicken Piccata

SERVES 2 TO 4 (DEPENDING ON YOUR APPETITE AND SIDES)
◆ PREP TIME: 15 MINUTES ◆ TOTAL TIME: 30 MINUTES

2 boneless, skinless chicken breasts (about 1¼ pounds total)

Kosher salt and freshly ground black pepper

¼ cup all-purpose flour

2 tablespoons extra-virgin olive oil

¾ cup chicken stock

¼ cup drained capers

4 garlic cloves, finely chopped

3 tablespoons unsalted butter, cut into small pieces

2 tablespoons fresh lemon juice

3 tablespoons chopped fresh parsley

This classic Italian American dish has always been a favorite of mine. The bright, briny flavors from the capers and lemon are so fresh and delicious, and it all comes together quickly in just one skillet. It's also my go-to method for achieving perfectly tender pan-seared chicken breasts. Slice the breasts in half horizontally to create thinner pieces, then gently pound them with a meat mallet for even cooking. A light coating of flour not only helps the sauce cling to the chicken but also gives it a silky texture.

I love serving this with Creamy Mashed Potatoes with Chives (page 232) to soak up the sauce, or a simple butter-Parmesan pasta.

1. Slice the chicken breasts horizontally (similar to a butterfly cut) all the way through to create two thinner, even pieces. To do this, place your hand flat on top of one chicken breast to keep it steady and use a sharp knife to carefully cut through the middle from one side to the other. Place the chicken pieces side by side on a cutting board and cover with plastic wrap. Gently pound with the smooth side of a meat mallet until the pieces are an even thickness. Season both sides of the chicken with salt and pepper.
2. Place the flour on a large plate. Working with one at a time, coat both sides of each piece of chicken with flour and transfer to a sheet pan or large plate.
3. In a large skillet, heat the olive oil over medium-high heat. When the oil is shimmering, add the chicken pieces in one layer and cook, undisturbed, until golden brown, about 3 minutes per side. Remove the skillet from the heat and transfer the chicken to a large plate.
4. Return the skillet to medium heat and pour in the stock. Stir, scraping up all the bits stuck to the skillet, then add the capers and garlic. Bring to a simmer and cook, stirring occasionally, until the sauce has reduced by about half, 3 to 4 minutes.
5. Add the butter and lemon juice and stir until the butter has melted. Taste the sauce and season with salt and/or pepper, if desired.
6. Return the chicken to the skillet, nestling it into the sauce. Simmer until the sauce has thickened slightly and the chicken is heated through, 1 to 2 minutes.
7. Transfer the chicken to a serving dish or large plate and spoon the sauce over. Sprinkle the parsley on top. Enjoy!

Honey-Mustard Salmon *with Pistachios and Dill*

SERVES 4 ◆ PREP TIME: 10 MINUTES ◆ TOTAL TIME: 30 MINUTES

HONEY-MUSTARD SALMON

4 (6-ounce) skin-on salmon fillets

Kosher salt and freshly ground black pepper

3 tablespoons Dijon mustard

2 tablespoons honey

1 teaspoon fresh lemon juice

Dash of cayenne pepper

PISTACHIO-DILL TOPPING

¼ cup shelled roasted and salted pistachios, chopped

¼ cup dill sprigs, coarsely chopped

1 teaspoon lemon zest

Big pinch of flaky sea salt, such as Maldon

Lemon wedges, for serving

I've been making this one on repeat

This dish is a spin on a classic honey-mustard salmon I've made countless times. To add some texture to the smooth, buttery roasted salmon, I created a simple yet vibrant topping. It's a mix of fresh dill (my favorite herb for fish!), toasted pistachios, and a pop of bright lemon zest. Not only is it incredibly easy to make, it also looks stunning sprinkled over the salmon. The topping adds an amazing crunch and takes this dish to the next level.

I love serving this salmon with The Simplest Broccoli (page 243), Buttery Lemon Rice with Herbs (page 227), or Mom and Dad's Spinach Salad with Eggs and Mushrooms (page 235).

1. **Make the honey-mustard salmon:** Preheat the oven to 400°F. Line a sheet pan with foil.
2. Place the salmon skin-side down on the prepared sheet pan and generously season the top and sides of the fillets with salt and black pepper.
3. In a small bowl, mix together the mustard, honey, lemon juice, cayenne, a pinch of salt, and a few grinds of black pepper. Spoon the honey-mustard mixture onto the salmon fillets to coat evenly.
4. Bake until the thickest part of the fillet registers 125°F on an instant-read thermometer for super-tender, medium-cooked salmon, about 12 minutes (or a few minutes longer for more well-done salmon).
5. **Meanwhile, make the pistachio-dill topping:** In a small bowl, combine the pistachios, dill, lemon zest, and flaky salt. Mix until all the ingredients are evenly distributed.
6. Remove the salmon from the oven and slide a spatula under the fillets to release them from the foil, leaving the skin behind. Transfer each fillet to a plate and spoon over the pistachio-dill topping to cover the fish. Serve with lemon wedges and enjoy!

Tuesday

let's make it in one pot, pan, or wok

Meals Made Entirely in One Cooking Vessel

It's still early in the week, and the last thing you need is a sink full of dirty dishes—you've got better things to do! That's where one-pot, -pan, and -wok dinners come to the rescue. Every recipe in this chapter is made in a single vessel. You'll find hearty soups and stews, along with one of my ultimate comfort foods: stir-fries (also a great way to eat a bunch of veggies). These recipes are perfect for sharing and feeding a whole family. Try my childhood favorites, like Nana's Broccoli and Swiss Cheese–Stuffed Chicken (page 79) and Mom's Japanese Curry Chicken with Radish and Cauliflower (page 67).

Shrimp and Broccoli Stir-Fry

SERVES 3 OR 4 ◆ PREP TIME: 15 MINUTES ◆ TOTAL TIME: 35 MINUTES

SHRIMP

1 pound large shrimp, peeled and deveined

1 tablespoon oyster sauce

1½ teaspoons cornstarch

½ teaspoon kosher salt

¼ teaspoon freshly ground black pepper

SAUCE

1 cup water

2 tablespoons cornstarch

2 tablespoons soy sauce

1 tablespoon oyster sauce

1 tablespoon rice vinegar

2 teaspoons toasted sesame oil

½ teaspoon sugar

¼ teaspoon freshly ground black pepper

BROCCOLI

Kosher salt

1 pound broccoli, crown cut into florets, stems sliced at an angle into ¼-inch-thick pieces

STIR-FRY

2 tablespoons avocado oil or other neutral oil, divided

3 tablespoons finely chopped fresh ginger

4 garlic cloves, finely chopped

3 scallions, thinly sliced

1 tablespoon rice vinegar

This stir-fry is one of my absolute favorites and an ode to bold Asian flavors. You start with what I call the holy trinity of Chinese cooking—ginger, garlic, and scallions—the three aromatics my mom always taught me to use when making a stir-fry. I especially love the broccoli in this dish as the florets mop up the sauce while the stems add crunch (you know I love texture!). My aunt Susan, who is an amazing cook, taught me to always mix the stir-fry sauce in a glass measuring cup ahead of time, so it's ready to go when you need it. Stir-fries are super easy, but the key is to prep everything before you turn on the heat so you're not running back and forth from the pantry or cutting board to the stove, which can feel a bit chaotic. If you get your prep done beforehand, the process can be fun and relaxing, as it is for me.

I love serving this with freshly cooked Jasmine Rice (page 231).

1. Fill a wok with 2 inches of water and bring to a boil over high heat.
2. **Prepare the shrimp:** In a medium bowl, stir together the shrimp, oyster sauce, cornstarch, salt, and pepper. Cover and refrigerate for up to 15 minutes while you prepare the sauce and cook the broccoli.
3. **Make the sauce:** In a glass measuring cup or small bowl, mix together the water, cornstarch, soy sauce, oyster sauce, vinegar, sesame oil, sugar, and pepper.
4. **Cook the broccoli:** When the water comes to a boil, season with salt and add the broccoli. Cook until bright green, about 1 minute. Drain and set aside.
5. **Make the stir-fry:** In the same wok, heat 1 tablespoon of the avocado oil. Add the shrimp and cook until cooked through and golden brown around the edges, 1 to 2 minutes per side. (The shrimp will turn pink on the outside and be opaque throughout.) Transfer to a large plate.
6. Add the remaining 1 tablespoon avocado oil to the wok. Add the ginger and cook, stirring, for 1 minute. Add the broccoli and garlic and cook, stirring, until the broccoli is crisp-tender, 2 to 3 minutes. (I like my broccoli a little al dente, but you can cook it for longer if you prefer a softer vegetable.)
7. Using a small whisk or spoon, mix the sauce (the cornstarch will have settled) and pour it onto the broccoli. Cook, stirring, until the sauce bubbles, thickens, and coats the broccoli, about 1 minute. Add the shrimp and scallions and cook, stirring, until the sauce coats everything, 1 to 2 minutes more. Remove from the heat and stir in the vinegar. Serve immediately and enjoy!

BUILD YOUR OWN

stir-fry

1 POUND PROTEIN

choose one from here

Chicken (boneless, skinless breasts), cut into ¼-inch-thick bite-size pieces (about 1 by 1½ inches)

Beef (flank steak), cut into ¼-inch-thick bite-size pieces (about 1 by 2 inches)

Shrimp (large), peeled and deveined

Tofu (firm), cut into ¼-inch-thick bite-size pieces (about 1 by 1½ inches)

BASE SAUCE

1 cup water

2 tablespoons cornstarch

2 tablespoons soy sauce

1 tablespoon rice vinegar

2 teaspoons toasted sesame oil

½ teaspoon sugar

¼ teaspoon freshly ground black pepper

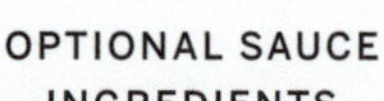

OPTIONAL SAUCE INGREDIENTS

1 tablespoon oyster sauce, for extra umami and depth of flavor (I usually add this)

1 to 2 tablespoons chili garlic sauce, to make it spicy

2 tablespoons creamy natural peanut butter, for a peanut stir-fry

1 to 2 tablespoons gochujang, for a spicy Korean stir-fry

Add one or more of these for extra flavor

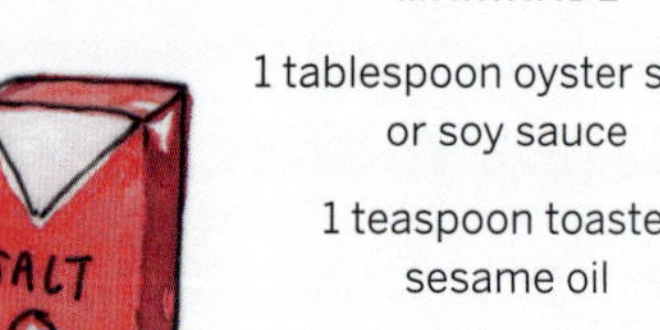

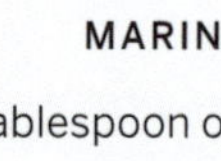

MARINADE

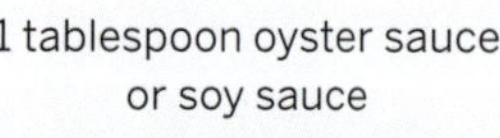

1 tablespoon oyster sauce or soy sauce

1 teaspoon toasted sesame oil

1½ teaspoons cornstarch

½ teaspoon kosher salt

½ teaspoon freshly ground black pepper

The cornstarch helps tenderize the protein

AROMATICS

3 tablespoons finely chopped fresh ginger

3 to 4 garlic cloves, finely chopped

3 scallions, thinly sliced

I always use all three! I call them the holy trinity of Chinese cooking.

FOR COOKING & SERVING

Avocado oil or other neutral oil, such as grapeseed

Kosher salt and freshly ground black pepper

Rice vinegar (optional)

Jasmine Rice (page 231)

1. In a medium bowl, stir together the marinade ingredients and the protein. Marinate at room temperature for 15 minutes or covered in the refrigerator for up to 4 hours. (Shrimp should only be marinated for up to 15 minutes.)

1 TO 2 POUNDS VEGGIES

Carrot, cut at an angle into ¼-inch-thick ovals

Onion, cut into large dice

Celery, cut at an angle into ¼-inch-thick slices

Bell pepper, cut into large dice

Zucchini, cut into ½-inch-thick half-moons

Broccoli florets, blanched in boiling water until bright green, about 1 minute

Water chestnuts (these are hearty, but don't need much time in the wok)

Shiitake mushrooms, sliced

Snow peas

Bean sprouts

These are listed in the order that I would add them to the stir-fry, from hearty to delicate. Mix and match however you like!

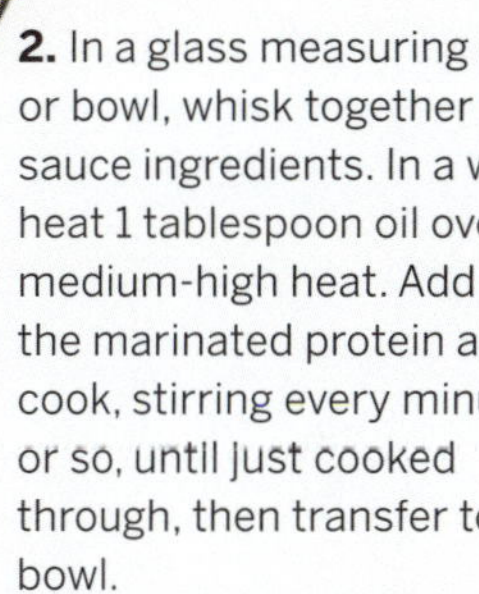

2. In a glass measuring cup or bowl, whisk together the sauce ingredients. In a wok, heat 1 tablespoon oil over medium-high heat. Add the marinated protein and cook, stirring every minute or so, until just cooked through, then transfer to a bowl.

3. Add 1 tablespoon oil and the ginger. Cook, stirring, for 1 minute. Add the garlic and veggies in the order listed, letting the heartier veggies cook for a few minutes before adding the more delicate veggies. Season with salt and pepper. Cook, stirring, until almost to your desired tenderness. Stir the sauce and add it to the wok. Cook until the sauce bubbles and thickens, then return the protein to the wok.

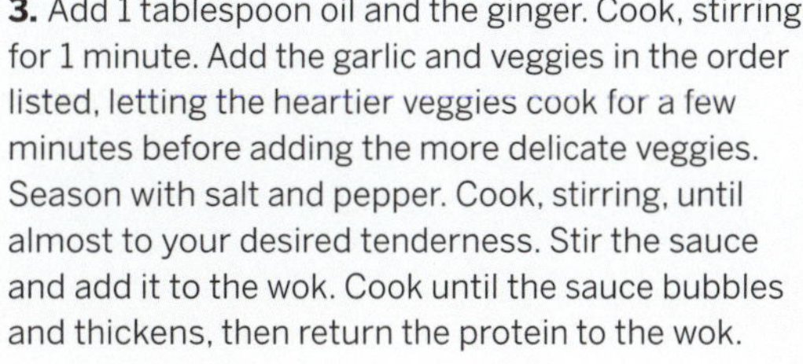

4. Add the scallions and cook, stirring, until everything is coated in sauce. Taste and adjust the seasoning. Add 1 tablespoon rice vinegar, if desired, for a pop of acid and serve over rice.

Enjoy!

Mom's "Beef Pepper Steak" Stir-Fry

SERVES 4 ◆ PREP TIME: 25 MINUTES ◆ TOTAL TIME: 50 MINUTES

MARINATED FLANK STEAK

1 pound flank steak, cut against the grain into ¼-inch thick, bite-size pieces

1 tablespoon soy sauce

1½ teaspoons cornstarch

1 teaspoon toasted sesame oil

½ teaspoon kosher salt

½ teaspoon freshly ground black pepper

SAUCE

¾ cup water

2 tablespoons oyster sauce

1 tablespoon black bean garlic sauce (see Tip)

1 tablespoon cornstarch

1 tablespoon rice vinegar

1 tablespoon soy sauce

½ teaspoon freshly ground black pepper

½ teaspoon sugar

TIP

If you can't find black bean garlic sauce, use 1 tablespoon more oyster sauce.

My mom started cooking when she was just eleven years old. Once a month, her mom worked a late-night hospital shift, and as the eldest of three, my mom was in charge of dinner. My grandma would prep everything ahead of time—the beef and veggies were sliced, the rice measured out—so all my mom had to do was cook. This stir-fry was one of her go-to dishes, and it's been a family favorite ever since. The name of this recipe might not make much sense to anyone outside our family, but that's what we've always called it.

It may seem unusual to add tomatoes to a stir-fry, but they're an essential ingredient that make the dish. They almost melt into the sauce, creating a rich, umami-packed gravy. A spoonful of black bean garlic sauce, a classic Chinese condiment, adds an extra layer of savory depth. Then there are strips of incredibly tender steak and crunchy bell peppers.

I love serving this with freshly cooked Jasmine Rice (page 231) to soak up all that delicious sauce.

STIR-FRY

3 tablespoons avocado oil or other neutral oil, such as grapeseed, divided

3 tablespoons finely chopped fresh ginger, divided

3 garlic cloves, finely chopped, divided

3 green bell peppers (14 ounces), cut into 1-inch squares

Kosher salt and freshly ground black pepper

1 medium yellow onion (10 ounces), cut into small dice

4 medium Roma (plum) tomatoes (1 pound), quartered

2 scallions, sliced

1. **Marinate the flank steak:** In a medium bowl, combine the steak, soy sauce, cornstarch, sesame oil, salt, and black pepper. Mix until the beef is evenly coated, then marinate in the refrigerator for at least 15 minutes or up to 4 hours.
2. **Make the sauce:** In a small glass measuring cup or bowl, combine the water, oyster sauce, black bean garlic sauce, cornstarch, vinegar, soy sauce, black pepper, and sugar. Whisk until the cornstarch has dissolved and set aside.
3. **Make the stir-fry:** In a wok or large nonstick skillet, heat 1 tablespoon of the avocado oil over medium-high heat. Spread the meat over the wok in one layer (as much as possible, depending on the surface of your wok/skillet) and cook, undisturbed, until golden brown, 2 to 3 minutes. Continue to cook, stirring occasionally, until the steak is almost cooked through, 1 to 2 minutes more. Transfer to a large bowl and set aside.
4. Add 1 tablespoon more of the avocado oil to the wok. Add half the ginger and garlic, the bell peppers, and a sprinkle each of salt and black pepper. Cook, stirring occasionally, until the peppers are starting to soften and blister but still have a bite, 3 to 4 minutes. Transfer the peppers to the bowl with the meat.
5. Add the remaining 1 tablespoon avocado oil to the wok, then add the onion. Season with salt and black pepper and cook, stirring occasionally, until tender, 3 to 4 minutes. Transfer to the bowl with the peppers and meat.
6. Add the tomatoes and the remaining garlic and ginger to the wok. Cook, stirring, until starting to soften, 2 to 3 minutes. Return the peppers, onion, and meat to the wok.
7. Whisk the sauce (the cornstarch will have settled) and pour it into the wok. Increase the heat to high and bring the sauce to a simmer. Cook, stirring, until the sauce thickens, 1 to 2 minutes.
8. Stir in the scallions and remove from the heat. Serve immediately and enjoy!

↖ A very special dish in my family ♡

Crustless Supreme Pizza Skillet

SERVES 4 ◆ PREP TIME: 15 MINUTES ◆ TOTAL TIME: 45 MINUTES

1 tablespoon extra-virgin olive oil

1 pound mild Italian chicken or pork sausage, casings removed

1 medium yellow onion (10 ounces), thinly sliced

1 green bell pepper (6 ounces), cut into ½-inch pieces

3 garlic cloves, thinly sliced

1 teaspoon dried oregano

1 teaspoon kosher salt

½ teaspoon crushed red pepper flakes

8 ounces cremini mushrooms, sliced

1 cup pizza sauce, store-bought or homemade (see page 189)

2 cups (8 ounces) shredded mozzarella cheese

⅓ cup pepperoni

Fresh basil leaves, for serving

While I love a good Neapolitan pizza, I'll always have a soft spot for a supreme pizza loaded with all the toppings. It was my go-to frozen pizza of choice as a kid, and honestly, it still hits the spot. This recipe is a lighter, more grown-up take—no crust, just all the toppings and flavors you love, cooked together in a skillet. The chicken sausage, bell peppers, mushrooms, and onion are coated in a delicious tomato sauce. And, of course, there's a generous layer of melted cheese and plenty of crispy pepperoni on top. Doug loved it so much that he ate the leftovers for lunch two days in a row!

1. In a large ovenproof skillet, heat the olive oil over medium-high heat. Add the sausage and cook, breaking it up into smaller pieces with a spatula, until golden brown and cooked through, about 5 minutes. Transfer the sausage to a large plate or bowl and set aside.
2. Add the onion, bell pepper, garlic, oregano, salt, and red pepper flakes to the skillet. Cook, stirring, until the vegetables are starting to soften, about 4 minutes. Add the mushrooms and cook, stirring, until everything is almost tender but not quite, about 4 minutes more. Return the sausage to the skillet and stir to combine. Scoop out ½ cup of the sausage and vegetable mixture and set it aside for topping (in step 5).
3. Add the pizza sauce to the skillet and cook, stirring, until heated through, 1 to 2 minutes. Remove from the heat and spread the contents of the skillet in an even layer.
4. Position a rack in the upper third of the oven and turn on the broiler.
5. Sprinkle the mozzarella in an even layer over the skillet. Add the reserved sausage and vegetables on top, spacing them evenly as you would if you were topping a pizza. Place the pepperoni on top.
6. Transfer the skillet to the top rack in the oven and broil until the pepperoni is curled and crispy and the cheese is deep golden brown, 5 to 7 minutes. Check every few minutes to make sure the top isn't browning too much. Remove from the oven and allow to cool for 5 minutes before serving.
7. Top with basil leaves and enjoy!

Creamy White Chicken Chili

SERVES 4 ◆ PREP TIME: 25 MINUTES ◆ TOTAL TIME: 1 HOUR 10 MINUTES

2 tablespoons extra-virgin olive oil

2 poblano peppers (about 6 ounces), stemmed, seeded, and finely chopped

1 large yellow onion (12 ounces), cut into small dice

4 garlic cloves, finely chopped

1 (4-ounce) can diced mild green chilies

2 teaspoons kosher salt

1½ teaspoons ground cumin

½ teaspoon dried oregano

½ teaspoon freshly ground black pepper

4 cups chicken stock

1 pound boneless, skinless chicken breast, cut in half

2 (15-ounce) cans cannellini beans or other white beans, drained and rinsed

½ cup light sour cream

3 tablespoons finely chopped fresh cilantro

1 lime, halved

FOR SERVING

Shredded Mexican-style cheese blend

Sliced avocado

Tortilla chips

Coarsely chopped fresh cilantro

This white bean chicken chili is comfort in a bowl—warm, hearty, and just light enough to enjoy any time of year, whether it's a chilly winter evening or a warm spring day. It has tons of flavor and a gentle kick from the green chilies, poblanos, and dried spices, like cumin and oregano. Most important, don't skip the toppings! They're essential to making the dish truly shine. Tortilla chips add a nice crunch, while sour cream and cheese melt into the broth. A sprinkle of cilantro and a squeeze of lime juice brighten the chili with a fresh pop.

1. In a large pot, heat the olive oil over medium-high heat. Add the poblanos, onion, and garlic. Cook, stirring, until the onion starts to become translucent, 3 to 4 minutes. Add the green chilies with their juices, the salt, cumin, oregano, and black pepper. Cook, stirring, until fragrant, 1 to 2 minutes. Stir in the stock and chicken breast.

2. Bring to a boil over high heat, then reduce the heat to low, cover, and simmer, stirring once or twice, until the chicken is cooked through and an instant-read thermometer inserted into the thickest part registers 165°F, about 15 minutes. Transfer the chicken to a plate and set aside until cool enough to handle.

3. Place the beans in the pot, increase the heat to high, and bring to a boil. Cook for 3 minutes, smashing some of the beans with a wooden spoon to break them down. (You want about a quarter of the beans to get broken down.) Reduce the heat to low and simmer for 5 minutes.

4. Meanwhile, using your fingers or two forks, shred the chicken into small bite-size pieces. Return the chicken to the pot and cook until heated through, about 1 minute. Remove from the heat and stir in the sour cream and cilantro. Squeeze in some lime juice to taste (start with the juice of ½ lime and add more, if you like).

5. **To serve:** Divide the chicken chili among four bowls and top with a generous amount of cheese, slices of avocado, a few tortilla chips, and a sprinkle of cilantro. Enjoy!

Thai Red Curry Poached Cod *with Bok Choy*

SERVES 4 ◆ PREP TIME: 10 MINUTES ◆ TOTAL TIME: 30 MINUTES

4 (5- to 6-ounce) skinless cod fillets

Kosher salt

1 tablespoon avocado oil or other neutral oil, such as grapeseed

2 tablespoons red curry paste, preferably Mae Ploy or Maesri

1 (13.5-ounce) can full-fat coconut milk

1½ cups water

1 tablespoon fish sauce

1 tablespoon sugar

2 baby bok choy (9 ounces total), quartered through the bulb

Juice of ½ lime

½ cup (½ ounce) fresh basil leaves, plus more for serving

Thinly sliced Thai (spicy) or Fresno (less spicy) chili, for serving (optional)

This one is *so* yummy & great for a busy night

This fish curry strikes a perfect balance of flavors, and the result is mind-blowingly good. It's got a nice spicy kick from curry paste, creaminess from the coconut milk, and a bright finish from fresh basil and a squeeze of lime. Best of all, it's ready in just 30 minutes.

Curry paste is the star ingredient here, and my favorite brand is Mae Ploy. Packed with a blend of aromatics, herbs, and chilies, just a few tablespoons transforms the broth into an incredibly fragrant curry with a gentle, lingering heat. The fish is poached directly in the broth, a simple and foolproof method that keeps it tender. Cod is delicate, so don't worry if it flakes apart a bit, it'll mix in with the curry and only make it more delicious.

I love serving this with freshly cooked Jasmine Rice (page 231).

1. Generously season both sides of the cod with salt.
2. In a large pot with a lid, heat the avocado oil over medium-high heat. Add the curry paste and cook, stirring, until fragrant and sizzling, about 1 minute.
3. Add the coconut milk, water, fish sauce, and sugar. Stir to dissolve the curry paste and add the bok choy. Bring to a simmer over high heat, then reduce the heat to low.
4. Place the cod fillets over the bok choy, gently pushing down to partially submerge them. Cover and simmer until the fish is cooked through and the bok choy is tender (the bulb should be slightly firm and the greens wilted), 8 to 10 minutes.
5. Remove from the heat and gently stir in the lime juice and basil leaves.
6. Divide the fish and bok choy among bowls. Spoon the red curry sauce over the top. Garnish with more basil leaves and chili slices, if desired, and enjoy!

Sheet Pan Mediterranean Chicken Plate *with Chickpeas and Tzatziki*

SERVES 4 ◆ PREP TIME: 20 MINUTES
◆ TOTAL TIME: 1 HOUR 10 MINUTES, PLUS 1 HOUR FOR MARINATING

MARINATED CHICKEN

3 tablespoons extra-virgin olive oil

Juice of ½ lemon

3 garlic cloves, finely chopped

1½ teaspoons paprika

1½ teaspoons ground cumin

1½ teaspoons kosher salt

1 teaspoon dried oregano

½ teaspoon freshly ground black pepper

1½ pounds boneless, skinless chicken thighs

TZATZIKI

1 large English cucumber (12 ounces), halved crosswise

2 cups plain full-fat or 2% Greek yogurt

1 garlic clove, grated

2 tablespoons fresh lemon juice, plus more if needed

1 tablespoon extra-virgin olive oil

½ teaspoon kosher salt, plus more if needed

This Mediterranean chicken plate comes together on a single sheet pan for the easiest cleanup. A simple marinade of spices, garlic, and lemon infuses the chicken with loads of flavor while keeping it tender. It roasts alongside chickpeas and red onion, which turns soft and sweet, almost caramelized, with beautifully charred edges after a quick broil.

At the end, the pita gets tossed in the leftover spice-infused oil and crisps up in the oven while you slice the chicken. To balance it all out, there's a refreshing tzatziki—Doug's favorite. (If tzatziki is involved, I know he's going to love the meal!)

1. **Marinate the chicken:** In a large bowl, combine the olive oil, lemon juice, garlic, paprika, cumin, salt, oregano, and pepper. Mix until well combined. Add the chicken and toss to coat evenly in the marinade. Cover and refrigerate for at least 1 hour or up to 6 hours.
2. Position racks in the middle and upper third of the oven and preheat to 425°F.
3. **Make the tzatziki:** Slice half the cucumber and set it aside for serving. Grate the other half into a medium bowl. Add the yogurt, garlic, lemon juice, olive oil, and salt. Mix until combined, then taste and add more lemon juice and/or salt, if you like. The tzatziki can be stored in an airtight container in the refrigerator for up to 4 days.
4. **Prepare the chickpeas:** Pour the chickpeas onto a sheet pan and pat dry with paper towels. Add the onion, olive oil, cumin, and salt. Using your hands, mix everything together until evenly coated and spread the ingredients into a single layer on the pan.
5. Add the chicken to the sheet pan, nestling it among the chickpeas and ensuring that each piece of chicken is making contact with the pan. Using a spatula, scrape out any marinade left in the bowl onto the sheet pan, drizzling it onto the chicken and chickpeas.
6. Roast on the middle rack until the chicken is cooked through and an instant-read thermometer inserted into the thickest part registers 165°F, about 30 minutes. Move the sheet pan to the top rack and turn on the broiler. Broil until the chicken is golden brown and a bit charred, 3 to 5 minutes.

CHICKPEAS

2 (15-ounce) cans chickpeas, drained and rinsed

1 medium red onion (10 ounces), thinly sliced

3 tablespoons extra-virgin olive oil

1 tablespoon ground cumin

1 teaspoon kosher salt

PITAS AND FOR SERVING

2 pitas

Extra-virgin olive oil (optional)

Chopped fresh parsley (optional)

7. Remove the sheet pan from the oven and transfer the chicken to a plate; keep the broiler on. Cover the chicken with foil and let rest while you toast the pitas.

8. **Toast the pitas:** Push the chickpeas to the sides of the sheet pan, making room in the center of the pan. Working with one piece at a time, toss the pitas in the oil remaining on the sheet pan until lightly coated. If the pan seems a bit dry, you can drizzle the pitas with a little olive oil. Place the pan back on the top rack and broil until the pitas are golden brown and warmed through and some of the onion is charred, 1 to 3 minutes. Meanwhile, slice the chicken.

9. **To serve:** Cut each pita into 6 triangles and divide among four plates (3 triangles per plate). Divide the chicken, chickpeas, and onion among the plates. Add the cucumber slices and top with a generous dollop of tzatziki. Sprinkle with the parsley, if you like, and serve the remaining tzatziki on the side. Enjoy!

This was the final recipe I developed for the book and it's such a winner! →

Mom's Japanese Curry Chicken *with Radish and Cauliflower*

SERVES 4 OR 5 ◆ PREP TIME: 15 MINUTES ◆ TOTAL TIME: 1 HOUR

2 tablespoons avocado oil or other neutral oil, such as grapeseed, divided

1 pound boneless, skinless chicken breasts, cut into large dice

2 teaspoons kosher salt, divided

1 medium yellow onion (10 ounces), cut into large dice

2 tablespoons finely chopped fresh ginger

3 carrots (about 8 ounces), cut into ½-inch-thick rounds

3 celery stalks (about 6 ounces), cut into 1-inch pieces

5 ounces radishes (from 1 bunch), halved

2 small Yukon Gold potatoes (about 10 ounces), cut into 1 by ½-inch pieces

7 ounces cauliflower, cut into bite-size florets

3 cups water

1 (3.2-ounce) box Golden Curry by S&B Japanese curry mix (I like medium-hot), broken into small pieces

1 tablespoon rice vinegar (optional, but recommended!)

Jasmine Rice (page 231), for serving

This Japanese curry is the first recipe my mom ever learned to cook. Whenever her parents worked late at the hospital (both were pharmacists), she would make dinner for her younger sisters. Naturally, this dish became a regular part of our dinner rotation when I was growing up. My dad even took over making it when my mom was busy with work, since he often had more time in the evenings. (By the way, when my mom retested the recipe for my cookbook and my dad got to taste it, he said it was the best he's ever had—way better than when he used to make it himself!) We especially love this version because it has so many veggies. The radishes are a standout: They soften as they cook, losing their spicy bite and transforming into something like a lighter, milder potato. It's a nourishing dinner that I hope will find its way into your family's rotation, too.

1. In a large pot, heat 1 tablespoon of the avocado oil over medium-high heat. Add the chicken in one layer and sprinkle with 1 teaspoon of the salt. Cook, stirring occasionally, until golden and cooked through, 4 to 6 minutes. Transfer the chicken to a large plate or bowl.
2. Add the remaining 1 tablespoon avocado oil to the skillet, then add the onion and ginger. Cook, stirring, until fragrant, about 1 minute. Add the carrots, celery, radishes, and remaining 1 teaspoon salt. Cook, stirring, for 1 minute. Add the potatoes and cauliflower and cook, stirring, for 1 minute more.
3. Add the water and bring to a boil over high heat. Reduce the heat to low, cover, and simmer until the vegetables are almost tender, 10 to 15 minutes.
4. Uncover the pot and add the chicken and curry mix. Increase the heat to medium and cook, stirring, until the curry mix has dissolved, 3 to 5 minutes.
5. Remove from the heat and stir in the vinegar, if desired. Divide the rice among bowls and spoon the curry over rice. Enjoy!

Grandpa's Jjigae

my ultimate comfort food

SERVES 4 ◆ PREP TIME: 15 MINUTES ◆ TOTAL TIME: 1 HOUR

3 ounces sweet potato (glass) noodles

4 cups water, plus more for soaking the noodles

8 ounces green cabbage, cut into 1-inch squares (2 cups)

8 ounces daikon, cut into thin, bite-size pieces (2 cups)

1 tablespoon kosher salt, plus more if needed

1 large yellow onion (12 ounces), cut into large dice

1 pound boneless beef short ribs (or chuck roast), thinly sliced against the grain into bite-size pieces

5 large garlic cloves, finely chopped

¼ cup gochujang

2 tablespoons soy sauce

1 (14-ounce) package firm tofu, drained and cut into 1-inch cubes

3½ ounces enoki mushrooms, roots sliced off, or other mushrooms, such as sliced shiitake or oyster

6 scallions, halved lengthwise, then cut crosswise into 1-inch pieces

2 tablespoons rice vinegar

Whenever I'm missing home, this is the recipe I turn to. Even the process of making jjigae feels like a warm hug—it's so familiar and soothing. I know exactly how everything needs to be cut and always prep the ingredients in the same order. I could probably make it with my eyes closed!

This recipe comes from my grandpa, who's no longer with us. He was an incredible cook with a keen sense of taste—he was even in charge of developing the flavors of liquid medicine produced by Abbott Labs. He was also famously particular in the kitchen—constantly peeking over our shoulders, making sure everything was just right, from how we cut the vegetables to how much seasoning we added. His highest compliment was when he'd take a bite and say, "Just like downtown!," a reference to where the restaurants were when my mom was growing up. Many of our family recipes come from him, but this stew might be my favorite. Every time I make it, I feel like I'm honoring his memory. It's hearty, comforting, and packed with nourishing veggies, while the sweet potato noodles add a perfectly chewy texture. Just writing about it makes me want to make it all over again.

1. Place the sweet potato noodles in a large bowl and cover with warm water by 2 inches. Set aside to soak while you prepare the other ingredients. (This will prevent the noodles from absorbing too much liquid in the stew.)
2. In a large pot, combine the water, cabbage, daikon, and salt. Bring to a boil over high heat, then reduce the heat to low, cover, and simmer for 5 minutes.
3. Stir in the onion and increase the heat to high. Bring the mixture back to a boil, then reduce the heat to low, cover, and simmer for 5 minutes.
4. Stir in the short ribs and garlic, increase the heat to high, and return the mixture to a boil. Reduce the heat to low, cover, and simmer for 5 minutes.
5. In a small bowl, stir together the gochujang and soy sauce. Add a ladle of hot broth from the pot and stir to combine. Add the gochujang mixture to the pot and stir to combine. Stir in the tofu and mushrooms. Increase the heat to high and bring the mixture back to a boil, then reduce the heat to low, cover, and simmer for 5 minutes.
6. Drain the sweet potato noodles and stir them into the pot. Add the scallions and vinegar and stir to combine. Cover and simmer until the noodles are cooked to your desired tenderness, 3 to 5 minutes. Taste and season with more salt, if desired. Divide among four bowls and enjoy!

Mom's Skillet Chicken Pot Pie

SERVES 6 ◆ PREP TIME: 30 MINUTES ◆ TOTAL TIME: 1 HOUR 30 MINUTES

2 boneless, skinless chicken breasts (about 1¼ pounds total), cut into bite-size cubes

Kosher salt and freshly ground black pepper

1 tablespoon avocado oil or other neutral oil, such as grapeseed

1 tablespoon unsalted butter

1 small leek (5 ounces), halved lengthwise and thinly sliced, cleaned thoroughly

8 ounces cremini or button mushrooms, quartered

2 celery stalks (4 ounces), cut into ¼-inch-thick slices

1 medium onion (10 ounces), cut into large dice

1 medium carrot (5 ounces), cut into medium dice

4 ounces green beans, cut into 1-inch pieces (¾ cup)

My dad loves pot pie so much that he'll often put in a special request for it for dinner. To keep things a bit healthier during the week, my mom perfected her own "lightened-up" version. She swaps milk for cream, uses just one crust, and keeps it simple by making everything in one skillet. A store-bought crust is draped over the savory filling and baked until golden. The result is a cozy, veggie-packed stew with tender pieces of flaky crust. It's hearty yet balanced, and every bite reminds me of home.

To make this recipe quicker and easier, you can replace the celery, carrot, green beans, and peas with 12 ounces (3 cups) of your favorite frozen mixed vegetables. Add them in step 6 with the chicken.

3 garlic cloves, finely chopped

1 tablespoon finely chopped fresh thyme leaves

¼ cup plus 2 tablespoons all-purpose flour, plus more for dusting

1 cup whole milk

1½ cups chicken stock

¼ cup dry white wine

1 cup frozen peas

1 tablespoon fresh lemon juice

1 (7-ounce) refrigerated pie crust, such as Pillsbury

1 large egg, beaten with 1 tablespoon water, for egg wash (optional)

1. Preheat the oven to 425°F.
2. Season the chicken with 1 teaspoon salt and ½ teaspoon pepper.
3. In a large deep skillet (11 to 12 inches), heat the avocado oil over medium-high heat. Add the chicken in a single layer and cook until golden brown and almost cooked through, 6 to 8 minutes, flipping once halfway through. Transfer to a large plate.
4. Reduce the heat to medium and add the butter and leek to the skillet. Cook, stirring often, until the leek is starting to become tender, 2 to 3 minutes. Add the mushrooms, celery, onion, carrot, green beans, garlic, and thyme. Season with 1 teaspoon salt. Increase the heat to medium-high and cook, stirring often, until the onion starts to become translucent and the vegetables reduce a bit, 6 to 8 minutes.
5. Add the flour and cook, stirring, for 1 minute. Add the milk in two additions, stirring to incorporate before adding more. Add the stock, ½ cup at a time, stirring to incorporate before adding more.
6. Stir in the wine and peas, and return the chicken to the skillet. Bring to a boil over high heat, then reduce the heat to low and simmer until the sauce thickens and reduces slightly, 3 to 5 minutes. Stir in the lemon juice, taste, and season with salt and/or pepper, if desired. Remove the skillet from the heat and set aside to cool for 10 minutes.
7. On a lightly floured work surface, roll out the dough into a 13-inch round (slightly larger than the skillet). Lay the dough over the skillet, letting it overhang the edges slightly. Gently press the dough against the edges of the skillet, crimping it with your fingers to seal. Using a sharp paring knife, cut four slits in the dough to vent steam.

8. Brush the dough with the egg wash, if you like. Place the skillet on a sheet pan (to catch any drips) and transfer to the oven.
9. Bake until the crust is golden brown, about 30 minutes. (The crust may slide off the sides of the skillet—don't worry if that happens! Just break off the pieces on the edges and serve them with the filling.) Remove from the oven and let cool for 10 minutes before serving. Enjoy!

Hot and Sour Soup

SERVES 4 ◆ PREP TIME: 30 MINUTES
◆ TOTAL TIME: 1 HOUR, PLUS 20 MINUTES FOR SOAKING (SEE TIPS)

SHIITAKE MUSHROOMS

6 dried shiitake mushrooms

Boiling water, for soaking

MARINATED PORK

1 pork tenderloin (about 1 pound), cut into thin, bite-size strips (see Tips)

2 teaspoons soy sauce

1 tablespoon water

1 teaspoon cornstarch

1 teaspoon toasted sesame oil

½ teaspoon kosher salt

¼ teaspoon ground white pepper

Growing up, we loved going to our local Chinese restaurant after water polo games (my brothers and I all played competitively!), and we always started the meal with one of our favorite dishes—hot and sour soup. These days, when I'm craving something hearty and packed with bold Asian flavors, I make this homemade version. Sambal oelek, a spicy Indonesian chili sauce, and white pepper add just the right amount of heat (white pepper has a distinct, almost earthy kick that I love), while white vinegar brings that signature tangy finish. Be sure to taste before serving and adjust the seasonings to suit your preferences—add a little extra vinegar for more acidity or a bit more sambal oelek if you like it spicier.

SOUP

¼ cup cornstarch

¼ cup water

2 large eggs

2 tablespoons avocado oil or other neutral oil, such as grapeseed

1 small carrot (about 3 ounces), cut into matchsticks

1 (2-inch) piece fresh ginger, cut into thin matchsticks

4 garlic cloves, finely chopped

8 cups chicken stock

1 (8-ounce) can sliced bamboo shoots, drained

8 ounces extra-firm tofu, cut into bite-size rectangles

2 tablespoons soy sauce

1 tablespoon sambal oelek, plus more if needed

1 teaspoon ground white pepper

½ teaspoon kosher salt

½ teaspoon sugar

3 scallions, thinly sliced

¼ cup distilled white vinegar, plus more if needed

1 tablespoon toasted sesame oil

1. **Soak the mushrooms:** Place the shiitake mushrooms in a heatproof medium bowl. Cover with boiling water and set aside until rehydrated, about 20 minutes (see Tips). Drain, cut into ¼-inch-thick slices, and set aside.
2. **Marinate the pork:** In a medium bowl, combine the pork, soy sauce, water, cornstarch, sesame oil, salt, and white pepper. Mix well to coat the pork, cover, and refrigerate for up to 30 minutes while you start making the soup.
3. **Make the soup:** In a small bowl, whisk together the cornstarch and water until combined. Set aside.
4. In a separate small bowl, whisk together the eggs and set aside.
5. In a large pot, heat the avocado oil over medium-high heat. Add the rehydrated shiitakes, the carrot, ginger, and garlic. Cook, stirring, until the carrot starts to become tender, 1 to 2 minutes.
6. Add the stock, bamboo shoots, tofu, soy sauce, sambal oelek, white pepper, salt, and sugar. Stir and bring to a simmer over medium-high heat.
7. Stir in the pork and simmer until cooked through, about 3 minutes. (Reduce the heat if needed to maintain a gentle simmer.)
8. Whisk the cornstarch mixture (the cornstarch will have settled) and, while stirring, slowly pour it into the soup. Return the broth to a simmer and cook until slightly thickened, 2 to 3 minutes.
9. While gently stirring, drizzle the eggs into the soup to create ribbons.
10. Stir in the scallions, vinegar, and sesame oil, then remove from the heat. Taste and adjust with more sambal oelek to make it spicier and/or more vinegar to make it more sour. Divide among four bowls and enjoy!

TIPS

While the mushrooms are soaking, prep all the other ingredients. By the time the mushrooms are rehydrated, you should be all set to cook the soup!

You could also use pork shoulder or butt, which are fattier cuts than tenderloin.

Mom's Loaded Vegetable Soup

2 tablespoons extra-virgin olive oil, plus more for drizzling

1 small yellow onion (6 ounces), cut into medium dice

2 small carrots (4 ounces), halved lengthwise and cut into ¼-inch-thick half-moons

1 celery stalk (2 ounces), cut into medium dice

2 garlic cloves, finely chopped

1 large leek (8 ounces), halved lengthwise and thinly sliced crosswise, cleaned thoroughly

1 medium yellow squash or zucchini (8 ounces), cut into medium dice

4 cups chicken stock or vegetable stock

1 tablespoon Italian seasoning

1½ teaspoons kosher salt, plus more if needed

½ teaspoon freshly ground black pepper

½ teaspoon sugar

6 ounces green beans, cut into ½-inch pieces (1 heaping cup)

1 (14-ounce) can chickpeas, drained and rinsed

1 (28-ounce) can diced tomatoes

½ cup (½ ounce) fresh basil leaves, chopped

Freshly grated Parmesan cheese, for serving

SERVES 6 ◆ PREP TIME: 30 MINUTES ◆ TOTAL TIME: 1 HOUR

This is my mom's staple healthy soup—light, flavorful, and perfect for enjoying on repeat (my dad loves it, too!). She often makes a big batch to have on hand for easy, satisfying meals throughout the week. It's also super flexible—feel free to toss in whatever veggies you have available, or swap in different beans to make it your own. Just don't hold back on the grated Parm at the end. It adds a touch of richness as it melts into the soup and is always how my mom serves it!

1. In a large pot, heat the olive oil over medium heat. Add the onion, carrots, and celery. Cook, stirring, until the onion starts to become translucent, 3 to 4 minutes.
2. Add the garlic, leek, and squash. Cook, stirring, until the vegetables are starting to become tender, 2 to 3 minutes.
3. Add the stock, Italian seasoning, salt, pepper, and sugar. Stir to combine and bring to a boil over high heat. Add the green beans, chickpeas, and tomatoes with their juices. Reduce the heat to low, cover, and simmer until the vegetables are tender, 10 to 15 minutes.
4. Uncover and stir in the basil. Taste and season with more salt, if desired. Divide the soup among serving bowls. Drizzle with a little olive oil and top with a generous amount of Parmesan. Enjoy!

Cheesy Enchilada Skillet *with Crunchy Tortilla Chips*

SERVES 4 ◆ PREP TIME: 15 MINUTES ◆ TOTAL TIME: 40 MINUTES

1 tablespoon extra-virgin olive oil

½ medium yellow onion (5 ounces), cut into small dice

2 garlic cloves, finely chopped

1 pound lean ground beef or ground turkey

1½ teaspoons chili powder

1 teaspoon ground cumin

1 teaspoon kosher salt

Dash of cayenne pepper

1 (15-ounce) can black beans, drained and rinsed

1 (15-ounce) jar or can red enchilada sauce

1 (6-ounce) can diced mild green chilies

6 (5- to 6-inch) corn tortillas, cut into 8 small triangles each

1 cup (4 ounces) shredded Mexican-style cheese blend

FOR SERVING

2 tablespoons finely chopped fresh cilantro

Sour cream

Pickled jalapeños

Avocado slices

Lime wedges

Tortilla chips

This one-skillet meal is pure comfort food and couldn't be easier to make. Everything comes together in one vessel, making it a great recipe for beginners or anyone in the mood for a quick dinner. The tortillas soften and almost melt into the sauce, creating a cozy base for all the toppings—spicy pickled jalapeños, tangy sour cream, and crunchy tortilla chips. The best part is that you get to pick your own adventure. Doug likes to go nacho-style, scooping up the saucy enchilada filling with the chips, while I prefer crumbling them on top for a little crunch in every bite.

1. Position a rack in the upper third of the oven and preheat to 425°F.
2. In a large ovenproof skillet, heat the olive oil over medium heat. Add the onion and cook, stirring, until translucent and starting to become tender, 3 to 4 minutes. Add the garlic and cook, stirring, for 1 minute.
3. Add the ground beef, chili powder, cumin, salt, and cayenne and cook, breaking up the beef with a spatula, until cooked through, 3 to 4 minutes.
4. Add the beans, enchilada sauce, and chilies with their juices and stir to combine. Add the tortillas and stir to submerge them in the sauce. Cook until the sauce is bubbling, 3 to 4 minutes.
5. Sprinkle the cheese evenly over the mixture in the skillet and transfer to the oven. Bake until the cheese is melted and the sauce is bubbling, about 10 minutes. For a deeper golden brown top, broil for 1 to 2 minutes. Remove from the oven and let rest for 5 minutes.
6. **To serve:** Top the skillet with the cilantro. Serve with sour cream, pickled jalapeños, avocado slices, lime wedges, and tortilla chips for crumbling on top or scooping. Enjoy!

This is a great recipe for beginners

Nana's Broccoli and Swiss Cheese–Stuffed Chicken

SERVES 4 TO 6 ◆ PREP TIME: 30 MINUTES ◆ TOTAL TIME: 1 HOUR 30 MINUTES

3 tablespoons unsalted butter, cut into 6 equal pieces, plus more for greasing

3 large boneless, skinless chicken breasts (about 2 pounds total)

Kosher salt and freshly ground black pepper

½ cup Italian-style breadcrumbs

⅓ cup (1.3 ounces) grated Parmesan cheese

16 slices Swiss cheese (about 13 ounces; see Tip)

1 pound frozen broccoli florets

TIP

We love using aged Swiss cheese—if you can find it, try it!

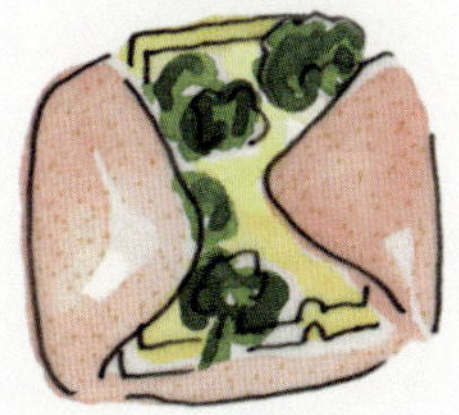

This is a cherished recipe from my dad's side of the family. My nana—a true New Yorker with impeccable style—was always effortlessly chic, her long blond hair just as stunning in her later years as it was in her youth. This stuffed chicken is one of her signature dishes, and it's become a beloved family staple. The cheese on top bakes to golden, crispy perfection, while the inside stays irresistibly melty. And while I usually prefer my veggies with a little bite, this is the one recipe where soft, tender broccoli is the way to go. It blends into the breadcrumb-and-Parmesan mixture, making every bite pure comfort.

1. Preheat the oven to 350°F. Lightly butter a 9 by 13-inch baking dish.
2. Working with one chicken breast at a time, place the chicken between two pieces of plastic wrap and pound with the flat side of a meat mallet (or a heavy skillet) to ¼-inch thickness. Slice each breast in half crosswise to create two equal-size pieces. Season both sides of the chicken with salt and pepper.
3. In a large shallow bowl, stir together the breadcrumbs and Parmesan. Place the Swiss cheese and broccoli close by for easy access.
4. Working with one piece of chicken at a time, coat both sides in the breadcrumb mixture, pressing it on with your fingers, then place in the prepared baking dish. Place one piece of Swiss cheese on top of the chicken, then place about ⅓ cup of the broccoli florets on top of the cheese. Roll up the chicken to enclose the broccoli and cheese and place it seam-side down in the dish. Don't worry if the broccoli spills out, just tuck it back in with your fingers. Repeat until all the chicken is stuffed.
5. Nestle any remaining broccoli around the chicken in the dish. Season any of the exposed broccoli with salt and pepper and sprinkle the remaining breadcrumb-Parmesan mixture on top.
6. Place one piece of butter on each piece of chicken. Cover everything completely with the remaining Swiss cheese, slightly overlapping the edges.
7. Bake until the internal temperature of the chicken registers 165°F on an instant-read thermometer, 55 to 60 minutes. Turn on the broiler and broil until the cheese is golden brown, 2 to 3 minutes. Remove from the oven and let rest for 5 minutes before serving. Enjoy!

Wednesday

let's have some fun

Vibrant Recipes to Spark Your Creativity: Sandwiches, Tacos, Wraps, and Colorful Bowls

By the time Wednesday rolls around, you might be craving a little excitement. These recipes are designed to pull you out of the midweek slump. Think handhelds like tacos and sandwiches, and colorful bowls with lots of elements so you can mix and match with every bite. Some of these dishes will feel more laid-back and casual, like Grandpa's Giant Baked Italian Sub (page 96), a beloved family staple. Others are interactive and fun, like my Healthy Shrimp Tacos with Cilantro-Lime Cabbage Slaw (page 106), where you can bring the skillet to the table and let everyone build their own tacos.

Rice Paper Egg Wrap *with Thai Peanut Slaw*

SERVES 1 ◆ PREP TIME: 10 MINUTES ◆ TOTAL TIME: 20 MINUTES

PEANUT SLAW

1 tablespoon creamy natural peanut butter

1 teaspoon rice vinegar

½ teaspoon soy sauce

½ teaspoon sriracha

1 teaspoon water

¾ cup thinly sliced red cabbage

¼ cup shredded or julienned carrot

WRAP

2 large eggs

Kosher salt and freshly ground black pepper

2 teaspoons avocado oil or other neutral oil, such as grapeseed

1 rice paper wrapper

1 scallion, thinly sliced

Chili crisp (optional)

FOR SERVING

6 to 8 fresh basil leaves

Toasted sesame seeds (optional)

This quick, simple meal for one is ideal for those nights when you're on your own and want something easy yet satisfying. Egg wraps are one of my go-to fuss-free dinners, but this time, I decided to switch things up with a Thai peanut slaw inspired by the peanut sauce that comes with chicken satay. I'll admit, I was a little unsure how peanut sauce would pair with eggs, but turns out it's incredible! The slaw is packed with crunch from the cabbage and carrots, a kick of heat from the sriracha, and a fragrant touch from the fresh basil. The combination is a delightful explosion of flavors and textures. Once wrapped up, it looks hearty and substantial yet somehow feels light. I can't wait for you to try it!

1. **Make the peanut slaw:** In a medium bowl, whisk together the peanut butter, vinegar, soy sauce, sriracha, and water until combined. Add the cabbage and carrot and mix until the sauce evenly coats the vegetables. Set aside.
2. **Make the wrap:** Crack the eggs into a small bowl, season with a sprinkle each of salt and pepper, and beat with a fork to combine.
3. Choose a skillet about the same size as the rice paper wrapper. In the skillet, heat the avocado oil over medium heat. Tilt the skillet to evenly coat, then place the rice paper wrapper in the skillet, textured-side down, and sprinkle the scallion evenly over the rice paper.
4. Pour the eggs into the center of the rice paper. Using chopsticks or a spoon, push them toward the perimeter of the rice paper so they cover the rice paper in an even layer. (Don't worry if the egg spills over the rice paper, just push it back toward the edges of the paper as it sets.) Cook, undisturbed, until the eggs are set, 2 to 3 minutes. Drizzle a little chili crisp on top, if desired.
5. **To serve:** Use a spatula to transfer the egg wrap to a large plate (or slide it directly off the skillet onto the plate). Place the slaw on top and spread it in an even layer, leaving some space around the edges. Top with the basil leaves and a sprinkle of sesame seeds, if desired. Roll the wrap up like a jelly roll and enjoy with your hands or a knife and fork!

an easy meal for one →

BBQ Pulled Chicken Sandwiches *with Chipotle Slaw*

SERVES 4 ◆ PREP TIME: 15 MINUTES ◆ TOTAL TIME: 1 HOUR 10 MINUTES

PULLED CHICKEN

1½ pounds boneless, skinless chicken breast

Kosher salt and freshly ground black pepper

1 tablespoon avocado oil or other neutral oil, such as grapeseed

1¼ cups BBQ sauce (I like Stubb's original)

½ cup chicken stock

1 tablespoon unsalted butter

SLAW

⅓ cup mayonnaise

2 tablespoons apple cider vinegar

1 tablespoon sugar

½ teaspoon kosher salt, plus more if needed

1 canned chipotle pepper in adobo sauce, finely chopped (1 scant tablespoon), plus 1 teaspoon adobo sauce from the can (see Tip)

¼ teaspoon celery seeds

8 ounces cabbage, thinly sliced (3 cups)

2 ounces carrot, cut into thin matchsticks (½ cup)

FOR ASSEMBLY

2 tablespoons unsalted butter, at room temperature

4 potato buns

Fresh cilantro leaves

I know you're not supposed to have a favorite child (or recipe), but this one is a standout in this book. The slaw gets its unique smoky flavor from chipotle peppers, while the chicken is a lighter, equally satisfying spin on pulled pork. A sprinkle of fresh cilantro at the end is a nod to a bánh mì and ties all the flavors together. One crucial tip: Don't skip toasting the buns with a little butter! That golden, rich surface is what takes this sandwich from good to unforgettable.

1. **Make the pulled chicken:** Generously season both sides of the chicken with salt and pepper.
2. In a medium pot, heat the avocado oil over medium-high heat. Add the chicken and cook until golden brown on the bottom, 4 to 6 minutes. Flip and cook until golden brown on the second side, 3 to 5 minutes. Add the BBQ sauce, stock, and ½ teaspoon salt. Reduce the heat to low, cover, and simmer for 10 minutes. Flip the chicken and cook, covered, until an instant-read thermometer inserted into the thickest part registers 165°F, about 10 minutes more. Transfer the chicken to a large plate and set aside to cool. Remove the pot from the heat and set aside.
3. When the chicken is cool enough to handle, shred it into small bite-size pieces with your fingers or two forks and return it to the pot with the sauce. Cook over medium heat, stirring often, until the sauce coats and infuses the chicken, 4 to 6 minutes. Remove from the heat and stir in the butter until melted.
4. **Meanwhile, make the slaw:** In a large bowl, whisk together the mayonnaise, vinegar, sugar, salt, chipotle, adobo sauce, and celery seeds. Add the cabbage and carrot and toss to coat evenly in the sauce. Taste and season with more salt, if desired. Set aside.
5. **Assemble the sandwiches:** Spread a thin layer of butter over the cut sides of the buns. Heat a large skillet over medium heat. Place the buns in the skillet, cut-side down, and toast until golden brown, 1 to 2 minutes. Press the buns down slightly if needed to ensure the cut side is making contact with the skillet.
6. Pile a generous serving of BBQ chicken on each bottom bun. Top with some slaw and a few cilantro leaves. Finish with the top buns and enjoy!

Hibachi Shrimp Bowl *with Sesame Soy Veggies*

SERVES 2 OR 3 ◆ PREP TIME: 10 MINUTES ◆ TOTAL TIME: 30 MINUTES

GARLIC BUTTER

3 tablespoons unsalted butter, at room temperature

1 garlic clove, finely chopped

ZUCCHINI AND ONION

2 teaspoons avocado oil or other neutral oil, such as grapeseed

1 small yellow onion (6 ounces), cut into ½ by 2-inch strips

Kosher salt and freshly ground black pepper

1 medium zucchini (8 ounces), cut into ½ by 2-inch strips (see Tip)

2 teaspoons soy sauce

1 teaspoon toasted sesame seeds

SHRIMP

1 tablespoon avocado oil or other neutral oil, such as grapeseed

1 pound large shrimp, peeled (tails left on), deveined, and patted dry with paper towels

Kosher salt and freshly ground black pepper

1 tablespoon soy sauce

Juice of ½ lemon

1 teaspoon toasted sesame seeds

Jasmine Rice (page 231), for serving

My mom worked as a waitress at Benihana during her college years. Our whole family—especially my grandparents—loved celebrating birthdays and special occasions there when I was growing up. We'd always order the Surf Side, a seafood trio grilled on the hibachi, along with fried rice and vegetables cooked in Benihana's signature garlic butter. Inspired by those flavors, I've created an easy, quick weeknight meal. The sautéed zucchini and onion also make a great side for other proteins, like chicken or fish.

1. **Make the garlic butter:** In a small bowl, mash together the butter and garlic until combined. Set aside.
2. **Make the zucchini and onion:** In a medium skillet, heat the avocado oil over medium-high heat. Add the onion and season with salt and pepper. Cook, stirring occasionally, until slightly tender and starting to brown, 2 to 3 minutes. Add the zucchini and cook, stirring occasionally, until tender, 4 to 5 minutes. Add 1 tablespoon of the garlic butter, the soy sauce, and sesame seeds. Stir to combine and cook until the butter melts and coats everything, about 1 minute. Transfer the zucchini and onion to a medium bowl and cover to keep warm; set aside.
3. **Make the shrimp:** In the same skillet, heat the avocado oil over medium-high heat. Add the shrimp and season with salt and pepper. Cook until golden brown, 1 to 2 minutes per side. Add the remaining 2 tablespoons garlic butter, the soy sauce, and lemon juice. Cook, stirring, until the butter melts and coats the shrimp, about 30 seconds. Remove from the heat and sprinkle with the sesame seeds.
4. Divide rice among the bowls and top with the shrimp and veggies. Spoon any extra sauce from the skillet over the shrimp and enjoy!

TIP

Cut the zucchini at an angle into ¼-inch-thick slices, then stack the slices and cut them into ½-inch-wide strips.

Lamb Kofta Bowls *with Couscous and Chopped Salad*

SERVES 4 ◆ PREP TIME: 40 MINUTES ◆ TOTAL TIME: 1 HOUR 30 MINUTES

LEMON-MINT YOGURT SAUCE

1 cup plain full-fat or 2% Greek yogurt

2 tablespoons fresh lemon juice

1 garlic clove, grated or finely chopped

1 tablespoon finely chopped fresh mint

1 tablespoon extra-virgin olive oil

¼ teaspoon kosher salt

CHOPPED SALAD

2 tomatoes (about 11 ounces), cut into small dice

1 English cucumber (12 ounces), cut into small dice

½ small red onion (3 ounces), cut into small dice

3 tablespoons finely chopped fresh parsley

Juice of 1 lemon (about 6 ounces)

2 tablespoons extra-virgin olive oil

Kosher salt and freshly ground black pepper

TIP

You can use ground beef or chicken instead of lamb, if you prefer.

I'll be honest—there's a fair bit of chopping in this one, but trust me, it's totally worth it! I've always found chopping to be one of the most relaxing parts of cooking, especially back when I worked in tech. On days when meetings wrapped up early, I'd unwind by heading to the kitchen and working through an ingredient list. There's something so satisfying about checking off each item, and it always feels like the day's worries fade away when I'm fully immersed in making a meal.

Now, on to the recipe! It's a flavorful, well-balanced meal featuring a refreshing chopped salad, warm couscous, and tender, spiced kofta. Once everything is prepped, the cooking itself is simple and low-effort—no need to stress over perfectly shaping the kofta; those rustic, jagged edges give them character. And as a bonus, the leftovers are fantastic! Just store the components separately and assemble when you're ready to enjoy them.

1. **Make the lemon-mint yogurt sauce:** In a small bowl, mix together the yogurt, lemon juice, garlic, mint, olive oil, and salt. Set aside in the refrigerator.
2. **Make the chopped salad:** In a medium bowl, mix together the tomatoes, cucumber, onion, parsley, lemon juice, and olive oil. Season with salt and black pepper. Set aside in the refrigerator.
3. **Make the lamb kofta:** In a medium bowl, combine the ground lamb, onion, parsley, mint, garlic, egg, coriander, cumin, salt, cinnamon, cayenne, and cloves. Mix until all the ingredients are evenly distributed. Set aside.
4. **Make the couscous:** In a small pot, combine the water, olive oil, and salt and bring to a boil. Remove from the heat, add the couscous, and stir to combine. Cover and let stand for 5 minutes, then fluff with a fork. Keep covered until ready to serve.
5. In a large nonstick skillet, heat the avocado oil over medium heat. Cook the koftas in batches to avoid overcrowding. Using a cookie scoop or two spoons, place dollops of the lamb mixture (about 2 tablespoons each) onto the skillet. Flatten slightly with a spatula and cook until browned and cooked through, 2 to 3 minutes per side. Transfer to a plate.
6. Divide the couscous and chopped salad among four bowls. Top with the lamb kofta and yogurt sauce. Enjoy!

makes amazing leftovers!

LAMB KOFTA

1 pound ground lamb (see Tip)

½ small red onion (3 ounces), finely chopped (about ½ cup)

¼ cup finely chopped fresh parsley

2 tablespoons finely chopped fresh mint

3 garlic cloves, finely chopped

1 large egg

1 tablespoon ground coriander

1½ teaspoons ground cumin

1 teaspoon kosher salt

½ teaspoon ground cinnamon

¼ teaspoon cayenne pepper

Pinch of ground cloves

COUSCOUS

1 cup water

1 tablespoon extra-virgin olive oil

¼ teaspoon kosher salt

1 cup couscous

1 tablespoon avocado oil or other neutral oil, such as grapeseed

Baked Crunchy Chicken Tacos

SERVES 4 (MAKES 12 TACOS) ◆ PREP TIME: 30 MINUTES ◆ TOTAL TIME: 1 HOUR 10 MINUTES

CHICKEN FILLING

1 tablespoon avocado oil or other neutral oil, such as grapeseed

1 small yellow onion (6 ounces), cut into small dice

1 teaspoon chili powder

1 teaspoon ground cumin

1 teaspoon kosher salt

½ teaspoon garlic powder

1 (4-ounce) can diced mild green chilies

½ cup mild green salsa

1 pound boneless, skinless chicken breasts, cut in half (see Tips)

FOR ASSEMBLY

12 (5- to 6-inch) corn tortillas (see Tips)

2 tablespoons avocado oil or another neutral oil, such as grapeseed, plus more if needed

1 cup (4 ounces) shredded Mexican-style cheese blend, plus more for serving

1 small head iceberg lettuce (about 9 ounces), thinly sliced

FOR SERVING (OPTIONAL)

Sour cream

Mild green salsa

Lime wedges

My favorite lunch spot in LA is, hands down, Tacos Delta, the cutest little outdoor joint in Silver Lake. I always order the hard tacos plate: two crunchy chicken tacos stuffed with shredded iceberg lettuce and cheese, served with refried beans and rice. It's truly the best thing ever—my mouth waters just thinking about it! And, of course, whenever my mom's in town, we go together. We love it so much that she even made me a Christmas ornament that says "Tacos Delta." Since she lives in Northern California and can only visit and enjoy these tacos every few months, I decided to develop a recipe that would satisfy her craving. I try to cook healthier at home, so I baked the tacos instead of frying them and was blown away by how crispy they got in the oven with just a light coating of oil. I made some other adjustments, like simmering the chicken in a punchy salsa sauce, but otherwise, the Tacos Delta spirit remains intact.

1. Preheat the oven to 425°F on convection mode (or 450°F on regular bake).
2. **Make the chicken filling:** In a medium pot, heat the avocado oil over medium heat. Add the onion, chili powder, cumin, salt, and garlic powder. Cook, stirring, until the onion starts to soften and becomes translucent, about 4 minutes. Add the green chilies with their juices, the salsa, and the chicken. Stir to combine.
3. Bring to a boil over high heat, then reduce the heat to low, cover, and simmer, stirring once or twice, until the chicken is cooked through and an instant-read thermometer inserted into the thickest part registers 165°F, about 20 minutes. Remove from the heat and transfer the chicken to a plate. Set the chicken aside until cool enough to handle.
4. Using your fingers or two forks, shred the chicken into small bite-size pieces. Return the chicken to the pot with the sauce and stir together.
5. **Assemble the tacos:** Place 6 tortillas between two damp paper towels and microwave until soft and pliable, 30 seconds to 1 minute. (Alternatively, wrap the tortillas in foil and place them in the oven while it preheats until they are warm and pliable, about 10 minutes.)
6. Coat a sheet pan with the oil. Working with one tortilla at a time (keeping the others between the damp paper towels or wrapped in foil), rub both sides in the oil. Sprinkle one side of the tortilla with 1 tablespoon of the cheese. Place

TIPS

I recommend Guerrero tortillas for this!

To speed things up, use rotisserie chicken instead of cooking the chicken breast. Just add 2 cups shredded rotisserie chicken in step 2 and simmer for 5 minutes.

You may have some leftover chicken filling—if so, save it for making a chicken taco salad the next day with shredded lettuce, tomatoes, onion, cheese, and tortilla chips.

2 heaping tablespoons of the shredded chicken in a line down the center of the tortilla, then fold the tortilla into a U-shape to create a taco. The chicken will be at the bottom of the U, with room above for toppings. Add more oil to the sheet pan, if needed. Warm the remaining 6 tortillas and repeat with the remaining cheese and chicken (see Tips).

7. Bake the tacos until pale golden brown and sizzling at the edges, 8 to 10 minutes. Remove from the oven and, using a thin spatula, carefully flip the tacos. Return them to the oven and bake until golden brown and crispy all over, 8 to 10 minutes.

8. Remove from the oven and let the tacos cool on the sheet pan for 5 minutes.

9. **To serve:** Gently pry open the tacos with your fingers and fill with the lettuce and additional cheese. Divide among four plates and serve with sour cream, salsa, and lime wedges for squeezing over, if desired. Enjoy!

Teriyaki Chicken Meatball Bowls

SERVES 4 ◆ PREP TIME: 20 MINUTES ◆ TOTAL TIME: 50 MINUTES

MEATBALLS

1 pound ground chicken (93/7 or similar; non-breast-only)

⅓ cup panko breadcrumbs

3 scallions, thinly sliced

1 large egg

2 tablespoons finely chopped fresh ginger

1 tablespoon toasted sesame oil

1 tablespoon soy sauce

½ teaspoon kosher salt

½ teaspoon freshly ground black pepper

1 garlic clove, finely chopped

2 tablespoons avocado oil or other neutral oil

TERIYAKI SAUCE

1 cup water

¼ cup lightly packed light brown sugar

¼ cup soy sauce

1 tablespoon cornstarch

2 teaspoons distilled white vinegar

1 teaspoon avocado oil or other neutral oil

1 teaspoon finely chopped fresh ginger

1 garlic clove, finely chopped

BROCCOLI

10 ounces broccoli crowns, cut into florets

Kosher salt

3 tablespoons water

FOR SERVING

Jasmine Rice (page 231)

Toasted sesame seeds

Everybody loves a teriyaki chicken bowl, right? This recipe is a spin on the classic, where instead of grilled chicken, you'll find meatballs packed with ginger, scallions, and garlic. If making meatballs seems like a lot of work, don't worry—I promise it's easier than you think! Just toss everything into a bowl, mix it up with your hands, and use a cookie scoop to shape them. Then pop them in the oven while you whip up an easy teriyaki sauce. The sauce coats the meatballs beautifully and seeps into the rice, infusing every bite with flavor.

1. Preheat the oven to 400°F on convection mode (or 425°F on regular bake).
2. **Make the meatballs:** In a large bowl, combine the ground chicken, panko, scallions, egg, ginger, sesame oil, soy sauce, salt, pepper, and garlic. Using your hands or a spoon, mix until all the ingredients are evenly distributed.
3. Drizzle a sheet pan with the avocado oil. Form the meat mixture into balls, about 1 heaping tablespoon each (I like to use a cookie scoop, then round them out with my hands) and place them on the prepared sheet pan. Dip your fingers in the oil on the pan or a little water if the meat mixture is sticking to them.
4. Bake until the meatballs are golden brown and the internal temperature registers 165°F on an instant-read thermometer, 12 to 15 minutes.
5. **Meanwhile, make the teriyaki sauce:** In a medium glass measuring cup or bowl, mix together the water, brown sugar, soy sauce, cornstarch, and vinegar.
6. In a medium pot, heat the avocado oil over medium heat. Add the ginger and garlic and cook, stirring, until fragrant, 1 to 2 minutes. Add the brown sugar mixture and whisk until it bubbles and thickens, 2 to 3 minutes. Reduce the heat to low.
7. Add the meatballs to the pot and roll them in the teriyaki sauce to coat. Remove from the heat, cover the pot, and set aside.
8. **Make the broccoli:** Place the broccoli in a large microwave-safe bowl. Drizzle with the water and sprinkle with a little salt. Cover the bowl with a plate and microwave until the broccoli is bright green and slightly tender, 3 to 4 minutes. (Alternatively, blanch the broccoli in boiling salted water for about 1 minute.)
9. **To serve:** Scoop some rice into four bowls and add the broccoli and meatballs on top. Spoon on some teriyaki sauce, sprinkle with sesame seeds, and enjoy!

Thai Basil Chicken Lettuce Cups

SERVES 2 OR 3 ◆ PREP TIME: 15 MINUTES ◆ TOTAL TIME: 40 MINUTES

SAUCE

¼ cup water

2 tablespoons oyster sauce

1 tablespoon dark soy sauce (see Tips)

1 tablespoon fish sauce

2 teaspoons sugar

BASIL CHICKEN

2 tablespoons avocado oil or other neutral oil, such as grapeseed

2 large shallots (5 ounces), thinly sliced

4 garlic cloves, finely chopped

1 red Fresno pepper or jalapeño, half the seeds removed, finely chopped (see Tips)

1 pound ground chicken (93/7 or similar; non-breast-only)

3 scallions, sliced

2 cups (2 ounces) fresh basil leaves, torn if large

Dark soy sauce (optional)

FOR SERVING

1 to 2 head(s) butter lettuce (see Tips), leaves separated

⅓ cup roasted salted cashews or peanuts, chopped

1 red Fresno pepper, thinly sliced into rounds (optional)

Jasmine Rice (page 231; optional)

These lettuce cups are inspired by one of my favorite Thai dishes, pad krapow gai—a spicy chicken and basil dish typically served with rice and a fried egg. I've kept all the bold flavors intact, with plenty of aromatics like shallots, garlic, ginger, and scallions, along with a sweet and savory sauce that soaks into the ground chicken. To keep things light, I like to serve it in refreshing lettuce cups, but if you're in the mood for something more filling, you can always add a spoonful of rice. Just don't skip the cashews, as they add a wonderful crunch and touch of richness to round out the dish!

If you've never cooked with dark soy sauce, I highly recommend you give it a try. It has a deep, caramel-like flavor and gives the dish a gorgeous dark color.

1. **Make the sauce:** In a small glass measuring cup or bowl, mix together the water, oyster sauce, soy sauce, fish sauce, and sugar until the sugar has dissolved. Set aside.
2. **Make the basil chicken:** In a large skillet, heat the avocado oil over medium-high heat. Add the shallots and cook, stirring, until starting to become tender, 2 to 3 minutes. Add the garlic and Fresno pepper and cook, stirring, for 1 minute. Add the ground chicken and cook, breaking it up into small pieces with a spatula, until cooked through, 3 to 5 minutes.
3. Add the sauce and scallions. Cook, stirring, until the sauce reduces and coats the chicken, 2 to 3 minutes. Remove from the heat and stir in the basil. Taste and season with more soy sauce, if desired.
4. **To serve:** Transfer the basil chicken to a serving bowl and serve with the lettuce leaves, cashews, and Fresno pepper (if using) on the side. To eat, add a spoonful of rice (if desired) onto a leaf of lettuce, spoon on some of the chicken, and top with cashews and a slice of pepper. Enjoy!

TIPS

Dark soy sauce is typically sold at Asian grocery stores (it's also available online). If you can't find it, use regular soy sauce! The dish will still be delicious, it just won't have the same rich, dark color.

For less heat, remove all the seeds from the Fresno pepper.

If you're serving three people, I recommend 2 heads of lettuce.

Grandpa's Giant Baked Italian Sub

SERVES 6 ◆ PREP TIME: 5 MINUTES ◆ TOTAL TIME: 25 MINUTES

1 (15-ounce/22-inch-long) French bread loaf, or 4 to 6 individual sub rolls (see Tip)

Extra-virgin olive oil, for drizzling

1¼ teaspoons Italian seasoning, divided

8 ounces sliced provolone cheese

14 ounces sliced deli ham

2½ ounces turkey pepperoni or regular pepperoni

¼ large head iceberg lettuce (about 5 ounces), thinly sliced

1 large tomato (about 6 ounces), sliced into thin rounds

1 cup whole peperoncini, stemmed

Italian dressing, such as Wish-Bone

TIP

French bread is wider and softer than a baguette, but you can use any soft sandwich sub roll to make individual sandwiches instead of a single big one, if you prefer.

This sub has been a beloved family staple for three generations! The recipe started with my Korean grandpa, who came to the US for pharmacy school, where he met my grandma. Together, they became die-hard Ohio State football fans and made a tradition of going to Tony's Subs before every game. After moving to Illinois for work, they began making subs at home, inspired by their favorite spot. Eventually, they passed the recipe down to my mom, who made it for my brothers and me throughout our childhood.

Depending on the size of your bread, you might want to scale back on the ham, the salad, or both. If you're after a lighter sandwich, feel free to adjust the amounts to your liking. In my family, we like to go all out with a sandwich that's packed to the brim—but you do you!

1. Preheat the oven to 375°F.
2. Using a bread knife, cut the bread in half lengthwise and place it cut-side up on your largest sheet pan. (The ends might hang off the edge slightly—that's OK!) Drizzle the cut sides of the bread with some olive oil and sprinkle with 1 teaspoon of the Italian seasoning.
3. Place the provolone in overlapping layers over the top half of the bread and sprinkle with the remaining ¼ teaspoon Italian seasoning. Place the ham in overlapping layers over the bottom half of the bread, followed by the pepperoni.
4. Bake until the cheese is melted with deep golden brown spots and the bread is crisp and toasted, about 18 minutes.
5. Meanwhile, in a large bowl, toss together the lettuce, tomato, and peperoncini. Generously drizzle with Italian dressing and toss to combine. Taste and add more dressing, if desired.
6. Remove the sub from the oven and layer the salad on top of the ham and pepperoni. Sandwich with the top half of the bread, cheesy-side down, then cut on a diagonal into six sections, and enjoy!

Lemongrass Pork Vermicelli Noodle Bowls

SERVES 4 ◆ PREP TIME: 20 MINUTES
◆ TOTAL TIME: 1 HOUR, PLUS 1 HOUR FOR MARINATING

This pork vermicelli bowl was one of my go-to take-out meals when I was single and living in a tiny studio apartment in New York City in my early twenties. I'd order it on repeat from a local Vietnamese spot whenever I didn't feel like cooking or was short on time. What I love most about it is how light yet satisfying it is, with a dynamic range of flavors and textures.

The pork is marinated in a sweet and savory lemongrass sauce that caramelizes in the skillet, giving it a smoky, charred finish. Paired with vermicelli noodles and a refreshing mix of raw and pickled veggies, it's a perfect harmony of bold and fresh. When I first made this dish at home, Doug couldn't stop raving about it—he devoured every bite. It tastes just like the one I used to order all those years ago.

MARINATED PORK

2 lemongrass stalks

2 tablespoons avocado oil or other neutral oil, such as grapeseed

2 tablespoons sugar

1 tablespoon fish sauce

1 tablespoon honey

1 tablespoon soy sauce

½ teaspoon freshly ground black pepper

¼ teaspoon kosher salt

1 large shallot (3 ounces), finely chopped

2 garlic cloves, finely chopped

1 pound pork shoulder, cut into thin, bite-size pieces

PICKLED VEGGIES

1 small carrot (2½ ounces), cut into thin matchsticks

1 (2-inch) piece daikon radish (3 ounces), peeled and cut into thin matchsticks

½ cup distilled white vinegar

½ cup water

1 tablespoon sugar

1 teaspoon kosher salt

NƯỚC CHẤM SAUCE

½ cup warm water

2 tablespoons fish sauce

2 tablespoons sugar

2 tablespoons fresh lime juice

2 garlic cloves, finely chopped

1. **Marinate the pork:** Cut off the top two-thirds and bottom 1 inch from the lemongrass stalks. Peel off the tough outer layer, smash the inner stalk with a meat mallet or a heavy skillet, then finely chop. (Lemongrass is fibrous, so it's important to chop it as finely as possible.) You should have about 1 heaping tablespoon; set aside.
2. In a large bowl, combine the avocado oil, sugar, fish sauce, honey, soy sauce, pepper, and salt. Mix until well combined. Add the lemongrass, shallot, garlic, and pork. Mix until the marinade coats the pork and the aromatics are evenly distributed. Cover and marinate in the refrigerator for at least 1 hour or up to overnight for the best flavor.
3. **Make the pickled veggies:** Place the carrot and daikon in a heatproof medium bowl. In a small pot, combine the vinegar, water, sugar, and salt. Bring to a simmer over high heat, stirring to dissolve the sugar and salt. Remove from the heat and pour over the vegetables. Set aside for at least 30 minutes while you prep the rest of the ingredients.
4. **Make the nước chấm sauce:** In a small glass measuring cup or bowl, combine the warm water, fish sauce, sugar, lime juice, and garlic. Mix until the sugar dissolves and set aside.
5. **Boil the noodles:** Bring a large pot of generously salted water to a boil. Add the vermicelli and cook according to the package directions, then drain and rinse under cold water.

TIP

The sugar from the pork may burn in the skillet—just soak the skillet in warm soapy water until the burnt bits loosen.

FOR NOODLES AND ASSEMBLY

Kosher salt

8 ounces dry vermicelli noodles

1 small head romaine lettuce (6 ounces), thinly sliced

Sliced cucumber

Fresh mint leaves

Avocado oil or other neutral oil, such as grapeseed, for cooking

FOR SERVING

¼ cup chopped roasted peanuts

Sriracha, for drizzling (optional)

6. **To assemble:** Divide the lettuce among four shallow bowls. Add the noodles, slightly overlapping the lettuce, then arrange the cucumber, mint, and pickled veggies in piles around the edge of the bowls.
7. In a large heavy skillet, heat 1 tablespoon avocado oil over medium-high heat. Add half the pork in one layer and cook until browned and cooked through, about 3 minutes per side. Transfer to a plate and cover with foil to keep warm. Repeat with the remaining pork, adding more oil to the skillet if needed. (See Tip.)
8. **To serve:** Divide the pork among the bowls, placing it over the noodles. Top with the peanuts and a generous drizzle of the nước chấm sauce. (Or put the sauce in small individual bowls, which is how it's usually served at restaurants.) Drizzle with some sriracha, if desired, and enjoy!

Mushroom Crispy Rice Bowl

SERVES 2 OR 3 ◆ PREP TIME: 10 MINUTES ◆ TOTAL TIME: 50 MINUTES

MUSHROOMS

2 tablespoons avocado oil or other neutral oil, such as grapeseed

1 pound mixed fresh mushrooms (oyster, king oyster, shiitake, and/or cremini), sliced

¼ teaspoon kosher salt

¼ teaspoon freshly ground black pepper

4 large garlic cloves, finely chopped

1 tablespoon soy sauce

1 tablespoon unsalted butter

1 tablespoon distilled white vinegar

CRISPY RICE

2 tablespoons unsalted butter

1 cup cooked Jasmine Rice (page 231)

Pinch of kosher salt

EGGS

2 teaspoons avocado oil or other neutral oil, such as grapeseed

2 or 3 large eggs (1 per person)

Kosher salt

FOR SERVING

2 to 3 cups cooked Jasmine Rice (page 231; about 1 cup per person)

1 scallion, sliced

Toasted sesame seeds

Toasted sesame oil

I love crisping rice in a skillet: Simply cook it with butter until it turns deeply golden. It's an easy technique that creates the most incredible crunchy bits to complement the fluffy softness of steamed rice. I've experimented with many different crispy rice bowls, but this version with sautéed mushrooms is hands down my favorite.

The mushrooms have a subtle Asian flavor from the soy sauce and are finished with a splash of vinegar for a bright tang. The real magic happens when you break the runny egg yolk and mix it into the rice, adding a lush richness to every bite. It's the kind of vegetarian dish that even a meat lover will devour.

1. **Make the mushrooms:** In a large skillet, heat the avocado oil over medium-high heat. Add the mushrooms and spread them in an even layer, then season with the salt and pepper. Cook, undisturbed, until deep golden brown on the bottom, 4 to 5 minutes. Add the garlic and soy sauce and cook, stirring often, until the mushrooms are tender, 3 to 4 minutes more. Remove from the heat and stir in the butter and vinegar. Transfer the mushrooms to a medium bowl and cover to keep warm.
2. **Make the crispy rice:** Without cleaning the skillet, add the butter and melt over medium heat. Add the rice and salt and stir to coat the rice with the melted butter. Cook, stirring often, until the rice is golden brown and crispy, 5 to 7 minutes. Remove from the heat.
3. **Make the eggs:** In a small nonstick skillet, heat the avocado oil over medium heat. Crack in the eggs and season with a little salt. Cook until the whites are set but the yolks are still runny, 2 to 3 minutes. If you like, you can tilt the skillet and use a spoon to spoon the hot oil onto the egg whites to help cook them through.
4. **To serve:** Divide the (not-crispy) rice among individual bowls. Top with the crispy rice, mushrooms, and a fried egg. Sprinkle with the scallion and some sesame seeds, and drizzle with a little sesame oil. I love breaking up the egg and mixing the yolk with the rice. Enjoy!

Veggie Ceviche Tostadas

MAKES 6 TOSTADAS (SERVES 2 AS A LIGHT MEAL)
◆ PREP TIME: 20 MINUTES ◆ TOTAL TIME: 30 MINUTES

TOSTADAS

2 tablespoons avocado oil or other neutral oil, such as grapeseed

6 (5- to 6-inch) corn tortillas (see Tips)

Kosher salt

CEVICHE

½ cup small-diced jicama or Asian pear (3 ounces)

½ cup small-diced red bell pepper (3 ounces)

1 large avocado, cut into small dice (9 ounces)

Kernels from 1 ear corn, or 1 cup thawed frozen corn kernels (5 ounces)

¼ cup small-diced red onion (1½ ounces)

½ jalapeño or serrano pepper, cut into small dice (remove the seeds first for less heat)

¼ cup finely chopped fresh cilantro

Juice of 3 limes

3 tablespoons extra-virgin olive oil

¼ teaspoon kosher salt, plus more if needed

¼ teaspoon freshly ground black pepper

1 garlic clove, grated

1 lime, cut into wedges, for serving

Doug and I can't get enough of these veggie tostadas, especially when we're craving something light and refreshing. Instead of frying, you bake the tortillas, which is not only easier but also healthier. They come out perfectly crispy every time.

The ceviche itself has a wonderful mix of textures, with creamy avocado and refreshing pieces of jicama and bell pepper. There's spice, sweetness, and brightness, with the lime dressing adding a tangy punch that ties everything together. And let's not forget how beautiful these tostadas look with their colorful toppings once they're assembled. They're not just a delicious weeknight meal—they'd also make a gorgeous appetizer for a dinner party. Serve one per person, and you're good to go!

1. **Make the tostadas:** Preheat the oven to 400°F on convection mode (or 425°F on regular bake). Coat a sheet pan with the avocado oil.
2. Place the tortillas on the prepared sheet pan and rub both sides in the oil. Season the top side with salt and bake for 6 minutes. Flip and bake until crispy and deep golden brown around the edges, 3 to 5 minutes more. Remove from the oven and set aside. (The tortillas will continue to crisp up as they cool.)
3. **Make the ceviche:** In a large bowl, combine the jicama, bell pepper, avocado, corn, onion, jalapeño, and cilantro.
4. In a small bowl, whisk together the lime juice, olive oil, salt, black pepper, and garlic until smooth and combined. Pour over the vegetables and mix to coat. Taste and season with more salt, if desired.
5. Divide the tostadas between two plates and spoon the veggie ceviche onto each tostada. Serve with the lime wedges for squeezing over. Enjoy!

TIPS

I love Guerrero white corn tortillas for this recipe. Freshly made tortillas may take a little longer to crisp up in the oven.

You'll probably have leftover veggies from making the ceviche. I like to use them in a scramble or salad the next day.

TIPS

For four servings, I recommend using 1½ cups uncooked rice, which will yield about 4 cups cooked rice.

If you don't like anchovies, replace them with ½ teaspoon kosher salt.

Steak Chimichurri Bowls

SERVES 4 ◆ PREP TIME: 25 MINUTES ◆ TOTAL TIME: 50 MINUTES

PICKLED ONION

½ medium red onion (5 ounces), thinly sliced

½ cup distilled white vinegar

½ cup water

1 tablespoon sugar

1 teaspoon kosher salt

CHIMICHURRI

Leaves and tender stems from ½ bunch cilantro (1.25 ounces), finely chopped

Leaves and tender stems from ½ bunch parsley (1.25 ounces), finely chopped

6 anchovy fillets, finely chopped (see Tips)

4 large garlic cloves, finely chopped

½ jalapeño, seeded and finely chopped

½ cup extra-virgin olive oil

Juice of 1 lime

1 tablespoon red wine vinegar

Kosher salt

STEAK

1 pound skirt steak

Kosher salt and freshly ground black pepper

1 tablespoon avocado oil or other neutral oil, such as grapeseed

Jasmine Rice (page 231; see Tips), for serving

This chimichurri recipe practically went viral in real life. It traveled through a chain of connections—through friends and acquaintances—and finally landed with my mom (shout-out to her friend Betsy). She passed it on to me, and that's when I truly fell in love with chimichurri.

For years, I thought chimichurri just wasn't for me, but this version changed everything. It's made with fresh jalapeños instead of red pepper flakes and uses lime juice and red wine vinegar for a brighter, tangier finish. Anchovies blend seamlessly into the herbs, adding a subtle umami depth that pairs beautifully with steak. The pickled onion brings tangy sweetness and satisfying crunch, balancing the richness of the meat. The best part is when the chimichurri seeps into the jasmine rice at the bottom of the bowl. So delish!

1. **Make the pickled onion:** Place the onion in a small heatproof bowl. In a small pot, combine the vinegar, water, sugar, and salt. Bring to a gentle boil, stirring to dissolve the sugar and salt. As soon as the liquid starts bubbling, pour it over the onion. Set aside for at least 15 minutes before using. (It can be stored in an airtight container in the refrigerator for up to 2 weeks.)
2. **Make the chimichurri:** In a medium bowl, stir together the cilantro, parsley, anchovies, garlic, jalapeño, olive oil, lime juice, and red wine vinegar to combine, then taste and season with salt. Set aside. (The chimichurri can be stored in an airtight container in the refrigerator for up to 5 days. It will lose its bright green color, but the flavors will meld the longer it sits.)
3. **Cook the steak:** Take the steak out of the fridge 30 minutes before cooking to let it come to room temperature. Cut it into large pieces that will fit in a skillet. Thoroughly pat the steak dry and generously season both sides with salt and pepper.
4. Heat a large cast-iron skillet or other heavy ovenproof skillet over high heat until smoking, 3 to 5 minutes. Add the avocado oil and tilt the pan to evenly coat.
5. Add the steak, being careful not to overcrowd the skillet (you may need to cook the steak in two batches). Cook until browned and cooked through (130°F on an instant-read thermometer for medium-rare), 2 to 3 minutes per side. Transfer the steak to a plate, cover with foil, and let rest for 5 minutes, then transfer to a cutting board and slice against the grain.
6. Divide the rice among four bowls and top with the steak and pickled onion. Spoon some chimichurri on top and enjoy!

Healthy Shrimp Tacos *with* *Cilantro-Lime Cabbage Slaw*

SERVES 3 OR 4 ◆ PREP TIME: 20 MINUTES ◆ TOTAL TIME: 1 HOUR

Pickled onion
(see page 105)

SLAW

½ cup plain full-fat or 2% Greek yogurt

¼ cup light sour cream

3 tablespoons finely chopped fresh cilantro

1 tablespoon water

1 garlic clove, finely chopped

¼ teaspoon kosher salt, plus more if needed

1 to 2 limes, halved

8 ounces red cabbage, thinly sliced (about 3 cups)

SHRIMP

1½ teaspoons chili powder

1½ teaspoons ground cumin

1 teaspoon kosher salt

½ teaspoon garlic powder

1 pound large shrimp, peeled and deveined

1 tablespoon extra-virgin olive oil

FOR SERVING

8 cassava flour tortillas, such as Siete Foods, or regular corn tortillas

1 avocado, halved and sliced

½ jalapeño, seeded and chopped small (optional)

Lime wedges

If I had to pick one go-to healthy recipe, this would be it. I know "healthy" can sometimes sound boring, but trust me, this dish is so much fun. It's packed with bold flavors, vibrant colors, and a variety of different textures. You've got crunchy slaw with a creamy cilantro-lime dressing, super-flavorful spiced shrimp, and an acid pop from pickled onion. I like to bring the skillet right to the table to keep the shrimp hot, and I warm the cassava tortillas one at a time so everyone can build their own tacos. It makes the meal interactive, which is exactly what I crave during the midweek slump.

1. Make the pickled onion so it can cool while you do everything else.
2. **Make the slaw:** In a large bowl, stir together the yogurt, sour cream, cilantro, water, garlic, and salt. Squeeze in the juice of 1 lime, taste, and add more lime juice, if desired. Add the cabbage and toss to combine. Taste and season with more salt, if desired. Set aside.
3. **Make the shrimp:** In a small bowl, stir together the chili powder, cumin, salt, and garlic powder. Place the shrimp in a medium bowl, sprinkle with the spice mixture, and toss to evenly coat.
4. In a large nonstick pan, heat the olive oil over medium-high heat. Add the shrimp in a single layer and cook until pink on the outside and cooked through, 1 to 2 minutes per side.
5. Heat a medium skillet over medium-high heat. Working with one at a time, toast the tortillas until golden brown in spots, about 1 minute per side.
6. **To serve:** Top the tortillas with some slaw, shrimp, pickled onion, a slice of avocado, some jalapeño (if desired), and a squeeze of lime juice. (I like to toast and assemble the tortillas one at a time right before eating them, so they're super fresh!) Enjoy!

my favorite healthy recipe

Thursday

let's indulge

Restaurant-Style Date-Night Dishes to Set the Mood

These are the recipes I turn to when Doug and I are staying in and I want to cook something a little more elevated and indulgent. New York is where we first fell in love, so it's no surprise that Italian became our go-to for birthday celebrations or a fancyish date night. If you're a pasta lover, this chapter is for you! The Spicy Creamy Shrimp Spaghetti (page 114), for instance, is loosely inspired by Carbone's famous spicy rigatoni. And for a nostalgic family favorite, there's Mom's Benihana Chicken Fried Rice (page 133). Growing up, my family celebrated all our birthdays at Benihana, so making this dish at home always feels super special and restaurant-worthy.

HOW TO COOK PASTA *like an italian*

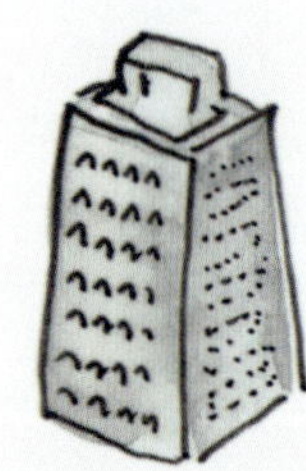

My family and I went to Tuscany, where we learned the art of pasta-making from two incredibly talented home cooks. They taught us to cook the pasta only partway in boiling water (before it's even al dente) and then finish it in the sauce. This method creates a cohesive dish—the pasta absorbs the sauce's flavors while its starches thicken the sauce for the silkiest coating. You'll find this technique in many of my pasta recipes.

1. Choose a pot big enough to fit the amount of pasta you're cooking (medium to large). Fill it halfway with water, cover, and bring to a boil over high heat. Generously season with kosher salt.

2. In a large skillet, make your sauce of choice.

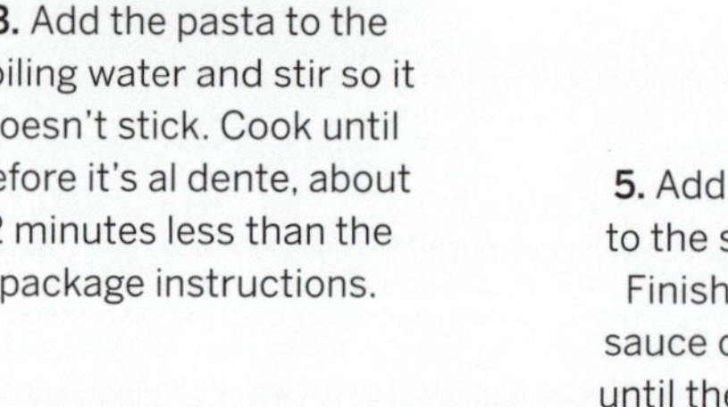

3. Add the pasta to the boiling water and stir so it doesn't stick. Cook until before it's al dente, about 2 minutes less than the package instructions.

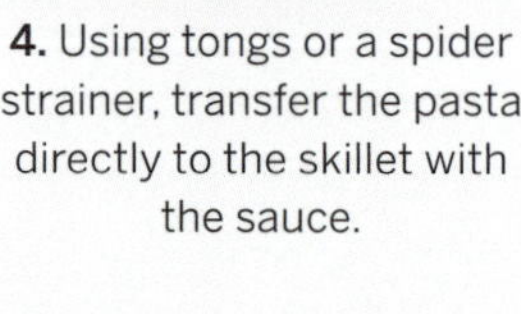

4. Using tongs or a spider strainer, transfer the pasta directly to the skillet with the sauce.

5. Add ¼ cup of the pasta water to the skillet and stir to combine. Finish cooking the pasta in the sauce over medium heat, stirring until the sauce reduces and coats the pasta and the pasta is to your desired tenderness, 2 to 3 minutes, adding more pasta water if needed.

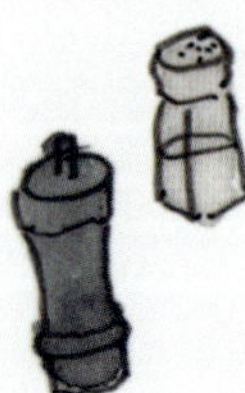

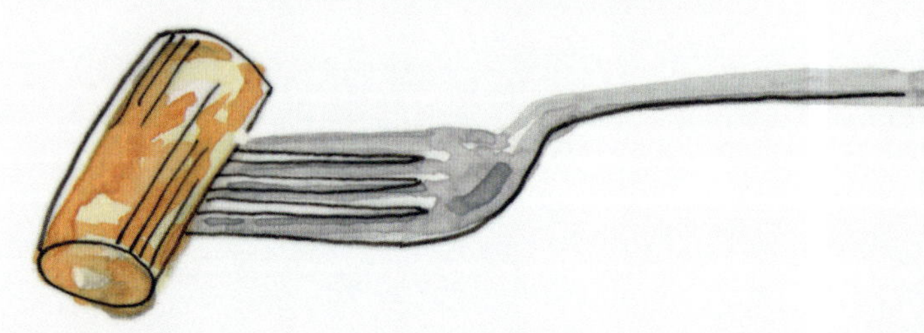

Strozzapreti *with Sausage and Crispy Sage*

SERVES 4 ◆ PREP TIME: 5 MINUTES ◆ TOTAL TIME: 40 MINUTES

Kosher salt

4 tablespoons (½ stick) unsalted butter, divided

40 fresh sage leaves (⅓ cup)

1 pound mild Italian sausage, casings removed

½ teaspoon crushed red pepper flakes, plus more for serving

5 garlic cloves, finely chopped

1 pound strozzapreti or other short pasta, such as gemelli, campanelle, or cavatelli

1 cup (4 ounces) grated Parmesan cheese, plus more for serving

My friend Sanaë told me about a pasta dish she loves from the restaurant Frankies 457 Spuntino in Brooklyn—cavatelli with sausage and sage. I've made crispy sage before, and I've also made pasta with sausage and a creamy cheese sauce emulsified with pasta water. So, I merged those ideas into an elegant, restaurant-worthy dish, and the result was absolutely incredible. The sage fries in butter until crisp, then half gets folded into the pasta while the rest is sprinkled on top for a final crunch.

1. Bring a large pot of generously salted water to a boil. Line a large plate with paper towels.
2. In a large skillet, melt 3 tablespoons of the butter over medium heat. Add the sage leaves in one layer. Cook until the butter is bubbling and starting to turn golden brown, about 2 minutes. (Be careful not to let the butter burn; lower the heat, if needed.) Remove from the heat and transfer the sage leaves to the paper towel–lined plate. Sprinkle lightly with salt and set aside.
3. Return the skillet to medium heat and add the sausage. Use a spatula to break it up into irregular chunks (about 1 teaspoon each) and increase the heat to medium-high. Cook, stirring occasionally, until browned and cooked through, 6 to 8 minutes. Add the red pepper flakes and garlic and cook, stirring, for 1 minute. Remove from the heat and set aside.
4. Cook the pasta until before it's al dente, 2 minutes less than the package directions. Using a spider strainer, transfer to the skillet with the sausage. (Alternatively, drain in a colander, making sure to reserve at least 2 cups of the pasta cooking water.)
5. Set the skillet over medium heat, then add ½ cup pasta water. Cook, stirring until the water has been absorbed. Add ½ cup more pasta water and cook, stirring and adding more pasta water as needed, until the pasta is almost to your desired tenderness. This whole process should take 3 to 5 minutes.
6. Remove from the heat and add the Parmesan and remaining 1 tablespoon butter. Stir until the butter has melted and the sauce is glossy. Add a little more pasta water to loosen the sauce, if needed. Add half the sage leaves and stir gently to fold them into the pasta.
7. Serve the pasta topped with some Parmesan, the remaining sage leaves, and a sprinkle of red pepper flakes. Enjoy!

Spicy Creamy Shrimp Spaghetti

SERVES 4 ◆ PREP TIME: 10 MINUTES ◆ TOTAL TIME: 1 HOUR

This recipe is loosely inspired by one of my favorite dishes from a restaurant: the spicy rigatoni vodka from Carbone. There are sweet bits of caramelized onion running through the tomatoes, a spicy kick from the Calabrian chili peppers, and a subtle richness from the heavy cream. My husband, Doug, and I *love* spicy food to the point that our stomachs can't handle it and our mouths are on fire (but don't worry, that won't be the case here), so we always make this pasta with two tablespoons of chilies. If you like a mellower heat that builds as you eat, start with one tablespoon.

Kosher salt

1 pound large shrimp, peeled and deveined

Freshly ground black pepper

2 tablespoons extra-virgin olive oil

1 tablespoon unsalted butter

1 medium sweet onion (10 ounces), finely chopped

4 garlic cloves, finely chopped

1 (28-ounce) can whole peeled San Marzano tomatoes (see Tip)

1 to 2 tablespoons crushed Calabrian chili peppers in oil

1 teaspoon sugar

½ cup heavy cream

1 pound spaghetti

Freshly grated Parmesan cheese, for serving

Torn or coarsely chopped fresh parsley or basil leaves, for serving (optional)

TIP

Look for DOP-certified San Marzano tomatoes from Italy.

1. Bring a large pot of generously salted water to a boil.
2. Pat the shrimp dry with paper towels and season with salt and pepper.
3. In a large skillet (with a lid), heat the olive oil over medium-high heat. Add the shrimp and cook until pink and opaque on the inside, 1 to 2 minutes per side. Transfer the shrimp to a large plate and set aside.
4. In the same skillet, melt the butter over medium-low heat. Add the onion, ¼ teaspoon salt, and ¼ teaspoon pepper. Cook, stirring often, until completely softened and translucent, 12 to 15 minutes. Add the garlic and cook, stirring, for 1 minute. Using your hands, crush the tomatoes to break them up as you drop them into the skillet, then pour in the juices from the can. Add the Calabrian chili peppers (use 1 tablespoon for mild heat), sugar, and 1 teaspoon salt.
5. Bring to a high simmer over medium-high heat, then reduce the heat to low, cover, and simmer until the tomatoes have broken down and the flavors have melded, about 15 minutes. Uncover and stir in the cream. Remove from the heat and keep covered while you cook the spaghetti.
6. Add the spaghetti to the boiling water and cook for 2 minutes less than the package directions. Using tongs, transfer the spaghetti directly to the skillet with the sauce. (Alternatively, reserve ½ cup of the pasta cooking water, then drain the spaghetti and add it to the skillet.)
7. Stir ¼ cup of the pasta water and the shrimp into the pasta and sauce. Cook over medium heat, stirring to coat the spaghetti in the sauce, until the sauce thickens and coats each strand of pasta and the pasta is al dente or cooked to your liking, 2 to 3 minutes. (Add more pasta water as needed to loosen the sauce.) Taste and season with more salt and/or pepper, if desired.
8. Immediately divide the hot spaghetti among four plates. Top with Parmesan and parsley or basil, if desired, and serve. Enjoy!

Crispy Parmesan Chicken Bruschetta

SERVES 4 ◆ PREP TIME: 30 MINUTES ◆ TOTAL TIME: 50 MINUTES

BRUSCHETTA TOPPING

¼ cup extra-virgin olive oil

¼ cup (¼ ounce) fresh basil leaves

1 tablespoon balsamic vinegar

1 garlic clove, grated or finely chopped

½ teaspoon sugar

½ teaspoon freshly ground black pepper, plus more if needed

2 pounds ripe tomatoes on the vine (about 6 medium), cut into ½-inch wedges

1 teaspoon kosher salt, plus more if needed

CRISPY CHICKEN

Avocado or olive oil spray or extra-virgin olive oil, for drizzling

4 boneless, skinless chicken breasts (about 2 pounds total)

Kosher salt and freshly ground black pepper

½ cup all-purpose flour

2 large eggs

½ cup panko breadcrumbs

½ cup Italian-style breadcrumbs

½ cup (2 ounces) grated Parmesan cheese

FOR SERVING

Flaky sea salt, such as Maldon

Freshly shaved Parmesan cheese (optional)

In my spin on classic bruschetta, I replace the slice of bread with a warm, crispy chicken cutlet and turn it into a full meal. The result is balanced, refreshing, and light—just what I'm craving on a weeknight. I love to make this in the summer, when tomatoes are at their ripest and sweetest, but you can also use halved cherry or grape tomatoes during the rest of the year. Instead of frying, I bake my chicken cutlets, but I promise you'll still get a crunchy and super-flavorful coating thanks to the Parmesan, panko, and Italian-style breadcrumbs.

To make crispy **Chicken Caesar Cutlets**, simply replace the bruschetta topping with the Lemony Caesar Salad on page 239. Or, for a chicken Milanese, top with arugula and shaved Parmesan dressed with lemon juice, olive oil, salt, and pepper.

TIP

For a less-punchy garlic flavor, infuse the olive oil with the garlic by heating them both in a small skillet over low heat until the garlic starts to sizzle.

1. Preheat the oven to 425°F on convection mode (or 450°F on regular bake).
2. **Make the bruschetta topping:** In a medium bowl, stir together the olive oil, basil, vinegar, garlic, sugar, and pepper. Set the dressing aside.
3. Place the tomatoes in a colander in the sink. Sprinkle with the salt and toss to combine. Let drain, stirring occasionally, while you prepare the chicken.
4. **Make the crispy chicken:** Spray a wire rack with some oil (or rub with olive oil) and place it over a sheet pan. If you don't have a wire rack, spray or drizzle a sheet pan with some oil.
5. Working with one chicken breast at a time, place the chicken between two pieces of plastic wrap and pound with the flat side of a meat mallet or the bottom of a heavy skillet to ¼-inch thickness. Season both sides with salt and pepper.
6. Place the flour in a large shallow bowl. Beat the eggs in a second large shallow bowl. In a third large shallow bowl, stir together the panko, Italian-style breadcrumbs, and Parmesan. Line up the bowls on the counter.
7. Working with one chicken breast at a time, dredge in the flour, coating both sides and shaking off any excess. Add the chicken to the eggs and turn to coat, then lift it out of the bowl, allowing the excess to drip back into the bowl. Dredge the chicken in the breadcrumb mixture to coat on both sides, pressing the crumbs with your fingers to adhere. Transfer to the oiled rack (or place directly on the oiled sheet pan).
8. Spray the breaded chicken with some oil or drizzle with a little olive oil. Bake until the chicken is golden brown and the internal temperature registers 165°F on an instant-read thermometer, 12 to 15 minutes. If the chicken is cooked through before it's golden brown, turn on the broiler and broil for 1 to 3 minutes.
9. Transfer the tomatoes to the bowl with the dressing and stir to combine. Taste and season with more salt and pepper, if needed.
10. **To serve:** Divide the chicken breasts among four plates. Spoon the bruschetta topping over the chicken. Sprinkle with a little flaky salt and top with some shaved Parmesan, if you like. Enjoy!

↖ Flip to page 1 to see the Chicken Caesar Cutlet

Seared Scallops *with Shaved Fennel and Citrus Salad*

SERVES 2 ◆ PREP TIME: 10 MINUTES ◆ TOTAL TIME: 40 MINUTES

FENNEL SALAD

2 tablespoons pine nuts

1 fennel bulb with the fronds (8 ounces)

¼ cup (1 ounce) shaved Parmesan cheese

1 grapefruit or pomelo

DRESSING

1 tablespoon plus 1 teaspoon red wine vinegar

1 teaspoon Dijon mustard

1 teaspoon honey

1 small garlic clove, grated

¼ teaspoon kosher salt, plus more if needed

¼ teaspoon freshly ground black pepper, plus more if needed

2 tablespoons extra-virgin olive oil

SCALLOPS

10 ounces large dry scallops (about 12)

Kosher salt and freshly ground black pepper

3 tablespoons all-purpose flour (see Tips)

2 tablespoons avocado oil or other neutral oil, such as grapeseed

2 tablespoons unsalted butter

Lemon wedges, for serving

I learned to make scallops from my dad. He's so good at cooking them and always coats them in a little flour for that restaurant-quality golden crust. Here I've paired them with a light, refreshing fennel salad. Raw fennel can have a strong licorice flavor, so I balance it out with a Dijon vinaigrette, toasted pine nuts, shaved Parmesan, and grapefruit for a touch of acidity.

1. **Make the fennel salad:** In a small skillet, toast the pine nuts over medium-low heat, stirring frequently, until golden and fragrant, 3 to 4 minutes. Transfer the pine nuts to a small bowl and set aside to cool.
2. Trim the fennel bulb, reserving some fennel fronds for serving, and slice it in half through the root end. Using a mandoline with a guard set to 1.5 mm, carefully slice the fennel (or use a sharp knife to thinly slice). Transfer to a large bowl and add the Parmesan.
3. Cut a small slice off the top and bottom of the grapefruit to create flat surfaces. Stand the fruit upright on a cutting board. Using a sharp knife, cut away the peel and white pith, following the curve of the grapefruit. Hold the grapefruit in one hand and slice along each membrane to separate the segments. Place the segments in a small bowl and set aside.

4. **Make the dressing:** In a small glass measuring cup or bowl, whisk together the vinegar, mustard, honey, garlic, salt, and pepper. While whisking, slowly drizzle in the olive oil and whisk until the dressing emulsifies and thickens. Set aside.
5. **Make the scallops:** Using your fingers, remove the small abductor muscle from the side of the scallops. Place the scallops on a large plate and pat them thoroughly dry with paper towels. Generously season both sides with salt and pepper. Place the flour in a small bowl and lightly coat each scallop in the flour, shaking off any excess, then return the scallops to the plate.

TIPS

For a gluten-free version, omit the flour.

If you're worried about the scallops sticking to your pan, you can use a nonstick skillet, you'll just have to lower the heat a bit, and you might not get as much of a golden crust on the scallops.

6. In a large cast-iron skillet or other heavy pan, heat the avocado oil over medium-high heat (see Tips). When the oil is shimmering, add the scallops, leaving a little space between them. Cook, undisturbed, until golden brown on the bottom, about 3 minutes. Using tongs or a thin spatula, flip the scallops and cook until golden brown on the second side, about 2 minutes. Remove the skillet from the heat and transfer the scallops to a large plate. If they stick a bit to the skillet, don't worry—just use the thin spatula to gently release them.
7. Add the butter to the skillet and let it melt, stirring and scraping up any brown bits stuck to the bottom of the skillet. Drizzle or spoon the butter over the scallops.
8. Add the pine nuts to the bowl with the fennel and Parmesan. Pour the dressing over and toss until evenly coated. Add the grapefruit segments and gently toss. Taste and season with more salt and/or pepper, if desired.
9. Serve the fennel salad alongside the scallops, spooning the butter on top. Sprinkle some fronds over everything and serve with lemon wedges. Enjoy!

Lamb Chops *with Herb Salsa and Lemon-Garlic Yogurt*

SERVES 4 ◆ PREP TIME: 20 MINUTES
◆ TOTAL TIME: 50 MINUTES, PLUS AT LEAST 1 HOUR FOR MARINATING

MARINATED LAMB

¼ cup extra-virgin olive oil

3 garlic cloves, finely chopped

Zest of 1 lemon

1 tablespoon finely chopped fresh rosemary

1½ teaspoons kosher salt

½ teaspoon freshly ground black pepper

1 frenched rack of lamb (about 2 pounds), cut into 8 rib chops

1 tablespoon avocado oil or other neutral oil, such as grapeseed, for cooking the lamb

HERB SALSA

⅓ cup extra-virgin olive oil

½ cup packed fresh parsley leaves, finely chopped

¼ cup packed fresh mint leaves, finely chopped

4 anchovy fillets, finely chopped

1 tablespoon fresh lemon juice

1 garlic clove, finely chopped

Kosher salt

FOR SERVING

Lemon-Garlic Yogurt (see page 199), for serving

Flaky sea salt, such as Maldon

If you've never cooked lamb before, this recipe is a great place to start. Lamb chops are quick and easy to make on the stove, and a rich layer of fat along the bone keeps them incredibly tender and juicy. I love a Mediterranean-inspired approach, like this one with rosemary, parsley, mint, and plenty of lemon. The lamb pairs beautifully with the creamy, tangy yogurt sauce and vibrant herb salsa, making for a meal that feels special yet is surprisingly easy to pull off.

I love serving this with Buttery Lemon Rice with Herbs (page 227).

1. **Marinate the lamb:** In a small bowl, combine the olive oil, garlic, lemon zest, rosemary, salt, and pepper. Arrange the lamb chops in a large dish and pour the marinade over them, ensuring they are evenly coated. Cover with plastic wrap and marinate in the refrigerator for at least 1 hour or up to 12 hours.
2. **Make the herb salsa:** In a small bowl, combine the olive oil, parsley, mint, anchovies, lemon juice, garlic, and a pinch of salt. Taste and season with more salt, if desired. Set aside.
3. **Cook the lamb:** Remove the lamb from the refrigerator and let stand at room temperature for 30 minutes before cooking.
4. Heat a large cast-iron pan or other heavy skillet over medium-high heat. Pour in the avocado oil and tilt the skillet to evenly coat. Add half the lamb chops (or as many as will fit in a single layer) and cook, undisturbed, until browned on the bottom, about 3 minutes. Flip and cook the chops to your desired doneness, 2 to 3 minutes for medium-rare (130° to 135°F on an instant-read thermometer). Transfer the chops to a plate and cover with foil. Repeat with the remaining lamb chops and transfer to the same plate. Cover with the foil and let rest for 5 minutes.
5. **To serve:** Place a generous dollop of lemon-garlic yogurt on each of four plates, then use the back of a spoon to spread it into a smooth half circle, covering about half the plate. Place 2 lamb chops on top of the yogurt and spoon the herb salsa over everything. Sprinkle with some flaky salt and enjoy!

Broiled Four-Cheese Mac and Cheese

SERVES 6 ◆ PREP TIME: 10 MINUTES ◆ TOTAL TIME: 1 HOUR

This mac and cheese has the best of all worlds. It's creamy and saucy, with al dente noodles and a melted cheesy topping. I usually steer clear of baked mac and cheese because it pains me when the noodles turn soggy. The fix is a quick broil that gives you that golden top without overcooking the pasta. For a more elevated take that reminds me of something you'd find at a modern American bistro, I use a blend of four cheeses and add a little mustard powder to enhance the cheesy flavor.

MAC AND CHEESE

Kosher salt

4 tablespoons (½ stick) unsalted butter

3 garlic cloves, finely chopped

¼ cup all-purpose flour

4 cups whole milk

½ teaspoon freshly ground black pepper

½ teaspoon mustard powder

Dash of cayenne pepper

Dash of ground nutmeg

1 (8-ounce) package cream cheese

1 cup (4 ounces) shredded white cheddar cheese

¾ cup (3 ounces) shredded mozzarella cheese

¼ cup (1 ounce) grated Parmesan cheese

1 pound medium shell pasta

TOPPINGS

1¼ cups (5 ounces) shredded mozzarella cheese

2 tablespoons grated Parmesan cheese

HOW TO MAKE A BÉCHAMEL

1. **Make the mac and cheese:** Bring a large pot of generously salted water to a boil.
2. In another large pot, melt the butter over medium heat. Add the garlic and flour and cook, whisking continuously, until smooth and bubbling, 1 to 2 minutes. Slowly pour in the milk, 1 cup at a time, whisking to incorporate after each addition. Increase the heat to medium-high and cook, whisking occasionally, until the sauce bubbles and thickens enough to coat the back of a spoon, about 6 minutes. Stir in 1¼ teaspoons salt, the black pepper, mustard powder, cayenne, and nutmeg.
3. Reduce the heat to low and add the cream cheese. Stir until melted, then whisk to fully incorporate into the sauce. Stir in the cheddar, mozzarella, and Parmesan. Keep the sauce warm over the lowest possible heat and stir it occasionally while you cook the pasta.
4. Add the pasta to the boiling water and stir to prevent the noodles from sticking together. Return the water to a boil and cook the pasta until before it's al dente, about 2 minutes less than the package directions.
5. Using a spider strainer, transfer the pasta directly to the pot with the cheese sauce, letting the excess water drip off (a little water clinging to the noodles is fine). Alternatively, drain the pasta and add it to the pot with the sauce.
6. Increase the heat to medium and cook the pasta in the sauce, stirring, until the pasta is cooked to your desired tenderness, about 2 minutes.
7. **Top the mac and cheese:** Position a rack in the upper third of the oven and turn on the broiler.
8. Transfer the mac and cheese to a 9 by 13-inch baking dish (or similar) and top with the mozzarella and Parmesan. Place on the top rack and broil until the cheese is melted with golden brown spots, 3 to 6 minutes. Enjoy!

Chicken Cordon Bleu *with Dijon Béchamel*

SERVES 2 ◆ PREP TIME: 25 MINUTES ◆ TOTAL TIME: 50 MINUTES

CHICKEN CORDON BLEU

Avocado oil spray or avocado oil, for the pan

2 boneless, skinless chicken breasts (about 1¼ pounds total)

Kosher salt and freshly ground black pepper

2 thin slices deli ham (2 ounces)

4 slices Swiss cheese (2½ ounces), torn in half

¼ cup all-purpose flour

1 large egg

¼ cup panko breadcrumbs

¼ cup breadcrumbs

DIJON BÉCHAMEL

1 tablespoon unsalted butter

1 tablespoon all-purpose flour

1 cup whole milk

1 tablespoon Dijon mustard

¼ teaspoon freshly ground black pepper

¼ teaspoon kosher salt, plus more if needed

Dash of cayenne pepper

Dash of ground nutmeg

Chopped fresh parsley, for serving

I developed this recipe for Doug after he mentioned how much he loves cordon bleu. Funny enough, I'd never made it before! I was surprised to learn that in France, it's actually pretty common—you can even find it premade in supermarkets. Meanwhile, here in the US, it's often thought of as a "fancy" meal. Despite its elegant, rolled-up presentation with the cheesy ham filling, it's quite simple to make. Since chicken breast can sometimes be on the dry side, I paired it with a creamy béchamel sauce infused with Dijon mustard for a bit of tang.

I love serving this with Mom and Dad's Spinach Salad with Eggs and Mushrooms (page 235) or The Simplest Broccoli (page 243).

1. **Make the chicken cordon bleu:** Preheat the oven to 425°F on convection mode (or 450°F on regular bake). Spray or drizzle a quarter-sheet pan with some oil.
2. Working with one chicken breast at a time, place the chicken between two pieces of plastic wrap and pound with the flat side of a meat mallet to ¼-inch thickness. Season both sides of the chicken breasts with salt and pepper.

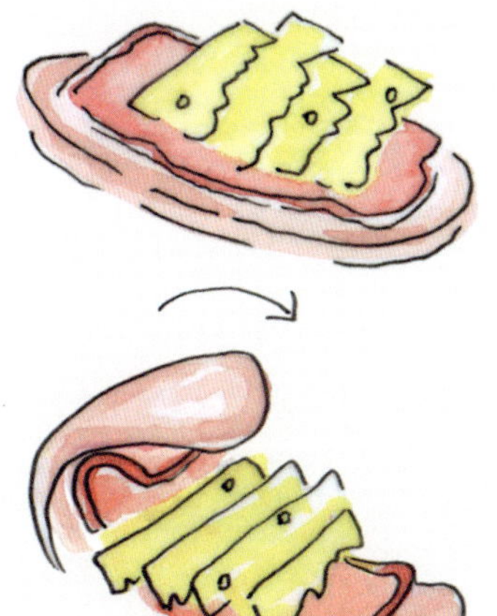

3. Place a slice of ham on one chicken breast, then place 4 half-pieces of cheese across the middle of the ham, stacking them. Starting at one short end, roll up the chicken breast to enclose the cheese and place it seam-side down on the cutting board. Repeat with the second chicken breast.
4. Place the flour in a large shallow bowl. Crack the egg into a second large shallow bowl and whisk with a fork to combine. In a third large shallow bowl, stir together the panko and breadcrumbs. Line up the bowls on the counter in this order: flour, egg, breadcrumbs.
5. With your hands, take a chicken roll, making sure the seam stays closed, and dredge it in the flour, gently rolling to coat all the sides and shaking off any excess. Dip it in the egg, gently rolling to coat, then lift away from the bowl, allowing the excess to drip back into the bowl. Roll it in the breadcrumb mixture to coat on all sides, pressing the crumbs with your fingers to adhere. Place the breaded chicken roll seam-side down on the prepared sheet pan. Repeat with the second chicken roll.
6. Generously spray (or drizzle) the chicken rolls with oil and bake until golden brown and the internal temperature registers 165°F on an instant-read thermometer, about 25 minutes. If the chicken is cooked through before it's golden brown, turn on the broiler and broil for 1 to 2 minutes.

HOW TO MAKE A BÉCHAMEL

7. **When the chicken has about 10 minutes left, make the Dijon béchamel:** In a small pot, melt the butter over medium-high heat. Add the flour and cook, whisking, for 1 minute. Add the milk, ¼ cup at a time, whisking to incorporate after each addition. Add the mustard, black pepper, salt, cayenne, and nutmeg. Cook, whisking often, until the mixture bubbles and thickens enough to coat the back of a spoon, about 2 minutes. Cover to keep warm if the chicken is still in the oven.
8. Serve the cordon bleu alongside the béchamel and garnish with some parsley. Enjoy!

Pan-Seared Fish *with Toasted Panko and Creamy Dill Sauce*

SERVES 2 ◆ PREP TIME: 10 MINUTES ◆ TOTAL TIME: 30 MINUTES

DILL SAUCE

2 tablespoons mayonnaise

2 tablespoons light sour cream

1 tablespoon chopped fresh dill

1 tablespoon fresh lemon juice

1 teaspoon drained capers, finely chopped

TOASTED PANKO

1 tablespoon unsalted butter

¼ cup panko breadcrumbs

Kosher salt

½ teaspoon lemon zest

FISH

2 (6-ounce) skin-on fish fillets, such as snapper, striped bass, or sockeye salmon

Kosher salt and freshly ground black pepper

1 tablespoon avocado oil or other neutral oil, such as grapeseed

1 tablespoon unsalted butter

Dill sprigs, for garnish

This recipe is a playful twist on fish and chips. It features a dill and caper sauce that reminds me of tartar sauce, and swaps out fried fish for pan-seared fish fillets sprinkled with toasted, buttery panko breadcrumbs. Despite its simplicity, the presentation makes it feel fancy while the crispy panko topping adds restaurant-worthy flair. You're guaranteed to impress with this dish.

I love serving this with Buttery Lemon Rice with Herbs (page 227) or Roasted Parmesan Asparagus (page 242).

1. **Make the dill sauce:** In a small bowl, combine the mayonnaise, sour cream, dill, lemon juice, and capers. Mix until well combined and set aside.
2. **Toast the panko:** In a large nonstick skillet, melt the butter over medium heat. Add the panko and a sprinkle of salt. Toast the panko, stirring continuously, until deep golden brown, 2 to 3 minutes. Transfer to a small bowl and mix in the lemon zest; set aside. Wipe out the skillet.
3. **Cook the fish:** Pat the fish fillets dry with paper towels and season both sides with salt and pepper.
4. In the same skillet, heat the avocado oil over medium-high heat. Add the fish fillets, skin-side down, and gently press with a spatula for 20 seconds. Cook until the skin is golden brown and the edges are opaque, 2 to 3 minutes. Flip the fillets and add the butter. Cook, tilting the skillet and using a spoon to baste the fish with the butter, until the fish is cooked through, 2 to 3 minutes more.
5. Divide the fish between two plates and add a dollop of dill sauce alongside. Sprinkle the toasted panko over the fish and sauce and garnish with dill. Enjoy!

Miso Carbonara Udon

SERVES 4 ◆ PREP TIME: 5 MINUTES ◆ TOTAL TIME: 35 MINUTES

6 large egg yolks (see Tips)

1 large egg

¼ cup (1 ounce) grated Pecorino Romano cheese

Freshly ground black pepper

8 ounces pancetta, guanciale, or bacon, cut into small dice

1 pound frozen udon noodles (see Tips)

2 tablespoons white miso paste

1 scallion, thinly sliced

I learned how to make carbonara from an Italian cook in Tuscany, who shared the secret to perfect pasta: Cook it only partway in boiling water (even less than al dente), then finish it in the sauce. This technique lets the noodles soak up more flavor while their starch naturally thickens the sauce. The ratios of egg, cheese, and pancetta come directly from his recipe, but the miso paste is my own little twist. It adds a deep, savory umami that makes the dish even more indulgent. (Doug couldn't get enough of this one!) For the best texture, I recommend using frozen udon noodles. They're thick and chewy, and they cook up super fast.

1. Bring a large pot of water to a boil. (No need to salt the water because you'll get plenty of salt from the other ingredients in this dish.)
2. In a medium bowl, beat the egg yolks and egg with the Pecorino Romano and a few grinds of pepper.
3. Heat a large skillet over medium-high heat. Add the pancetta and cook until golden brown and crispy, 6 to 8 minutes, then remove the skillet from the heat. Using a slotted spoon, transfer the pancetta to a plate, leaving the fat in the skillet. (Keep the skillet on the stove—you will use it again soon.)
4. While whisking continuously, drizzle 1 tablespoon of the hot fat into the eggs. (This will temper the eggs, keeping them from scrambling when added to the sauce.)
5. Add the udon to the boiling water, allow the water to return to a boil, and cook for 1 minute. Using tongs or a spider strainer, transfer the noodles directly to the skillet with the fat (or reserve 1 cup of the cooking water, then drain the noodles and transfer to the skillet). Add the miso, ¼ cup of the noodle cooking water, and 1 teaspoon pepper. Cook over medium-high heat, tossing the noodles, until coated in the sauce, about 1 minute. Add more noodle cooking water as needed to thin the sauce slightly so it better coats the noodles.
6. Remove the skillet from the heat. While mixing and tossing the udon with tongs, slowly pour in the egg mixture, then toss continuously until the sauce is silky and creamy (keep everything moving so the eggs don't cook from the heat of the skillet). Add more noodle cooking water as needed to loosen the sauce. Add all but 2 tablespoons of the pancetta and toss to combine with the noodles.
7. Divide among four plates, top with the scallion and reserved 2 tablespoons pancetta, and serve hot. Enjoy!

TIPS

Use the egg whites for the Egg White Frittata with Oyster Mushrooms and Goat Cheese on page 200.

You can use dried pasta (any shape) instead of frozen udon. Use 1 pound of pasta and increase the pancetta to 12 ounces. Boil the pasta for 3 minutes less than the package instructions, then drain it and cook in the skillet to the desired tenderness (for me, this is 3 to 4 minutes in the skillet, until al dente).

Mom's Benihana Chicken Fried Rice

SERVES 6 AS A SIDE OR 4 AS A MAIN
◆ PREP TIME: 20 MINUTES ◆ TOTAL TIME: 45 MINUTES

4 large eggs

Kosher salt and freshly ground black pepper

4 teaspoons avocado oil or other neutral oil, such as grapeseed, divided

1 boneless, skinless chicken breast (about 7 ounces), cut into ½-inch pieces

4 tablespoons soy sauce, divided

1 medium carrot (3 ounces), cut into small dice

½ medium yellow onion (5 ounces), cut into small dice

2 garlic cloves, finely chopped

4 cups Jasmine Rice (page 231; see Tip)

4 tablespoons (½ stick) unsalted butter, divided

2 tablespoons toasted sesame seeds

4 scallions, thinly sliced

TIP

Day-old rice is best, but fresh rice works, too. Use 1½ cups uncooked rice to make 4 cups cooked.

The best fried rice ever!

Buttery, salty, and packed with umami, this fried rice has been a family favorite for as long as I can remember. My mom based this recipe off the fried rice at Benihana, where she used to waitress in college, and it quickly became one of her signature dishes. When she was dating my dad in her early twenties, she'd surprise him after work with chocolate chip cookies and a big batch of this fried rice. (Safe to say, her cooking won him over!) What makes it even better is how versatile it is. Sometimes we swap the chicken for sliced mushrooms to keep it vegetarian, or go with bacon for a richer, more indulgent version.

1. In a small bowl, whisk the eggs with a sprinkle each of salt and pepper.
2. In a wok or large nonstick skillet, heat 2 teaspoons of the avocado oil over medium-high heat. Add the eggs and cook, stirring, until scrambled, 1 to 2 minutes. Transfer to a plate and set aside.
3. Add the remaining 2 teaspoons oil and the chicken to the skillet. Spread the chicken into an even layer and cook, undisturbed, until golden brown on the bottom, 3 to 4 minutes. Stir in 1 tablespoon of the soy sauce and cook, stirring, until almost cooked through, about 2 minutes.
4. Add the carrot, onion, and garlic. Cook, stirring, until the onion starts to soften and become translucent, about 3 minutes.
5. Add the rice, the remaining 3 tablespoons soy sauce, 2 tablespoons of the butter, the sesame seeds, 1 teaspoon pepper, and ½ teaspoon salt. Cook, stirring, until everything is combined, about 2 minutes.
6. Create a small well in the middle of the rice and add the remaining 2 tablespoons butter to the well. Cook, undisturbed, until the butter melts and the rice is crispy, 2 to 3 minutes. Stir the rice to mix up the buttery pieces. Cook, tossing once or twice, until there are more crispy bits, about 2 minutes.
7. Add the scrambled eggs and mix, breaking them up into smaller pieces with a spatula. Add the scallions and cook for about 1 minute, tossing two or three times until combined. Divide among bowls and enjoy!

Rotini *with Pesto and Frizzled Zucchini*

SERVES 4 ◆ PREP TIME: 5 MINUTES ◆ TOTAL TIME: 30 MINUTES

Kosher salt

¼ cup pine nuts

½ cup plus 2 tablespoons extra-virgin olive oil, divided

1 small, thin zucchini (3 ounces), sliced into ⅛-inch-thick rounds

2 cups (2 ounces) fresh basil leaves

½ cup (2 ounces) grated Parmesan cheese, plus more for serving

2 garlic cloves, peeled

1 tablespoon fresh lemon juice

1 pound rotini pasta or other corkscrew shape, such as fusilli

Flaky sea salt, such as Maldon

The first time I tasted real pesto was back in high school. I played water polo competitively, and our team traveled to Italy for matches against local teams. One of our stops was Genoa, in Liguria, a region famous for its pesto. In the evenings, we'd sit down for these amazing family-style dinners, often starting with pasta tossed in fresh, homemade pesto. That trip sparked a lifelong love for pesto, and now it's my go-to sauce for an easy and elegant pasta meal. I especially love pairing it with corkscrew pasta because the grooves catch every bit of sauce. For a special finish, I've added frizzled zucchini coins—they become slightly sweet and beautifully complement the vibrant pesto.

1. Bring a large pot of generously salted water to a boil.
2. In a small skillet, toast the pine nuts over medium-low heat, stirring frequently, until golden and fragrant, 3 to 4 minutes. Transfer to a small bowl to prevent them from burning and set aside.
3. Line a large plate with paper towels. In a large skillet, heat 2 tablespoons of the olive oil over medium heat. When the oil shimmers, add the zucchini in one layer (or as much of it as possible, depending on the size of your skillet) and season with salt. Cook until golden brown and crisped around the edges, 6 to 8 minutes, flipping it once halfway through. Using a spatula, transfer the zucchini to the paper towel–lined plate and set aside.
4. In a large food processor or blender, combine the remaining ½ cup olive oil, the basil, Parmesan, garlic, lemon juice, ½ teaspoon salt, and 2 tablespoons of the pine nuts. Process until smooth, 30 seconds to 1 minute, then transfer to a large bowl.
5. Add the pasta to the boiling water and cook according to the package directions until al dente (or to your liking), then drain in a colander. Immediately transfer the hot pasta to the bowl with the pesto and stir with a big spoon or spatula to evenly coat the pasta in the pesto.
6. Divide the pasta among four shallow bowls and top with the frizzled zucchini, a pinch of sea salt, and the remaining pine nuts. Serve with some Parmesan on top and enjoy!

Friday

let's come together

Small Bites for Sharing *with a Group of Loved Ones*

It's Friday and you've made it through the week—time to relax and maybe invite a few friends over to break bread. In my family, we sometimes skip a sit-down dinner when entertaining and instead serve a tapas-style meal with lots of small plates. Here you'll find small bites and appetizers, perfect for sharing and feeding a crowd. There's something for everyone, like my Potato Samosa Bites with Raita (page 142)—a flavorful, vegetarian option with some heat—and my mom's elegant shrimp scampi (page 154), which always looks stunning served in scallop shells. When I'm hosting, I like to prep as much as possible ahead of time, so many of these recipes can be made in advance and finished in the oven when guests arrive.

Mom's Healthy Rice Paper Dumplings

SERVES 8 TO 10 AS AN APPETIZER (MAKES 40 DUMPLINGS) ◆ PREP TIME: 30 MINUTES ◆ TOTAL TIME: 2 HOURS

FILLING

1 pound ground chicken (93/7 or similar; non-breast-only)

8 ounces peeled and deveined shrimp, cut into small dice

½ cup (2 ounces) finely chopped red cabbage

⅓ cup (1½ ounces) finely chopped carrot

3 tablespoons finely chopped fresh cilantro

2 tablespoons finely chopped fresh ginger

2 garlic cloves, finely chopped

3 scallions, sliced

1 large egg

2 tablespoons soy sauce

2 tablespoons toasted sesame oil

1½ teaspoons kosher salt

½ teaspoon freshly ground black pepper

FOR THE SERVING PLATE (OPTIONAL, BUT HIGHLY RECOMMENDED)

Chopped red cabbage

Chopped carrot

Chopped fresh cilantro

This is one of my mom's newer creations, and let me tell you, it's phenomenal. She had been raving about these rice paper dumplings for weeks, and honestly, I wasn't expecting much. She was so confident in them, that when she came to LA and we were cooking together, I told her nonchalantly to go ahead and make them. Then I took a bite, and I was completely blown away.

The outside has an incredibly crispy-chewy texture, while the filling is packed with flavor: chicken, shrimp, and loads of colorful veggies. These dumplings feel like a fusion of Vietnamese and Chinese cuisines, with the rice paper wrapper, nước chấm–inspired sauce, and potsticker-style filling. If you have time, I recommend lining the serving plate with chopped veggies. It prevents the dumplings from sticking and doubles as a slaw once you drizzle the sauce over the top.

1. **Make the filling:** In a large bowl, combine the ground chicken, shrimp, cabbage, carrot, cilantro, ginger, garlic, scallions, egg, soy sauce, sesame oil, salt, and pepper. Set aside.
2. **Prepare the serving plate, if desired:** Line a serving plate with cabbage, carrot, and cilantro, and set aside.
3. **Make the sauce:** In a small glass measuring cup or bowl, combine the warm water, fish sauce, sugar, lime juice, and cilantro. Stir until the sugar has dissolved and set aside.
4. **Make the dumplings:** Fill a pie dish or large bowl with warm water and place two damp paper towels on a cutting board, covering its surface, to prevent sticking. Line a sheet pan with damp paper towels. Working with one at a time, soak a rice paper wrapper in the water for 10 to 15 seconds, until pliable but still slightly firm (it will continue to soften as you work), then place it textured-side down on the damp paper towels.

SAUCE

¼ cup warm water

1 tablespoon fish sauce

1 tablespoon sugar

1 tablespoon fresh lime juice

1 tablespoon finely chopped fresh cilantro

DUMPLINGS

20 rice paper wrappers

3 tablespoons avocado oil or other neutral oil, such as grapeseed, plus more as needed

5. Cut the rice paper in half with a sharp knife and separate the two pieces. Add 1 slightly heaping tablespoon of filling to the center of each piece, fold the sides over the filling to form a triangle shape, fold the top tip of the triangle over, then flip the dumpling and fold the excess rice paper over the filling. (See page 141 for an illustrated step-by-step dumpling folding guide.) Place the dumplings on the paper towel–lined pan.
6. In a large nonstick skillet, heat 1 tablespoon of the avocado oil over medium heat. Working in batches, add the dumplings to the skillet, rubbing the bottoms in the oil and leaving a little space between each. (Careful—they can stick to one another if they're touching!) Cook until golden brown on the bottom, 4 to 6 minutes. Flip and cook until golden brown on the second side and cooked through (an instant-read thermometer should register 165°F), 2 to 4 minutes. Transfer the dumplings to the prepared serving plate, placing them on the chopped vegetables, if you like. (This prevents the dumplings from sticking to the plate as they sit.) Repeat with the remaining dumplings, adding 1 tablespoon of the oil to the skillet between each batch. The dumplings may cook faster as the skillet heats up, so check the bottoms frequently.
7. Drizzle some sauce on the dumplings and serve the rest on the side for dipping. Enjoy!

HOW TO FOLD A RICE PAPER DUMPLING

HOW TO FOLD A

rice paper dumpling

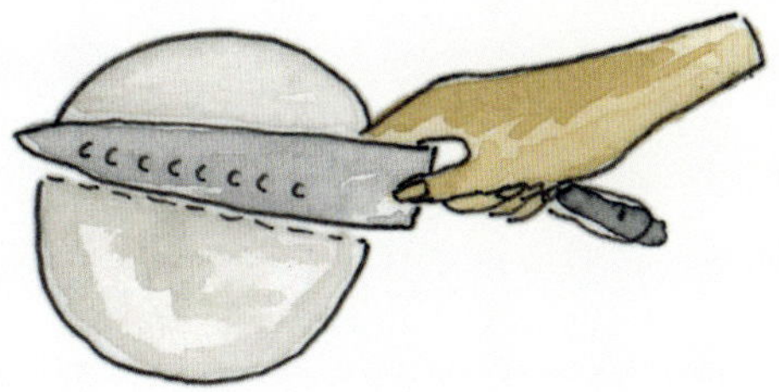

1. Cut the soaked rice paper wrapper in half with a sharp knife to create two equal pieces.

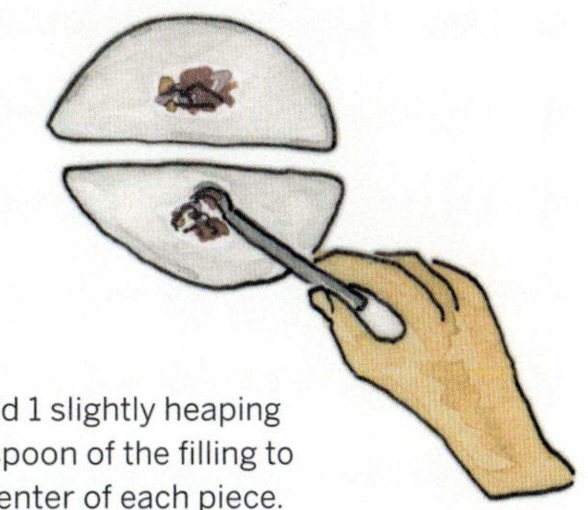

2. Add 1 slightly heaping tablespoon of the filling to the center of each piece.

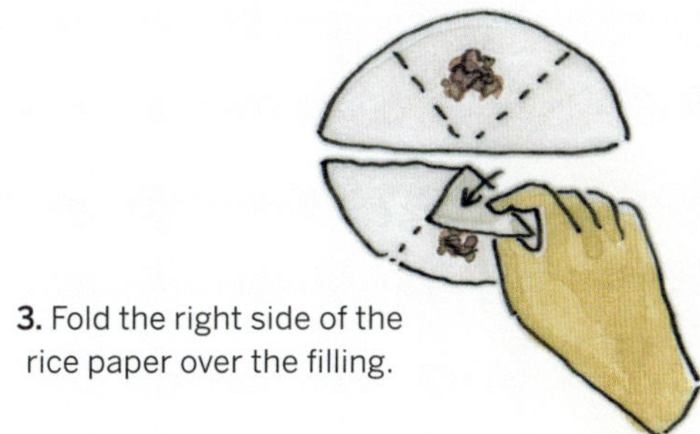

3. Fold the right side of the rice paper over the filling.

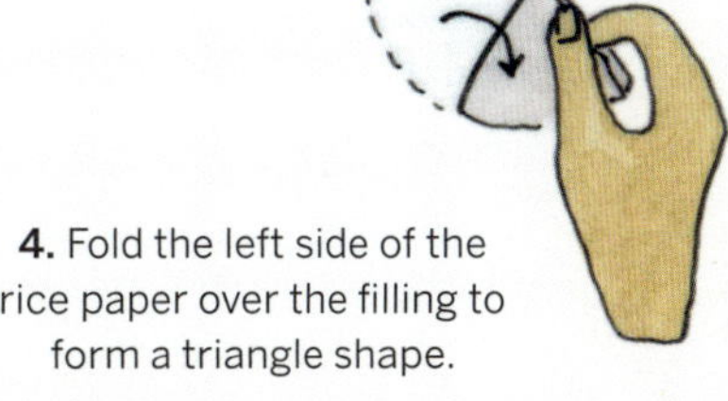

4. Fold the left side of the rice paper over the filling to form a triangle shape.

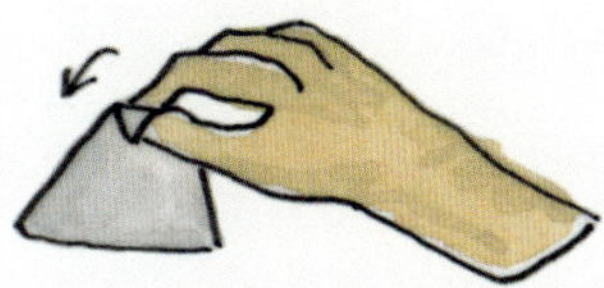

5. Fold the top tip of the triangle over.

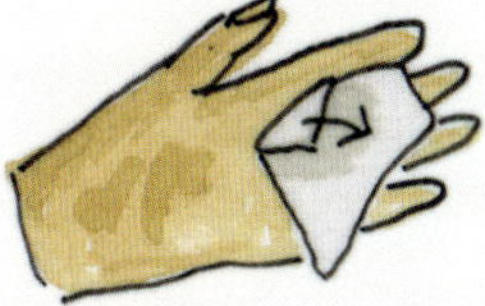

6. Pick up the dumpling and flip it over.

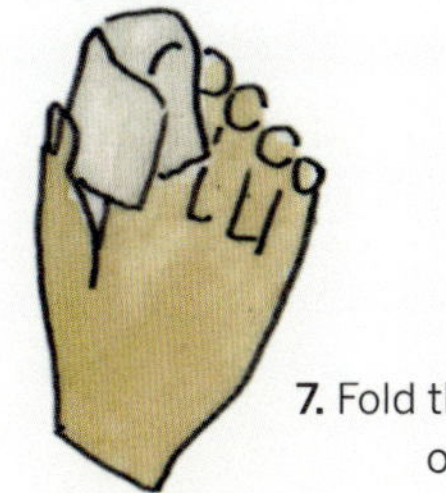

7. Fold the excess rice paper over the filling.

Potato Samosa Bites *with Raita*

SERVES 6 TO 8 AS AN APPETIZER (MAKES 24 BITES)
◆ PREP TIME: 25 MINUTES ◆ TOTAL TIME: 1 HOUR

SAMOSAS

Kosher salt

1 pound Yukon Gold potatoes, peeled and cut into 1½-inch pieces

1 tablespoon avocado oil or other neutral oil

1 tablespoon finely chopped fresh ginger

1 serrano pepper, seeded and finely chopped

½ cup frozen peas, thawed

1 teaspoon garam masala

½ teaspoon cumin seeds

½ teaspoon ground cumin

½ teaspoon ground turmeric

½ teaspoon kosher salt

2 tablespoons finely chopped fresh cilantro

All-purpose flour, for dusting

1 (8½- to 14-ounce) sheet frozen all-butter puff pastry dough, thawed in the refrigerator

2 tablespoons unsalted butter, melted

RAITA

1 cup plain full-fat or 2% Greek yogurt

2 Persian cucumbers (6 ounces), coarsely grated

1 garlic clove, grated or finely chopped

2 tablespoons finely chopped fresh cilantro

1 tablespoon fresh lemon juice

½ teaspoon ground cumin

Kosher salt

This recipe takes inspiration from one of my favorite Indian snacks: veggie samosas. The flaky crust of a samosa reminds me of puff pastry, so I used store-bought frozen puff pastry and a mini muffin pan to create these bite-size versions. The potato and pea filling is loaded with bold flavors like fresh ginger, garam masala, and cumin. I like to serve these warm alongside a cool cucumber raita—it's the perfect balance to the spices and really brings everything together.

1. Preheat the oven to 400°F.
2. **Make the samosas:** Bring a medium pot of salted water to a boil. Add the potatoes and boil until easily pierced with a fork, 15 to 20 minutes. Drain and let cool in the colander, then transfer to a large bowl and crumble into small pieces with your hands.
3. Rinse and dry out the pot, then pour in the avocado oil and heat over medium heat. Add the ginger and serrano pepper and cook, stirring, until fragrant, about 1 minute. Add the peas, garam masala, cumin seeds, ground cumin, turmeric, and salt. Cook, stirring, until the spices are fragrant, 1 to 2 minutes. Add the potatoes and cook for 1 minute, stirring to combine all the ingredients. Remove from the heat and stir in the cilantro.
4. Dust a clean work surface with flour. Unfold the puff pastry, then roll it out into an 8 by 12-inch rectangle. Cut the pastry into twenty-four 2-inch squares. (Cut the 8-inch end of the pastry into four 2-inch-wide strips and the 12-inch end into six 2-inch-wide strips to create 24 small squares.)
5. Lightly brush a 24-cup nonstick mini muffin pan with some of the melted butter. Place a puff pastry square in each of the cups, push the pastry down, and press it against the sides of the cup. Fill each cup with 1 tablespoon of the potato mixture. Brush the top of the potato filling and the exposed puff pastry with more melted butter. Bake until golden brown, 20 to 22 minutes.
6. **Meanwhile, make the raita:** In a medium bowl, stir together the yogurt, cucumber, garlic, cilantro, lemon juice, cumin, and ½ teaspoon salt. Taste and season with more salt, if desired.
7. Serve the samosa bites warm, with the raita on the side, and enjoy!

Cheesy Broccoli Bites

SERVES 8 TO 10 AS AN APPETIZER (MAKES 48 BITES) ◆ PREP TIME: 15 MINUTES ◆ TOTAL TIME: 2 HOURS

2 tablespoons unsalted butter, plus more for greasing

1 medium yellow onion (10 ounces), cut into small dice

1 garlic clove, finely chopped

Kosher salt and freshly ground black pepper

1 pound broccoli crowns, coarsely chopped into small pieces

1 cup (120 grams) all-purpose flour

1 cup (4 ounces) shredded mozzarella cheese

1 cup whole milk

2 large eggs

1 teaspoon baking powder

½ cup (2 ounces) plus 2 tablespoons grated Parmesan cheese

These broccoli bites are a twist on a recipe my mom used to make with spinach. We developed this version together, packing in a full pound of broccoli and two types of cheese for a combo that's sure to win over both kids and adults. They do take a bit of time since you bake them twice (the second bake gets those edges really crispy!), but they're super easy and ideal for making ahead. Just arrange them on a sheet pan, store them in the fridge, and pop them in the oven for their final bake when guests arrive. They're a crowd-pleasing appetizer everyone will love!

1. Preheat the oven to 375°F. Grease a 9 by 13-inch baking dish and a sheet pan with butter.
2. In a large skillet, melt the butter over medium heat. Add the onion and garlic, season with salt and pepper, and cook, stirring, until the onion is translucent, about 4 minutes.
3. Add the broccoli and cook, stirring, until bright green and slightly tender, about 5 minutes. Transfer the broccoli mixture to a large bowl and let cool for a few minutes.
4. Add the flour, mozzarella, milk, eggs, baking powder, and 2 teaspoons salt to the broccoli mixture and stir to combine.
5. Pour the mixture into the prepared baking dish and smooth the top into an even layer. Evenly sprinkle the Parmesan on top. Bake until golden brown and a toothpick inserted into the center comes out clean, 30 to 35 minutes. Let cool for 15 minutes.
6. Using a sharp knife, cut into 24 squares (make four lengthwise cuts, then six crosswise cuts). Cut each square in half on a diagonal to create two triangles. You should have 48 triangles total.
7. Using a small spatula, transfer the broccoli bites to the prepared sheet pan, leaving a little space between them. (At this stage, you can let the bites cool completely, then cover and refrigerate them until your guests arrive.) Bake the bites until slightly crisp around the edges, about 15 minutes. (This will also firm them up.) Let cool for 5 minutes, then transfer the bites to a platter or large plate and serve warm. Enjoy!

↖ These are great for kids and reheat well!

Honey-Soy Glazed Edamame

SERVES 4 AS AN APPETIZER ◆ PREP TIME: 5 MINUTES ◆ TOTAL TIME: 25 MINUTES

Kosher salt

2 tablespoons soy sauce

1 tablespoon plus 1 teaspoon honey

1 tablespoon toasted sesame seeds, plus more for serving

1 tablespoon rice vinegar

1 (14- to 16-ounce) package frozen edamame soybeans in pods

2 tablespoons unsalted butter

3 garlic cloves, finely chopped

½ teaspoon crushed red pepper flakes, plus more for serving

Flaky sea salt, such as Maldon

This quick and easy appetizer is seriously finger-licking good—you'll be fishing for every last edamame pod at the bottom of the bowl! It's bursting with bold, punchy flavors from a sweet and salty sauce, while a touch of butter adds the right amount of richness and helps the sesame seeds cling to the pods. Since edamame is high in protein, it's a healthy, satisfying, and well-balanced dish, making it an ideal starter for any Asian-inspired meal!

1. Bring a large pot of generously salted water to a boil.
2. Meanwhile, in a small bowl, mix together the soy sauce, honey, sesame seeds, vinegar, and ¼ teaspoon salt. Set aside.
3. Add the edamame to the boiling water. Cook at a gentle boil until the edamame are heated through and slightly tender, 4 to 5 minutes. Drain and set aside.
4. In the same pot, melt the butter over medium heat. Add the garlic and red pepper flakes and cook, stirring, until the garlic is fragrant and starting to turn golden brown, about 1 minute.
5. Add the honey-soy mixture and cook until the sauce thickens slightly, about 1 minute. Add the edamame and toss until completely coated in the sauce, about 1 minute.
6. Transfer the edamame to a serving bowl. Top with more red pepper flakes and sesame seeds and a sprinkle of flaky salt. Serve with a bowl on the side for discarding the pods and enjoy!

CROSSROADS

Smoked Trout Dip *with Pickled Onion*

SERVES 6 TO 8 AS AN APPETIZER ◆ PREP TIME: 20 MINUTES ◆ TOTAL TIME: 35 MINUTES

TROUT DIP

4 ounces (½ cup) cream cheese, softened

¼ cup light or full-fat sour cream

2 tablespoons chopped fresh chives

2 tablespoons chopped fresh dill

2 tablespoons pickled onion (see page 105), drained, patted dry, and finely chopped

1 teaspoon lemon zest (from 1 lemon)

2 tablespoons fresh lemon juice, plus more if needed

¼ teaspoon freshly ground black pepper, plus more if needed

8 ounces smoked trout, skin removed, flesh finely chopped or broken into small pieces

FOR SERVING

Chopped fresh chives

Dill sprigs

Extra-virgin olive oil, preferably a high-quality finishing oil

Flaky sea salt, such as Maldon

Pickled onion (see page 105)

Crackers, such as Ritz

I'm all about contrasting textures, so for this bright, creamy dip, I chose to hand-chop the trout and herbs instead of blending them with a food processor like it's often made. This approach not only lets the fresh flavors of lemon, chives, and dill shine but also gives the trout a nice rustic texture. The pickled onion, inspired by the trout dip at Found Oyster, one of my favorite spots in LA, brings an unexpected tang, a hint of sweetness, and an amazing crunch. Found Oyster pairs their dip with Ritz crackers, and it's a match made in heaven. The buttery, flaky crackers are the best complement to the salty, zesty flavors. Once you try it, you'll never want to serve trout dip any other way!

1. **Make the trout dip:** In a medium bowl, combine the cream cheese, sour cream, chives, dill, pickled onion, lemon zest, lemon juice, and pepper. Mix until all the ingredients are evenly distributed. Add the trout and mix, breaking it up into smaller pieces, until well combined. Taste and season with more pepper and/or lemon juice, if desired. (The trout dip can be stored in an airtight container in the refrigerator for up to 4 days; see Tip.)
2. **To serve:** Transfer the dip to a serving bowl. Sprinkle with chives and a few sprigs of dill. Drizzle with some high-quality olive oil and sprinkle with some flaky salt. Place a small mound of pickled onion on top of the dip. Serve with crackers and a knife for spreading and enjoy!

TIP

If you have leftover trout dip, save it for an open-face sandwich. Simply spread it on toasted bread and top with some pickled onion. It makes an easy and delicious lunch!

Spicy Whipped Feta Dip *with Toasted Pita*

SERVES 4 TO 6 AS AN APPETIZER ◆ PREP TIME: 10 MINUTES ◆ TOTAL TIME: 15 MINUTES, PLUS 1 HOUR FOR RESTING

1 (8-ounce) block feta cheese, broken into pieces

¾ cup plain full-fat or 2% Greek yogurt

1 tablespoon fresh lemon juice, plus more if needed

¼ cup extra-virgin olive oil, plus more as needed

1 tablespoon finely chopped fresh dill, plus a few sprigs for garnish

2 teaspoons crushed Calabrian chili peppers in oil (see Tip), plus more as needed

4 pita breads

TIP

For a bigger spread, serve the dip with some colorful crudités like Persian cucumbers, carrots, endives, and radishes.

A good dip always hits the spot, but oftentimes I find they can feel a bit heavy—think a spinach and artichoke or queso. I wanted to create something light, refreshing, *and* satisfying, and this whipped feta dip is just that! Tangy and cool with a spicy kick from Calabrian chilies (yum), it's served with warm toasted pita for a wonderful contrast of flavors and temperatures.

The Greek yogurt creates a luscious and silky texture that complements the brininess of feta cheese. And I love that you can prepare this dish hours in advance because, believe it or not, I get a little bit stressed when hosting. I'm always on the lookout for recipes like this one that I can make ahead and stash in the fridge until guests arrive.

1. In a food processor or blender, combine the feta, yogurt, and lemon juice. Pulse until the feta breaks down and blends with the yogurt, about 1 minute. With the food processor running, slowly stream in the olive oil and pulse until smooth, 1 to 2 minutes more.
2. If the mixture is looking a bit grainy, place a fine-mesh sieve over a medium bowl. Pour the feta mixture into the sieve (working in batches, if needed) and use a silicone spatula to press it against the sieve. Discard the bits of cheese that do not make it through the strainer. (This will give you the creamiest, silkiest feta, but you can skip this step if you prefer.)
3. Stir the dill and Calabrian chili peppers into the whipped feta. Taste and add more chilies and/or lemon juice, if you desire.
4. Cover and refrigerate the dip for at least 1 hour or up to overnight. (It will thicken the longer it chills.)
5. When you are ready to serve, brush both sides of the pitas with some olive oil. Heat a medium skillet over medium-high heat. Working with one at a time, add the pitas and cook until hot and toasted, 1 to 2 minutes per side. Cut into 6 to 8 wedges each.
6. Give the dip a stir, then drizzle with a little olive oil. Garnish with some fresh dill and a small dollop of Calabrian chili peppers, if you like, and enjoy!

Bacon and Parsley Stuffed Mushrooms *with Crispy Tops*

SERVES 6 AS AN APPETIZER (MAKES 18 TO 20 STUFFED MUSHROOMS, DEPENDING ON THE SIZE OF YOUR MUSHROOMS!)
◆ PREP TIME: 15 MINUTES ◆ TOTAL TIME: 1 HOUR 10 MINUTES

4 slices bacon

1 pound cremini or white button mushrooms, ideally small and evenly sized

4 ounces (½ cup) cream cheese, at room temperature

¼ cup finely chopped fresh parsley, plus more for serving

3 tablespoons grated Parmesan cheese

2 tablespoons Italian-style breadcrumbs

2 garlic cloves, finely chopped

Kosher salt and freshly ground black pepper

3 tablespoons unsalted butter, melted

¼ cup panko breadcrumbs

These stuffed mushrooms are inspired by the way my mom always made them when I was growing up—filled with bacon, parsley, cream cheese, and finely chopped mushroom stems for extra tenderness. The filling is rich, creamy, and salty, with fresh parsley running through to brighten it up. But I felt it needed one more thing: a little crunch! So I took her already amazing recipe and added a buttery panko topping for a crispy finish. It's just the right amount of texture pop.

You can prep and stuff the mushrooms up to a day in advance and keep them in the fridge until ready to bake.

1. Preheat the oven to 400°F. Line a large plate with paper towels.
2. Place the bacon in a large skillet in a single layer. Cook over medium heat until crispy, 8 to 12 minutes, flipping once halfway through. Transfer to the paper towel–lined plate to drain excess fat and cool slightly. When cool enough to handle, finely chop the bacon and place it in a large bowl.
3. Remove the mushroom stems from the caps. Finely chop half the stems and add them to the bowl with the bacon (discard the remaining stems). Add the cream cheese, parsley, Parmesan, Italian-style breadcrumbs, garlic, ¼ teaspoon salt, and ¼ teaspoon pepper. Mix until all the ingredients are evenly distributed.
4. Place the mushroom caps gill-side down on a sheet pan. Brush with half the melted butter and sprinkle with a little salt and pepper.
5. Place the panko in a small bowl. Working with one mushroom at a time, stuff the gill-side cavity with the filling (it should heap out like a dome). Roll the stuffed side in the panko to coat, then return the mushroom to the sheet pan, panko-side up. (You may have a little extra filling, depending on the size of the mushrooms, which you can save in the refrigerator for scrambling with some eggs the next morning!)
6. Brush or drizzle the panko with the remaining melted butter and bake until the mushrooms are tender and the topping is golden brown, 25 to 30 minutes.
7. Transfer to a serving plate, sprinkle with a little parsley, and enjoy warm!

Mom's Garlic-Butter Shrimp Scampi

SERVES 2 AS A MAIN OR 4 AS AN APPETIZER ◆ PREP TIME: 10 MINUTES ◆ TOTAL TIME: 35 MINUTES

1 pound large shrimp, peeled (tails left on) and deveined

Kosher salt and freshly ground black pepper

¼ cup Italian-style breadcrumbs

4 tablespoons (½ stick) unsalted butter

2 garlic cloves, finely chopped

¼ cup (1 ounce) grated Parmesan cheese

Lemon wedges, for serving

1 tablespoon finely chopped fresh parsley (optional)

This shrimp scampi is a staple in my kitchen and my go-to appetizer for dinner parties. The garlic butter soaks into the breadcrumbs and Parmesan, creating a delicious golden crust over the shrimp. Best of all, it's incredibly easy to prepare but looks impressively elegant, especially when served in individual scallop shells. (You can find them online—just search for "scallop shells for baking"!) For a crowd, double the recipe and assemble it in a larger dish, keeping the shrimp in a single layer for even baking.

1. Preheat the oven to 375°F.
2. Pat the shrimp dry and lightly season both sides with salt and pepper. Place them in a 9-inch baking dish in one layer and top with the breadcrumbs. (If you are using individual scallop shells, put 4 or 5 shrimps on each shell, arranging them in a circular pattern with the heads toward the center and the tails facing the edge.)
3. In a small skillet, melt the butter over medium-low heat. Add the garlic and cook, stirring, until the garlic just starts to sizzle, about 1 minute. Spoon the garlic butter over the shrimp and sprinkle the Parmesan on top.
4. Bake until golden brown, 18 to 20 minutes. Remove from the oven and squeeze some lemon juice over the top. Sprinkle with the parsley, if using, and serve with more lemon wedges on the side. Enjoy!

My go-to for dinner parties

Grandpa's Korean Vegetable Pancakes

SERVES 4 AS AN APPETIZER (MAKES ABOUT 10 PANCAKES)
◆ PREP TIME: 20 MINUTES ◆ TOTAL TIME: 45 MINUTES

DIPPING SAUCE

2 tablespoons soy sauce

1 tablespoon fresh lemon juice

1 tablespoon toasted sesame oil

1 teaspoon toasted sesame seeds

1 teaspoon water

½ teaspoon sugar

PANCAKES

1 cup all-purpose flour

1 cup water

½ teaspoon kosher salt

1 cup thinly sliced leek greens (from 1 large leek)

½ cup (2 ounces) coarsely grated or julienned carrot

½ cup (1½ ounces) thinly sliced red cabbage

3 scallions, halved lengthwise, then cut crosswise into 1-inch pieces

1 jalapeño, seeded and thinly sliced into 1-inch-long strips

2 tablespoons avocado oil or other neutral oil, such as grapeseed, plus more if needed

My Korean grandpa was an incredible cook, and these pancakes were one of his specialties. He came to the US for pharmacy school, fell in love with my grandma, and then lived in America for the rest of his life. He loved this country and was so proud to have immigrated and raised a family here. What made his cooking so special was his sense of taste: He was a super-taster, meaning he had an enhanced ability to detect subtle flavors and nuances that most people might miss. He could perfectly recreate a recipe from memory, like he once did for the Benihana ginger salad dressing.

Despite his love for the Costco hot dog, McDonald's Egg McMuffin, and Taco Bell Enchirito, he never forgot about his favorite Korean dishes. I have countless memories of him huddled over the range at my parents' house, his little Korean pancake factory churning out one slice of heaven after another. Grandpa used to make large, pan-size pancakes, but I like individual ones for maximum crispiness around the edges. Although he's no longer with us, his legacy lives on with this family recipe and many others. I know he would be proud.

1. **Make the dipping sauce:** In a small bowl, stir together the soy sauce, lemon juice, sesame oil, sesame seeds, water, and sugar until the sugar dissolves. Set aside.
2. **Make the pancakes:** Line a sheet pan with paper towels.
3. In a large bowl, whisk together the flour, water, and salt. Add the leek, carrot, cabbage, scallions, and jalapeño. Mix to combine.
4. In a large skillet, heat the avocado oil over medium heat. Working in batches, dollop ¼ cup of the batter onto the skillet for each pancake, leaving a little space between the dollops. Using a spatula, spread the vegetables in each pancake into an even layer. Cook until golden brown, 2 to 3 minutes per side. Transfer the pancakes to the prepared sheet pan to drain excess oil. Repeat with the remaining batter, adding more oil to the skillet between batches if it looks dry.
5. Serve immediately as you go, while the pancakes are hot and fresh, with the sauce on the side for dipping. Enjoy!

Crispy Zucchini Coins *with Creamy Lemon-Dill Sauce*

SERVES 4 AS AN APPETIZER (MAKES 23 TO 25 COINS)
◆ PREP TIME: 15 MINUTES ◆ TOTAL TIME: 45 MINUTES

LEMON-DILL DIPPING SAUCE

½ cup plain full-fat or 2% Greek yogurt

3 tablespoons mayonnaise

2 tablespoons finely chopped fresh dill

1 tablespoon fresh lemon juice, plus more if needed

¼ teaspoon kosher salt, plus more if needed

ZUCCHINI COINS

1 medium zucchini (8 ounces), sliced into ¼-inch rounds (look for a longer, thinner zucchini)

Kosher salt and freshly ground black pepper

¼ cup rice flour

BATTER

⅓ cup all-purpose flour

3 tablespoons rice flour

¼ teaspoon kosher salt, plus more for sprinkling

½ cup plus 2 tablespoons seltzer

Peanut oil or other neutral oil, such as grapeseed, for frying

These zucchini coins are incredibly crispy on the outside, while the inside stays soft and tender. The light, rice flour batter reminds me of tempura—it crisps up without weighing the zucchini down. You can prep everything in advance and mix the batter just before frying for the best texture. Serve them warm with a refreshing lemon-dill yogurt sauce, made extra creamy with a touch of mayo.

1. **Make the lemon-dill dipping sauce:** In a small bowl, mix together the yogurt, mayonnaise, dill, lemon juice, and salt. Taste and add more lemon juice and/or salt, if you like. Set aside in the refrigerator.
2. **Make the zucchini coins:** Place the zucchini on a cutting board or sheet pan and season lightly with salt and pepper on both sides. Place the rice flour in a small bowl. Line a large plate or sheet pan with paper towels.
3. **Make the batter:** In a medium bowl, mix together the all-purpose flour, rice flour, and salt.
4. When you're ready to cook the zucchini, add the seltzer and whisk to combine.
5. Fill a large heavy skillet with ¼ inch of peanut oil and heat over medium-high heat to 350°F. (Use an instant-read thermometer to check the oil temperature, or test it by dipping the edge of a zucchini round into the oil—if it bubbles immediately, the oil is hot enough.)
6. Working with one zucchini coin at a time, dredge in the rice flour, then dip in the batter to coat. Let the excess batter drip off, then slip the battered zucchini into the hot oil. Repeat until the skillet is full, leaving some space between the coins. Fry until golden brown, 2 to 3 minutes per side, using tongs to flip them halfway through. Transfer to the prepared plate and sprinkle with some salt. Repeat with the remaining zucchini coins.
7. Serve immediately, while the zucchini coins are hot and fresh, with the lemon-dill dipping sauce on the side. Enjoy!

one of my faves ↗

French Onion Crostini

CARAMELIZED ONIONS

3 tablespoons unsalted butter

2 pounds yellow onions (about 3 medium), thinly sliced

¾ teaspoon kosher salt

¼ teaspoon freshly ground black pepper

WHITE SAUCE

1 tablespoon unsalted butter

1 garlic clove, finely chopped

1 tablespoon plus 1 teaspoon all-purpose flour

1 cup whole milk

1 teaspoon fresh thyme leaves, or ¼ teaspoon dried

¼ teaspoon kosher salt

¼ teaspoon freshly ground black pepper

3 ounces Gruyère cheese, grated (¾ cup)

CROSTINI

6 tablespoons extra-virgin olive oil

1 French baguette (about 10 ounces), sliced into ½-inch-thick rounds

3 ounces Gruyère cheese, grated (¾ cup)

Fresh thyme leaves, for garnish

HOW TO MAKE A BÉCHAMEL

SERVES 6 TO 8 AS AN APPETIZER (MAKES ABOUT 30 CROSTINI)
◆ PREP TIME: 15 MINUTES ◆ TOTAL TIME: 2 HOURS

I love this method for crostini because it makes the bread so incredibly crispy. You slice a baguette into thin rounds, rub the bottoms with olive oil on a sheet pan, add your topping, and bake until deeply golden. In each bite, you get the crunch of toasted bread against the creamy softness of a caramelized onion white sauce. Inspired by French onion soup, these crostini combine the natural sweetness of caramelized onions with the earthy sharpness of Gruyère cheese. Whenever I make them, I can't stop going back for more!

1. **Make the caramelized onions:** In a large pot, melt the butter over medium heat. Add the onions, salt, and pepper and cook, stirring, until the onions start to soften, about 10 minutes. Reduce the heat to medium-low and cook, stirring occasionally, until golden brown, tender, and caramelized, 40 to 50 minutes more. Transfer the onions to a medium bowl. (No need to wash the pot; you'll use it in the next step!)
2. Preheat the oven to 425°F.
3. **Make the white sauce:** In the same pot, melt the butter over medium heat. Add the garlic and flour and cook, stirring, until bubbling and fragrant, 30 seconds to 1 minute. Add the milk, ¼ cup at a time, whisking to incorporate after each addition. Add the thyme, salt, and pepper and cook, whisking continuously, until the sauce bubbles and thickens, about 2 minutes. Stir in the Gruyère and cook until melted, about 1 minute. Remove from the heat and stir in the caramelized onions. Let cool for a few minutes while you prepare the crostini. (The onions and sauce can be stored in an airtight container in the refrigerator for up to 3 days.)
4. **Assemble the crostini:** Coat a sheet pan with the olive oil. Spread a layer of the onion mixture over each baguette round, placing them on the prepared sheet pan as you go and rubbing the underside of each round in the oil to ensure it is nicely coated. Leave a sliver of space between the crostini.
5. Sprinkle the Gruyère over the crostini and bake until golden brown and crispy and the cheese has melted, 15 to 18 minutes. For a deeper golden brown, you can broil the crostini for 1 to 2 minutes.
6. Remove from the oven and sprinkle with some fresh thyme. Let cool for 5 minutes, then transfer to a serving plate or platter. Enjoy warm!

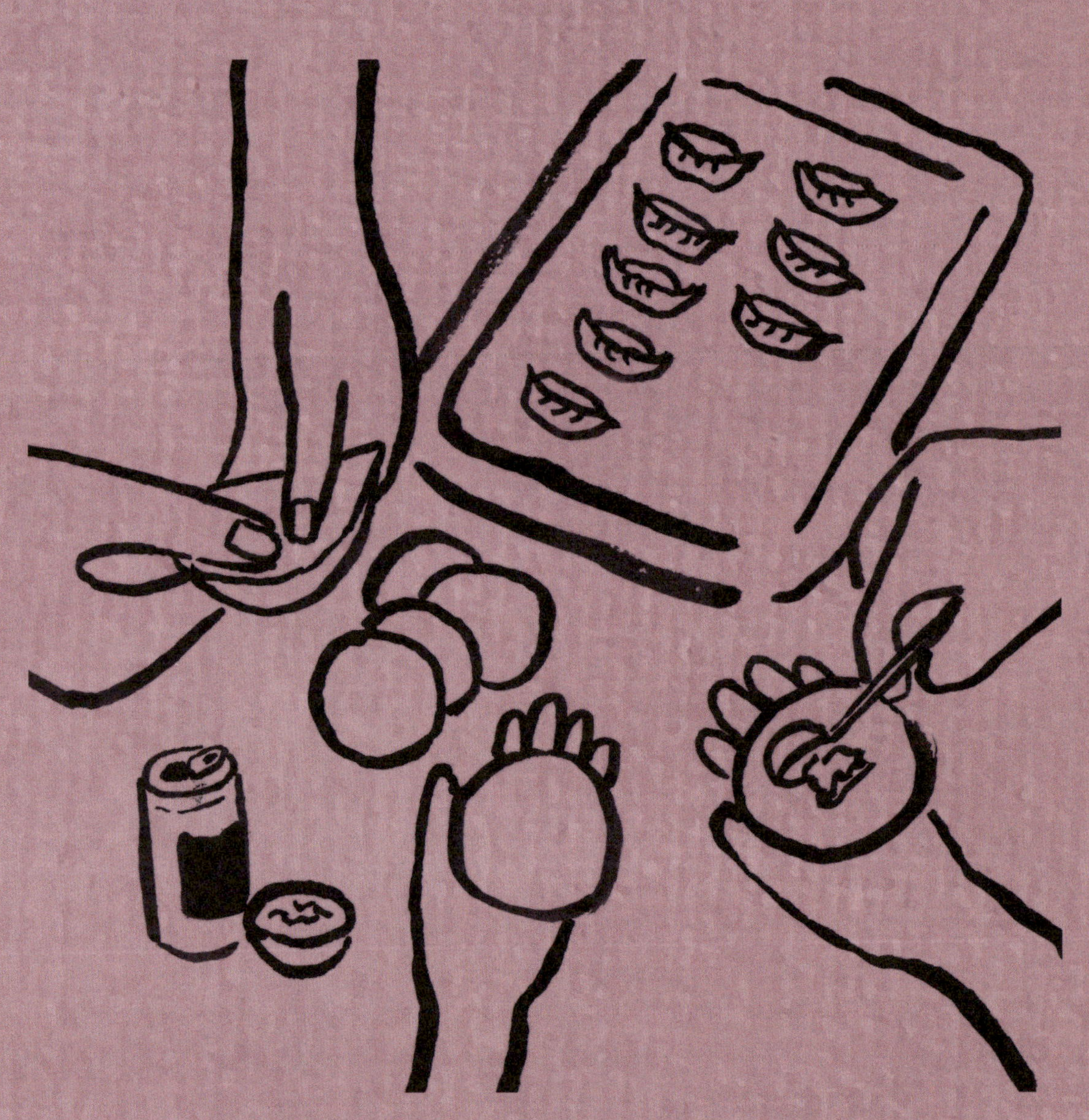

Saturday

let's adventure

Immersive and Enjoyable Recipes *for a Fun Weekend Activity*

Now that it's the weekend and you've got some extra time, why not tackle a fun, creative cooking project? These recipes are perfect for snow days, holiday gatherings when everyone's hanging out at home, or those lazy Saturdays when you finally feel ready to make artisan bread (page 178—it's SO much easier than it looks). In this chapter, you'll find my childhood favorites like potstickers (page 172) and wontons (page 192)—recipes that are even more fun when made with a group. You'll also get the chance to try your hand at homemade pork buns, pasta, and Chinese hand-pulled noodles. No special skills are required, and I'll guide you through every step with detailed illustrations. Just be ready to roll up your sleeves, set aside a few hours, and maybe invite some friends or family over for a little extra help.

Chinese Hand-Pulled Noodles *with Chili Oil and Scallions*

SERVES 4 ◆ PREP TIME: 15 MINUTES ◆ TOTAL TIME: 1 HOUR 15 MINUTES, PLUS 1 HOUR 30 MINUTES FOR RESTING

NOODLE DOUGH

3 cups (360 grams) all-purpose flour

½ teaspoon kosher salt

¾ cup water, plus more if needed

2 tablespoons avocado oil or other neutral oil, such as grapeseed

SAUCE

3 tablespoons soy sauce

3 tablespoons rice vinegar

2 tablespoons toasted sesame oil

1 garlic clove, finely chopped

¼ teaspoon sugar

FOR COOKING AND SERVING

Kosher salt

Chili oil crisp

Sliced scallions

Chopped fresh cilantro

Toasted sesame seeds

You might think hand-pulled noodles are really hard to make, but they're actually easier to master than you'd expect! These noodles have an amazing chew and bounce (because you know I can't stand a soggy noodle). And since they're the star of the show, all they need is a simple, punchy sauce and fresh herbs.

The dough can be made ahead and stored in the fridge, making this the perfect recipe for impressing guests. Prep everything in advance (herbs washed, sauce mixed) then pull the noodles to order, just like at a Chinese noodle shop. Get ready to wow with your skills!

1. **Make the noodle dough:** In a medium bowl, whisk together the flour and salt.
2. Make a well in the center of the flour mixture, then gradually pour the water into the middle of the well, stirring with chopsticks (or a spoon) to incorporate before adding more. Mix until a shaggy dough starts to form, then use your hands to knead the dough in the bowl, folding and rotating the dough, until all the flour has been incorporated, 2 to 3 minutes. If there is still flour left in the bowl, add a little water, 1 teaspoon at a time, until all the flour is incorporated. Shape the dough into a ball. Cover the bowl with a clean dish towel and let rest for 30 minutes.
3. Turn the dough out onto a clean work surface and knead until smooth and elastic, about 10 minutes. Cover and let rest for 5 minutes more. (Alternatively, knead the dough in the bowl of a stand mixer fitted with the dough hook; knead on medium-low speed until smooth and elastic, 8 to 10 minutes.)
4. Transfer the dough to a large cutting board or clean work surface and roll it out to a rectangle about 5 by 16 inches and about ¼ inch thick. Using a sharp knife, cut the dough into eight 5 by 2-inch pieces.
5. Drizzle the avocado oil onto a large plate. Working with one piece of dough at a time, rub both sides of the dough in the oil and arrange the pieces on the plate, slightly overlapping one another. Cover with plastic wrap and let rest for 1 hour. (The dough pieces can be stored in the refrigerator for up to 3 days; bring to room temperature before forming the noodles.)

(recipe continues)

6. **While the dough is resting, make the sauce:** In a small bowl, whisk together the soy sauce, vinegar, sesame oil, garlic, and sugar. Set aside so the flavors meld.

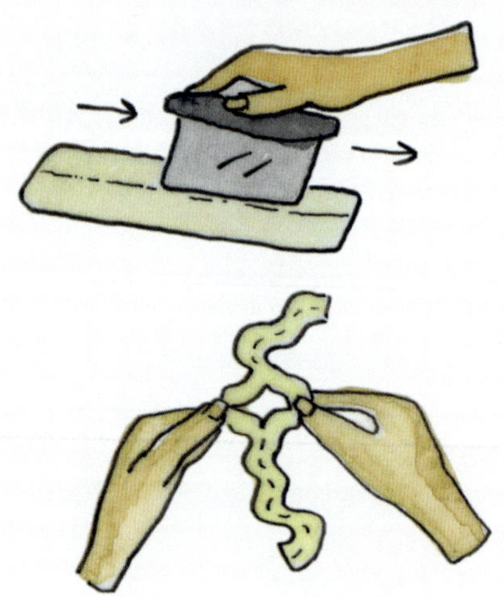

7. **Shape and cook the noodles:** Bring a large pot of salted water to a boil. When the water reaches a boil, transfer one piece of dough to a clean cutting board (keeping the other pieces covered with plastic wrap). Using a bench scraper or the back of a knife, make an indentation lengthwise down the center of the dough. Holding either side of the dough gently but firmly between your thumbs and fingers, slowly stretch the dough to shoulder width, then slap it against the cutting board by flicking both wrists down until the noodle is about 1 inch wide. Move your hands to the middle of the noodle and use the indentation to separate it with your fingers into two strands. You can either leave the noodles attached at the ends, creating one big "O," or fully separate them into two noodles. Set them aside on the cutting board and repeat with the remaining pieces of dough.

HOW TO PULL THE NOODLES

8. Add four noodles (or two attached noodles) to the boiling water (this is one serving), moving them around with tongs or chopsticks to prevent them from sticking together. Allow the water to return to a boil and cook until the noodles are firm and chewy, 1 to 2 minutes. Using a spider strainer, transfer the noodles to a medium bowl.

9. **To serve:** Stir the sauce and add a few spoonfuls to the bowl with the noodles. Add a small spoonful of chili crisp (or just a drizzle for less heat) and use tongs to mix the noodles with the sauce. Transfer to a plate and generously top with scallions and cilantro. Sprinkle with some sesame seeds and enjoy! Follow the same process to cook and serve the remaining noodles.

TIP

If you'd like to add veggies, such as chopped cabbage or bok choy, throw some into the boiling water with the noodles. It will take about the same amount of time to blanch the vegetables as it does for the noodles to cook. Toss everything together with the sauce and enjoy!

Mom's Red and White Lasagna

SERVES 6 TO 8 ◆ PREP TIME: 30 MINUTES ◆ TOTAL TIME: 2 HOURS 10 MINUTES

RED SAUCE

2 tablespoons extra-virgin olive oil

½ medium yellow onion (5 ounces), cut into small dice

1 large carrot (5 ounces), coarsely chopped

2 celery stalks (4 ounces), coarsely chopped

4 garlic cloves, finely chopped

1 pound ground beef

1 pound hot Italian sausage (see Tip), casings removed

1 (28-ounce) can whole peeled San Marzano tomatoes

1 (14-ounce) can crushed tomatoes

½ cup red wine

1 tablespoon Italian seasoning

1½ teaspoons kosher salt, plus more if needed

1 teaspoon sugar

½ teaspoon freshly ground black pepper, plus more if needed

Alrighty, folks, this is a special one: my mom's lasagna! It's so good that nearly everyone who tries it asks for the recipe. Creamy and decadent yet somehow not too heavy, it's made with a béchamel and doesn't go overboard on the cheese (no ricotta, either!).

My mom loves Italy, and being the lively extrovert that she is (she's the only person on earth who makes me look like a wallflower), she befriends people wherever she goes. Her friend Lorenzo owns a café in Florence called Fantasie Gastronomiche. They are known for their delicious lasagna: A stunning tray is displayed in a refrigerated case, and they cut and heat pieces to order. Many years ago, on one of my mom's visits, Lorenzo showed her exactly how to make his signature dish, and ever since then, it's been one of our family favorites. Our version is almost identical, with one tweak: My dad requested a little extra cheese, so we added a sprinkling of mozzarella on top for a melted cheesy crust. We typically serve this with my Lemony Caesar Salad (page 239) and The Best Garlic Bread (page 240). I hope you love this one as much as we do!

1. **Make the red sauce:** In a large pot, heat the olive oil over medium-high heat. Add the onion, carrot, celery, and garlic and cook, stirring, until the onion is translucent and the carrots and celery are starting to soften, 3 to 5 minutes. Add the ground beef and sausage and cook, stirring and breaking up the meat with a wooden spoon, until cooked through, 3 to 5 minutes. Using your hands, crush the whole tomatoes to break them up as you drop them into the pot, then pour in the juices from the can. Add the crushed tomatoes, wine, Italian seasoning, salt, sugar, and black pepper. Stir to combine, then bring to a boil. Reduce the heat to low, cover, and simmer until the sauce is deeply aromatic, the ingredients have melded together, and the tomatoes have broken down, about 30 minutes. Taste and season with more salt and/or black pepper, if desired.

(recipe and ingredients continue)

TIP

Use mild Italian sausage if you prefer no heat.

the dreamiest lasagna →

BÉCHAMEL

4 tablespoons (½ stick) unsalted butter

¼ cup all-purpose flour

4 cups whole milk

1½ teaspoons kosher salt

½ teaspoon freshly ground black pepper

⅛ teaspoon ground nutmeg

Dash of cayenne pepper

FOR COOKING AND ASSEMBLY

Extra-virgin olive oil

Kosher salt

1 (10- to 16-ounce) package lasagna noodles (oven-ready/no-boil or regular)

1½ cups (6 ounces) grated Parmesan cheese

1¼ cups (5 ounces) shredded mozzarella cheese

Olive oil or avocado oil spray, for greasing

HOW TO MAKE A BÉCHAMEL

2. **Meanwhile, make the béchamel:** In a medium pot, melt the butter over medium heat. Whisk in the flour and cook, whisking continuously, until smooth and bubbling, 1 to 2 minutes. Slowly pour in the milk, 1 cup at a time, whisking to incorporate after each addition. Increase the heat to medium-high and cook, whisking occasionally, until the sauce bubbles and thickens enough to coat the back of a spoon, about 5 minutes. Stir in the salt, black pepper, nutmeg, and cayenne. Remove from the heat and cover the pot. Give the béchamel a stir before using it to assemble the lasagna in step 5.
3. Preheat the oven to 375°F.
4. **Cook the lasagna noodles:** (If using oven-ready/no-boil noodles, skip to step 5.) Generously coat a sheet pan with olive oil and set aside. Bring a large pot of generously salted water to a boil. Add the lasagna noodles and cook until al dente according to the package instructions. Drain the noodles and transfer to the prepared sheet pan. Turn the noodles to coat in the oil so they don't stick together.
5. **Assemble the lasagna:** Set aside ½ cup of the Parmesan for the final topping. Spread a thin layer of red sauce over the bottom of a 9 by 13-inch baking dish. Cover with a layer of lasagna noodles, breaking or tearing them to fill any gaps. Spoon about ⅓ of the remaining red sauce over the noodles, followed by ⅓ of the béchamel. Sprinkle with ⅓ of the remaining Parmesan (⅓ cup). Repeat the layering (noodles, red sauce, béchamel, Parmesan) two more times, then finish with the mozzarella on top. Sprinkle with the reserved ½ cup Parmesan.
6. Tear off a piece of foil slightly larger than the baking dish and coat one side of the foil with a thin layer of olive oil or spray with oil (this will keep the foil from sticking to the lasagna as it bakes). Cover the lasagna with the foil, oiled-side down, and place the baking dish on a sheet pan. Bake for 25 minutes, then remove the foil and bake until the lasagna is bubbling and the top is golden brown, 20 to 25 minutes more. Remove from the oven.
7. Let the lasagna rest for 10 minutes before serving, then enjoy!

Korean Braised Short Ribs *with Daikon*

SERVES 5 OR 6 ◆ PREP TIME: 15 MINUTES ◆ TOTAL TIME: 4 HOURS 15 MINUTES

4 pounds bone-in short ribs

Kosher salt and freshly ground black pepper

2 tablespoons avocado oil or other neutral oil, such as grapeseed

1 large sweet onion (12 ounces), halved and cut into ¼-inch-thick slices

¼ cup (1 ounce) finely chopped fresh ginger

5 garlic cloves, finely chopped

3 cups beef stock

½ cup soy sauce

⅓ cup plus 2 tablespoons packed light brown sugar

1 tablespoon fish sauce

¼ cup plus 2 tablespoons rice vinegar, divided

1½ pounds daikon radish (1 large), peeled and cut into 1 by 2-inch chunks

FOR SERVING

Jasmine Rice (page 231)

4 scallions, sliced at an angle

I made these short ribs for my mom when she came to visit, and we both loved them! They take a few hours to cook, but most of that time is hands-off in the oven. The key is to finish the short ribs, uncovered, at high heat. This sears the exterior while keeping the inside fall-apart tender, intensifying the broth's sweet and savory flavors, and giving the meat a gorgeous, deep brown crust.

1. Preheat the oven to 325°F. Place the short ribs on a sheet pan and season all over with salt and pepper.
2. In a large Dutch oven or ovenproof pot with a lid, heat the avocado oil over medium-high heat. When the oil is shimmering, working in batches to avoid overcrowding the pot, add the short ribs, meat-side down, and cook until browned on all sides, 7 to 9 minutes. Return the ribs to the sheet pan. If there is excess grease in the pot, carefully drain off all but about 2 tablespoons.
3. Reduce the heat to medium and add the onion and ginger. Cook, stirring, until the onion starts to become tender, 3 to 5 minutes. Add the garlic and cook, stirring, for 1 minute. Add the stock, soy sauce, brown sugar, fish sauce, and ¼ cup of the vinegar. Stir to combine. Add the short ribs, meat-side down, ensuring most of the meat is submerged in the liquid. Bring to a simmer over high heat. Remove from the heat and add the daikon, placing it on top of the short ribs (it's okay if the daikon isn't submerged).
4. Cover the pot with a lid and transfer to the oven. Bake until the meat is falling off the bone and shreds easily with a fork, about 2½ hours. Remove the pot from the oven and increase the oven temperature to 450°F.
5. Remove the lid from the pot. Using tongs, lift the short ribs above the liquid, positioning them meat-side up on top of the daikon, ensuring that as much meat as possible is exposed. Return the pot to the oven and bake, uncovered, until the meat is browned and the sauce has reduced a bit, 20 to 25 minutes.
6. Remove the pot from the oven and stir in the remaining 2 tablespoons vinegar. Let cool for 10 minutes. If a lot of fat rises to the surface, you can skim some of it off with a spoon.
7. **To serve:** Scoop some rice into shallow bowls and top with the short ribs and daikon. Spoon the sauce over everything and top with the scallions. Enjoy!

Mom's Golden Crispy Chicken Potstickers

MAKES 40 POTSTICKERS ◆ PREP TIME: 30 MINUTES ◆ TOTAL TIME: 2 HOURS 45 MINUTES

DOUGH (SEE TIP)

3 cups plus 2 tablespoons (376 grams) all-purpose flour, plus more if needed

½ cup plus 2 tablespoons (80 grams) cornstarch

½ teaspoon kosher salt

1¼ cups just-boiled water, plus more if needed

FILLING

1 pound ground chicken (93/7 or similar; non-breast-only)

1 cup (4 ounces) finely chopped napa cabbage or green cabbage

3 scallions, chopped

3 tablespoons finely chopped fresh ginger

1 garlic clove, finely chopped

1 large egg

1 tablespoon Shaoxing cooking wine (optional)

1 tablespoon soy sauce

1 tablespoon toasted sesame oil

1 teaspoon kosher salt

½ teaspoon freshly ground black pepper

2 tablespoons cornstarch

2 tablespoons water

TIP

You can substitute 2 (12-ounce) packages store-bought potsticker skins for the homemade dough.

We often make these on holidays, turning our kitchen into a little dumpling factory. While my mom and I fold and pleat, the rest of the family gathers around the kitchen island, eagerly waiting for batch after batch to come off the skillet. It's a bit of a labor of love, but the result is so delicious—crispy on the outside, with just the right amount of chew. To guide you through the process, I've included an illustrated step-by-step guide on page 175. But don't stress if your potstickers aren't perfect (just be sure the filling is tucked inside). And if you're short on time, skip making your own dough and use store-bought wrappers instead!

1. **Make the dough:** In a food processor, combine the flour, cornstarch, and salt. Pulse to combine. With the food processor running, slowly add the just-boiled water and pulse until a dough ball forms. It should be smooth and slightly sticky to the touch. (If the dough is too wet, add a little more flour. Alternatively, if the mixture is too dry and not coming together into a ball, add more water, 1 teaspoon at a time.) Remove the dough ball from the food processor and wrap tightly in plastic. Let rest at room temperature for at least 15 minutes or up to 2 hours while you prepare the filling and sauce.
2. **Make the filling:** In a large bowl, combine the ground chicken, cabbage, scallions, ginger, garlic, egg, Shaoxing wine (if using), soy sauce, sesame oil, salt, and pepper. Mix with a spoon or your hand until all the ingredients are evenly distributed.
3. In a small bowl, whisk together the cornstarch and water until dissolved. Pour into the filling and mix until evenly distributed. Set aside.
4. **Make the sauce:** In a small bowl, mix together the soy sauce, vinegar, sesame oil, chili oil (if using), sesame seeds, and sugar. Set aside.
5. **Assemble the potstickers:** Unwrap the dough ball and place it on a lightly floured work surface. Using a bench scraper or sharp knife, cut it in half. (You can weigh the dough on a digital scale to ensure the pieces are of equal weight; each piece should weigh about 360 grams.) Wrap one half tightly in plastic wrap (to prevent it from drying out) and set aside. Roll the other half of the dough into a log and cut it in half. Divide each half into 5 equal pieces, then cut each piece in half again to create 20 equal pieces (each piece should weigh about 18 grams).

SAUCE

3 tablespoons soy sauce

2 tablespoons rice vinegar

2 tablespoons toasted sesame oil

1 tablespoon chili oil or chili garlic sauce (optional)

1 teaspoon toasted sesame seeds

½ teaspoon sugar

FOR ASSEMBLY AND SERVING

All-purpose flour, for dusting

4 tablespoons avocado oil or other neutral oil, such as grapeseed, plus more as needed, divided

1 cup water, divided

Finely chopped napa or green cabbage (optional)

6. Line a sheet pan with parchment paper. Take one piece of dough and roll it into a ball. Use a small rolling pin to roll it into a thin round about 4 inches in diameter. Place 1 tablespoon of the filling in the middle of the round. (If using store-bought wrappers, moisten the perimeter of the wrapper with some water to make it stick. No need to do this with the fresh dough.) Fold the wrapper in half over the filling, pinching it at the center to seal. Starting from the midpoint, make two small pleats on each side, folding the edges toward the center and pressing firmly to secure. Transfer to the prepared sheet pan. See page 175 for a step-by-step illustrated guide on how to fold potstickers. Repeat to roll and fill the remaining dough pieces.
7. Pour 2 tablespoons of the avocado oil into a cold large nonstick skillet with a lid. Add half the potstickers, seam-side up, rubbing the bottoms in the oil and leaving some space between each. Add ½ cup of the water, cover the skillet, and place over medium heat. Cook until all the water has evaporated, 7 to 9 minutes. Uncover the skillet, reduce the heat to medium-low, and cook, undisturbed, until the bottoms of the potstickers are golden brown, 3 to 4 minutes. Flip the potstickers so the pleated side is against the skillet and cook until golden brown, 3 to 4 minutes more. Transfer to a plate. Repeat with the remaining 2 tablespoons oil, ½ cup water, and potstickers.
8. **To serve:** Place the potstickers on a bed of chopped cabbage, if you like. Spoon the sauce on top and enjoy!

HOW TO FOLD A POTSTICKER

HOW TO FOLD A *potsticker*

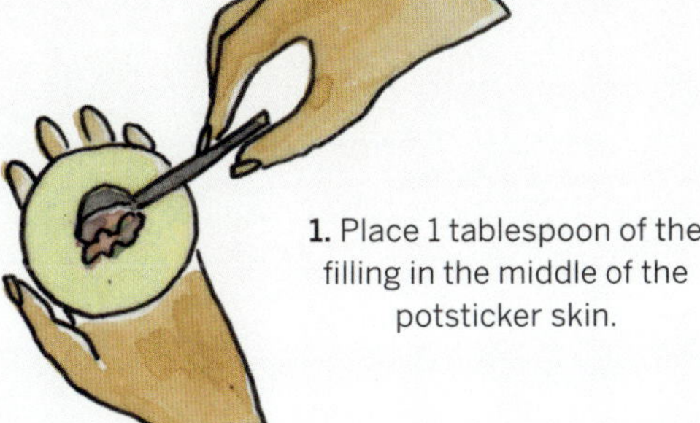

1. Place 1 tablespoon of the filling in the middle of the potsticker skin.

2. If using store-bought wrappers, moisten the perimeter of the skin with some water to make it stick. (No need to do this with fresh dough.)

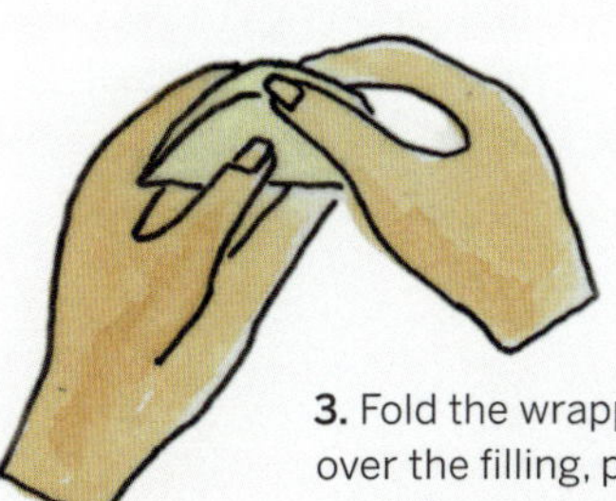

3. Fold the wrapper in half over the filling, pinching it at the center to seal.

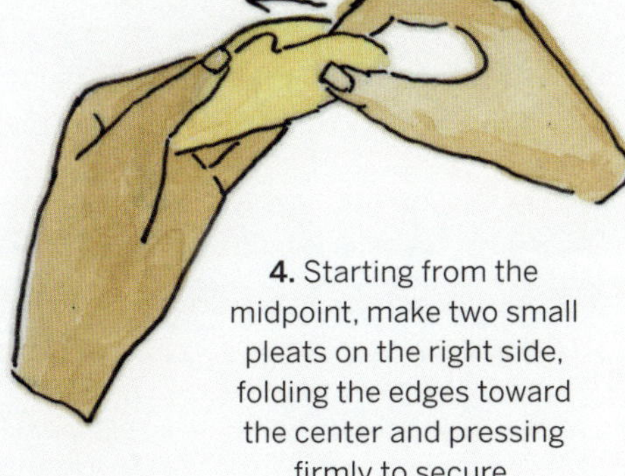

4. Starting from the midpoint, make two small pleats on the right side, folding the edges toward the center and pressing firmly to secure.

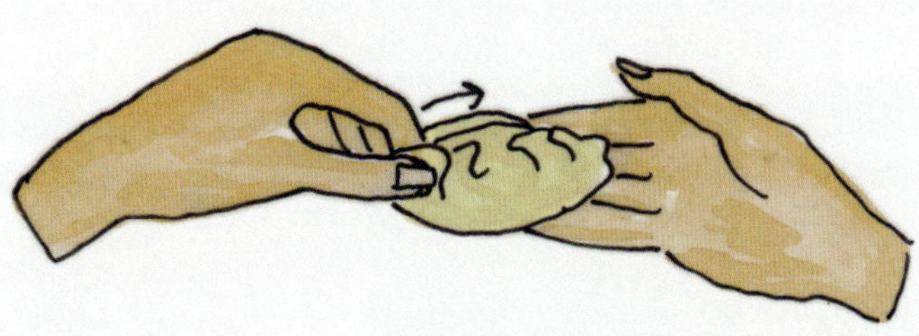

5. Repeat on the left side, making two small pleats.

HOW TO MAKE A BÉCHAMEL

Creamy Lemon Spinach and Ricotta Stuffed Shells

SERVES 4 ◆ PREP TIME: 15 MINUTES ◆ TOTAL TIME: 1 HOUR 45 MINUTES

My mom and I love making stuffed shells, and we came up with this version together—a creamy, lemony take that has quickly become a new favorite. There's something a little fancy about the combination of a fragrant lemon béchamel and leeks. The shells come out of the oven with a golden brown Parmesan crust, and once they're plated and drizzled with sauce, they're a real showstopper. When my dad first tried them, he said, "This tastes like something you'd get at a restaurant!"

SHELLS

Kosher salt

20 jumbo pasta shells (about 6 ounces total)

2 teaspoons extra-virgin olive oil

FILLING

2 tablespoons unsalted butter

1 large leek (8 ounces), thinly sliced

5 ounces baby spinach, chopped

2 garlic cloves, finely chopped

½ teaspoon dried oregano

Kosher salt and freshly ground black pepper

1¼ cups whole-milk ricotta cheese

½ cup (2 ounces) shredded mozzarella cheese

1 large egg

LEMONY BÉCHAMEL

3 tablespoons unsalted butter

3 tablespoons all-purpose flour

3 cups whole milk

1 teaspoon kosher salt

¼ teaspoon freshly ground black pepper

¼ cup (1 ounce) grated Parmesan cheese

1 teaspoon lemon zest

2 tablespoons fresh lemon juice

½ cup (2 ounces) grated Parmesan cheese

1. **Make the shells:** Bring a large pot of generously salted water to a boil. Add the shells and cook according to the package directions until al dente. Drain and transfer to a large bowl. Drizzle with the olive oil and toss to coat (this is so they don't stick). Preheat the oven to 375°F.
2. **Make the filling:** In a large skillet, melt the butter over medium heat. Add the leek and cook, stirring, until almost tender, 3 to 5 minutes. Add the spinach, garlic, oregano, ½ teaspoon salt, and ¼ teaspoon pepper. Cook, stirring, until the spinach is wilted and bright green, 2 to 4 minutes.
3. Transfer the vegetables to a large bowl and add the ricotta, mozzarella, and egg. Mix until combined.
4. **Make the lemony béchamel:** In the same large skillet, melt the butter over medium heat. Add the flour and cook, stirring, for 1 minute. Slowly add the milk, about ½ cup at a time, whisking continuously to fully incorporate after each addition. Add the salt and pepper and increase the heat to medium-high. Cook, stirring, until the sauce bubbles and thickens slightly, about 5 minutes. Remove from the heat and stir in the Parmesan, lemon zest, and lemon juice. Pour the sauce into a 9 by 13-inch baking dish.
5. Working with one at a time, use a spoon to stuff each shell with about 2 tablespoons of the ricotta filling. Place the stuffed shells seam-side up in the baking dish. Sprinkle the shells with the Parmesan and cover the dish with foil.
6. Bake for 20 minutes, then remove the foil and bake until bubbling, 10 to 15 minutes more. Turn on the broiler and broil until the tops of the shells are golden brown, 2 to 3 minutes.
7. Serve the shells with the creamy sauce drizzled on top and enjoy!

Easy Artisan Bread

MAKES 1 LOAF ◆ PREP TIME: 5 MINUTES ◆ TOTAL TIME: 1 HOUR, PLUS 2 HOURS 30 MINUTES FOR RESTING

3 cups (360 grams) bread flour (preferred) or all-purpose flour, plus more for dusting

1½ teaspoons (7 grams) kosher salt

1 teaspoon (3 grams) instant yeast

1¼ cups (300 ml) warm water (110° to 120°F; see Tips)

Salted butter, such as Kerrygold, at room temperature, for serving

Flaky sea salt, such as Maldon

TIPS

I use warm water from the faucet and check the temperature with an instant-read thermometer to make sure it's not too hot for the yeast.

Technically you're not supposed to slice bread until it's cooled down, but I can never resist!

HOW TO KNEAD AND SHAPE THE DOUGH

Everyone should know how easy it is to make delicious artisan bread at home! I'm talking about a rustic, crusty loaf with a chewy interior—the kind that looks like it came straight from a bakery. Even if you've never baked bread before and feel a little intimidated, this recipe might surprise you with how easy it is. It's an especially fun thing to make if you're hosting a dinner party. Time it so the bread comes out of the oven just as your guests arrive, and not only will they be super impressed, your kitchen will smell amazing, too.

1. In a large bowl, combine the flour, kosher salt, and yeast and mix with a wooden spoon. Add the warm water and mix until a shaggy dough forms, about 1 minute. Cover with a clean dish towel and let rise in a warm place until it doubles in size, about 2 hours.
2. Dust a large cutting board or clean work surface with flour. Lightly dust your hands with flour to prevent the dough from sticking, then turn the dough out onto the floured surface. Knead the dough, pressing down with the heels of your hands and pushing the dough away from you. Fold it back over itself, give it a quarter turn, and repeat. Knead until the dough is smooth, about 3 minutes. Cup your hands around the dough and gently tuck the edges under while rotating the dough on the work surface to help form a tight, smooth ball.
3. Line a large bowl with parchment paper and place the dough in the bowl, smooth-side up (or use a proofing basket, if you have one). Dust the top with some flour. Cover with a clean dish towel and let rise for 30 minutes.
4. Meanwhile, preheat the oven to 450°F. Place a 5- to 6-quart Dutch oven or a lidded large ovenproof pot in the oven (with the lid on) to preheat as well.
5. Using a knife, cut a ¼-inch-deep slit across the top of the dough. Remove the hot Dutch oven from the oven and uncover. Using the parchment paper, lift the dough from the bowl and carefully lower it into the pot. Cover with the lid and bake for 30 minutes. Remove the lid and bake until the bread is deep golden brown, 15 to 20 minutes more.
6. Using the parchment paper, lift the bread out of the Dutch oven and transfer it to a wire rack to cool for 5 minutes (see Tips). Serve it with butter and a sprinkle of flaky salt, and enjoy!

so much easier than you think!

Baked Pork Buns

MAKES 12 BUNS ◆ PREP TIME: 30 MINUTES
◆ TOTAL TIME: 2 HOURS 30 MINUTES, PLUS 2 HOURS 45 MINUTES FOR RESTING

MARINATED PORK

2 tablespoons light brown sugar

2 tablespoons hoisin sauce

2 tablespoons red wine, sherry cooking wine, or water

1 tablespoon oyster sauce

1 tablespoon soy sauce

¼ teaspoon kosher salt

¼ teaspoon freshly ground black pepper

1 garlic clove, finely chopped

1 pound boneless fatty pork chops, shoulder, or butt (see Tip)

Avocado oil or avocado oil spray

TIP

If you don't eat pork, boneless, skinless chicken thighs work just as well! Use the same amount and follow the recipe as written.

Baked pork buns, or char siu bao, are one of my favorite things to order at a dim sum restaurant. My mom and I developed this recipe together when I was home for Thanksgiving one year, and after a few tries, we were thrilled to finally nail it. When my dad tried the buns, he said they were the best he'd ever had. Honestly, I agree—they're so good that my mom can't stop making them for her friends!

Don't be intimidated by the dough. It's surprisingly easy to work with, as it's not sticky and it seals perfectly around the filling. While there are a few steps to this recipe and it takes some patience, nothing is overly complicated or technically demanding. Plus, the payoff is so worth it: Breaking into a fresh, steaming bun feels like such a treat!

1. **Marinate the pork:** In a small glass measuring cup or bowl, mix together the brown sugar, hoisin sauce, wine, oyster sauce, soy sauce, salt, pepper, and garlic. If using pork shoulder or butt, cut it into 3 large pieces. Place the pork in a large dish (or a zip-top bag), pour the marinade over the pork, and turn to evenly coat. Cover (or seal the bag) and marinate in the refrigerator for at least 1 hour or up to overnight.
2. Preheat the oven to 350°F. Lightly spray or rub a wire rack with avocado oil and place it over a sheet pan. (You can line the sheet pan with foil first for easier cleanup, if you like.)
3. Place the pork on the oiled rack (or directly on the oiled sheet pan), spacing the chops or pieces evenly apart. Spoon some of the marinade on top of the pork; reserve the rest of the marinade. Roast for 20 minutes, then flip the pork and spoon more of the marinade over the top. Roast until the pork is cooked through and its internal temperature registers 145°F on an instant-read thermometer, about 20 minutes more. Set aside until cool enough to handle, then transfer to a cutting board. Cut the pork into ¼- to ½-inch pieces.

(recipe and ingredients continue)

DOUGH

1 cup whole milk, plus more if needed

1 (¼-ounce) packet active dry yeast (2¼ teaspoons)

¼ cup (50 grams) granulated sugar

1 large egg

3 tablespoons unsalted butter, melted

1 teaspoon kosher salt

3⅓ cups (400 grams) bread flour, plus more if needed

Avocado oil or other neutral oil, such as grapeseed

SAUCE

⅓ cup water

3 tablespoons hoisin sauce

2 tablespoons oyster sauce

1 tablespoon cornstarch

1 tablespoon granulated sugar

1 tablespoon soy sauce

1 teaspoon toasted sesame oil

4. **Meanwhile, make the dough:** In a small pot, heat the milk over medium heat until it reaches 110°F (or microwave in a heatproof bowl). Check the temperature with an instant-read thermometer, if you have one; it should be warm, not hot, to the touch.
5. Pour the milk into the bowl of a stand mixer fitted with the paddle attachment. Sprinkle the yeast over the milk and mix on medium speed for 1 minute. (Alternatively, transfer the milk to a large bowl, sprinkle with the yeast, and stir with a wooden spoon to combine.) Add the granulated sugar, egg, melted butter, and salt. Mix until combined.
6. Add the flour and mix until a shaggy dough forms. Switch to the dough hook (or transfer to a lightly floured surface, if kneading by hand). Knead the dough on medium speed until smooth and elastic, 6 to 8 minutes (8 to 10 minutes by hand). The dough should be soft and slightly sticky. Add a little more flour if the dough seems too sticky or a little more milk if it seems too dry.
7. Lightly coat a large bowl with avocado oil. Place the dough ball in the bowl and cover with a clean dish towel or plastic wrap. Let rise in a warm place until the dough has doubled in size, 1 to 1½ hours.
8. **Make the sauce:** In a medium glass measuring cup or bowl, mix together the water, hoisin sauce, oyster sauce, cornstarch, granulated sugar, soy sauce, and sesame oil. Set aside.
9. **Cook the filling:** In a large skillet, heat the avocado oil over medium heat. Add the onion and cook, stirring, until translucent and tender, 4 to 6 minutes. Add the pork and cook, stirring often, until browned, 3 to 5 minutes. Reduce the heat to low.
10. Whisk the sauce (the cornstarch will have settled) and pour it into the skillet. Cook until the sauce thickens and coats the pork, 1 to 2 minutes. Remove from the heat and set aside.
11. Line two sheet pans with parchment paper and lightly dust a work surface with flour. Place the dough on the work surface and roll it into a log. Cut the log into 4 equal pieces, then cut each piece into thirds so you have 12 equal pieces (I like to use a kitchen scale to check the weight—each piece of dough should weigh about 66 grams).

COOKING

1 tablespoon avocado oil or other neutral oil, such as grapeseed

½ medium yellow onion (5 ounces), finely chopped

EGG WASH

1 large egg

1 tablespoon whole milk

1 teaspoon granulated sugar

HOW TO SHAPE THE PORK BUNS

12. Working with one piece of dough at a time, use a small rolling pin to roll the dough into a 5-inch round. Place 2 tablespoons of the filling in the center. Bring two opposite sides of the dough together at the center and pinch them to seal. Then bring the remaining two sides together and pinch to form an X. Continue pinching and gathering the edges around the filling, twisting slightly at the top to completely seal the bun. Make sure there are no gaps to ensure the filling will not leak during baking.

13. Place the buns seam-side down on the prepared sheet pans (6 buns per sheet), leaving some space between each. Cover the sheet pans with clean dish towels and let rise in a warm place until slightly puffed, 30 to 45 minutes.

14. Position the racks in the upper and lower thirds of the oven and preheat to 350°F.

15. **Make the egg wash:** In a small bowl, whisk together the egg, milk, and granulated sugar with a fork until well combined. Using a pastry brush, brush the tops and sides of the buns with the egg wash.

16. Bake the buns until the tops are golden, rotating the pans and switching the racks from top to bottom halfway through, 18 to 22 minutes. Remove the buns from the oven and let them cool for a few minutes. Enjoy warm! Leftover buns can be stored in an airtight container in the refrigerator for up to 4 days or in the freezer for up to 3 months. Reheat from frozen in the microwave until heated through, 1 to 2 minutes. (They make great leftovers!)

Mom's Spaghetti and Meatballs

SERVES 6 ◆ PREP TIME: 25 MINUTES ◆ TOTAL TIME: 2 HOURS 30 MINUTES

My mom's spaghetti and meatballs are one of my favorite comfort foods. Like many of her other Italian recipes, she learned to make these meatballs while traveling in Italy. To me, the perfect meatball walks a fine line—it's gotta be tender and juicy, but not too soft, and meaty enough without feeling heavy or dense. The secret is making a panade, soft white bread soaked in milk, and using equal parts ground beef and hot Italian sausage. The sausage, combined with plenty of garlic, Parmesan, and a whole bunch of parsley, creates the juiciest, most flavorful meatballs. Browning the meatballs on the stove gives them a deep golden crust, though they're still delicious baked in the oven.

MEATBALLS

2 ounces soft white bread, torn into small pieces (about 1 cup; see Tips)

1 cup whole milk

1 pound ground beef (90/10)

1 pound hot Italian sausage (see Tips), casings removed

Leaves from 1 bunch parsley, finely chopped (about 1 cup)

4 garlic cloves, finely chopped

2 large eggs

½ cup dry white wine

¼ cup (1 ounce) grated Parmesan cheese

1½ teaspoons kosher salt

¼ teaspoon freshly ground black pepper

2 tablespoons extra-virgin olive oil, plus more for your hands

1. **Make the meatballs:** Place the bread in a medium bowl and add the milk. Let sit until the bread softens and is soaked with the milk, about 15 minutes.
2. Meanwhile, in a large bowl, combine the ground beef, sausage, parsley, garlic, eggs, wine, Parmesan, salt, and pepper. Drain off any milk that did not get absorbed into the bread, then add the milk-soaked bread to the bowl with the meat mixture. Mix with your hands until the ingredients are evenly distributed.
3. Form the meat mixture into 2½-inch balls, coating your hands with a little olive oil to prevent the mixture from sticking. (You should have about 13 meatballs.)
4. In a large pot, heat the olive oil over medium heat. Working in batches to avoid crowding the pot, cook the meatballs until browned on most sides, about 2 minutes per side. Transfer the meatballs to a large plate. (They will finish cooking in the sauce. See Tips for baking the meatballs in the oven.)
5. **Make the sauce:** In the same pot, combine the olive oil and onion and cook over medium heat, stirring, until the onion starts to become tender and translucent, 3 to 5 minutes. Add the garlic and cook, stirring, for 1 minute more. Using your hands, crush the whole tomatoes to break them up as you drop them into the pot, then pour in the juices from the can. Add the wine, Italian seasoning, salt, sugar, and red pepper flakes. Bring to a boil over high heat, then reduce the heat to low, cover, and simmer until the tomatoes break down, about 20 minutes.
6. Add the meatballs and stir to coat in the sauce. Cover and simmer over low heat until the internal temperature of the meatballs registers 160°F on an instant-read thermometer, about 30 minutes. You can serve the meatballs or simmer over very low heat for up to 3 hours so the flavors continue to deepen.

SAUCE (SEE TIPS)

¼ cup extra-virgin olive oil

1 medium yellow onion (10 ounces), cut into small dice

4 garlic cloves, finely chopped

2 (28-ounce) cans whole peeled San Marzano tomatoes

½ cup red wine

2 teaspoons Italian seasoning

2 teaspoons kosher salt

1 teaspoon sugar

½ teaspoon crushed red pepper flakes

FOR SERVING

Kosher salt

1½ pounds uncooked spaghetti

Freshly grated Parmesan cheese

Chopped fresh parsley

7. **To serve:** Bring a large pot of generously salted water to a boil. Cook the spaghetti until before it's al dente (2 minutes less than the package directions). Reserve 1 cup of the pasta water, then drain the pasta and return it to the pot over medium heat. Add a few ladles of the tomato sauce and ¼ cup of the pasta water, and cook, tossing the pasta in the sauce with tongs, until each strand is coated and the pasta is cooked to your desired tenderness, 2 to 3 minutes. Add more pasta water and sauce as needed.
8. Divide the spaghetti among six plates or shallow bowls and top each with two meatballs and some extra sauce. Sprinkle with Parmesan and parsley and enjoy!

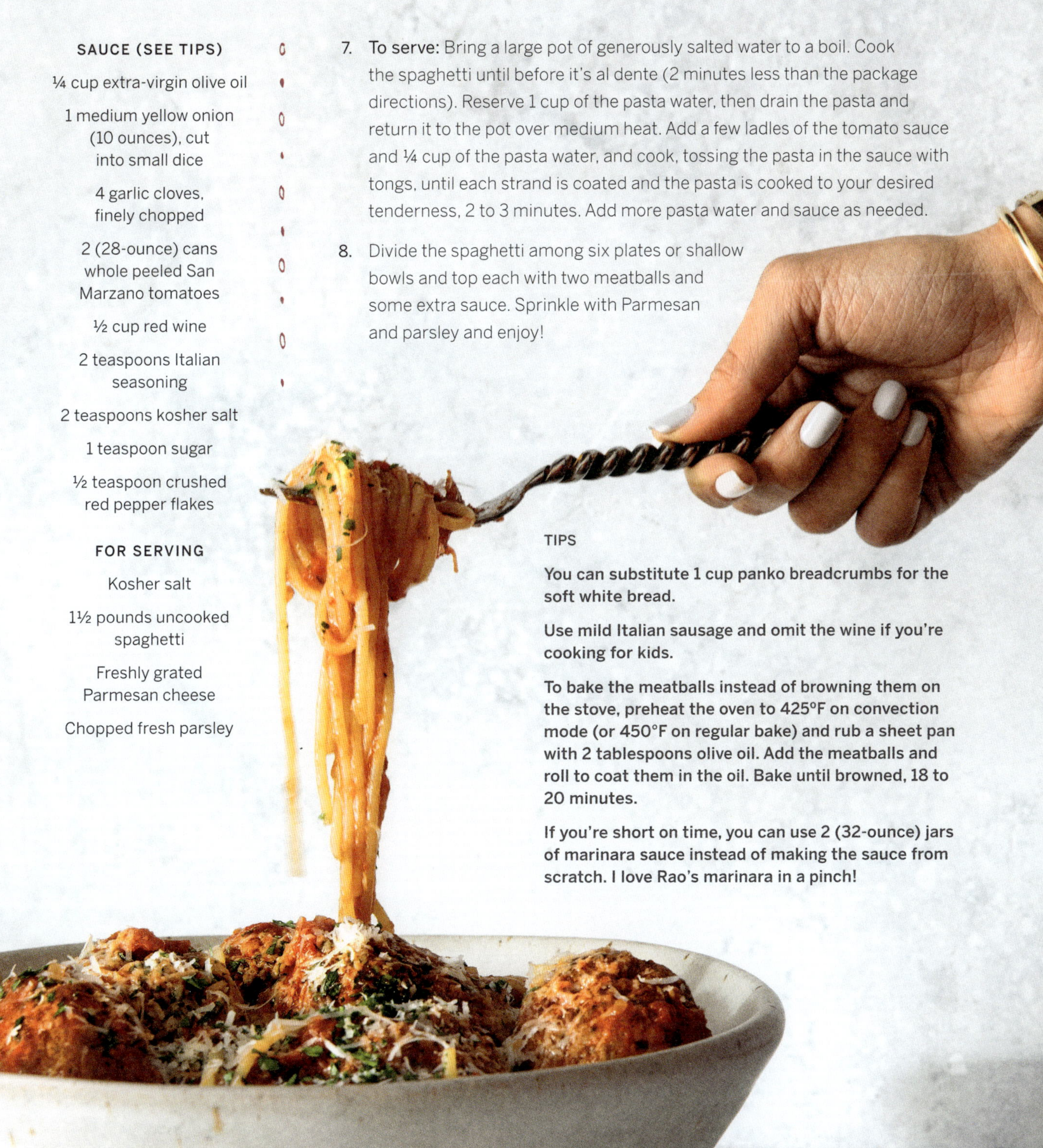

TIPS

You can substitute 1 cup panko breadcrumbs for the soft white bread.

Use mild Italian sausage and omit the wine if you're cooking for kids.

To bake the meatballs instead of browning them on the stove, preheat the oven to 425°F on convection mode (or 450°F on regular bake) and rub a sheet pan with 2 tablespoons olive oil. Add the meatballs and roll to coat them in the oil. Bake until browned, 18 to 20 minutes.

If you're short on time, you can use 2 (32-ounce) jars of marinara sauce instead of making the sauce from scratch. I love Rao's marinara in a pinch!

Handmade Pici Cacio e Pepe

SERVES 3 ◆ PREP TIME: 5 MINUTES
◆ TOTAL TIME: 1 HOUR 15 MINUTES, PLUS 30 MINUTES RESTING

PICI PASTA (SEE TIP)

1½ cups (180 grams) all-purpose flour, plus more if needed

⅔ cup (120 grams) semolina flour, plus more for dusting

Kosher salt

¾ cup lukewarm water, plus more if needed

2 teaspoons extra-virgin olive oil

CACIO E PEPE SAUCE

¾ cup (3 ounces) grated Pecorino Romano, plus freshly grated to serve

1 teaspoon freshly ground black pepper (coarse grind), plus more for serving

2 tablespoons unsalted butter

TIP

I recommend weighing the flour with a digital kitchen scale, if you have one.

HOW TO SHAPE THE PICI PASTA

I love thick, chewy noodles, and pici—a pasta from Tuscany—is exactly that. The strands of pici are like thick spaghetti but with a rustic texture that stands up beautifully to a rich sauce like cacio e pepe. You don't need any fancy equipment to make pici. Just roll out the dough, slice it into strips, and shape each strand by hand. Shaping takes a little time, but it's a fun, meditative activity. (Or at least, I think so!) A light coating of oil helps the dough glide easily as you roll and stretch it.

I learned to make this cacio e pepe sauce from a chef in Rome, who taught me the ideal technique and ratios for a glossy sauce that clings to every strand of pasta. It's simple, decadent, and absolutely worth mastering—I can't wait for you to try it!

1. **Make the pici pasta:** In a large bowl, mix together the all-purpose flour, semolina, and ½ teaspoon salt until combined. Create a well in the center and pour in the water. Using a fork, scrape the flour from the sides of the well and beat it into the water until a thick batter forms in the center. Continue incorporating the flour until a shaggy dough begins to form, then switch to using your hands to press and knead the dough against the sides of the bowl until all the flour is fully incorporated. If the dough feels too dry, add more water, 1 teaspoon at a time; if it's too sticky, sprinkle in a little more flour.
2. Dust a clean work surface with some semolina. Transfer the dough to the work surface and knead by folding the dough onto itself, rotating it 90 degrees, and repeating this fold until the dough becomes smooth and elastic, about 10 minutes. To check if the dough is ready, press it gently with your finger; if the dough springs back, it's good to go. Cover the dough tightly with plastic wrap and let rest at room temperature for 30 minutes.
3. Coat a sheet pan with semolina. Unwrap the dough and place it on a work surface lightly dusted with semolina. Roll the dough into a rectangle of about 16 by 6 inches and brush the surface lightly with the olive oil. Starting from the shorter 6-inch side, cut the dough into strips about 6 inches long and ½ inch wide. Roll each strip against the work surface with your palms to form long strands, about ¼ inch thick. As you roll, gently move your hands away from each other, encouraging the strands to stretch. Place the pici on

(recipe continues)

the prepared sheet pan and roll in the semolina to prevent sticking. Repeat with the remaining strips. (The pici can sit at room temperature for up to 2 hours before cooking or can be covered with plastic wrap and stored in the refrigerator for up to 2 days.)

4. When ready to cook, bring a large pot of generously salted water to a boil.

5. **Meanwhile, make the cacio e pepe sauce:** Place the pecorino in a medium bowl. Whisk 1 tablespoon of the boiling water from the pot into the cheese. Continue adding water, 1 tablespoon at a time, until the sauce has the consistency of mashed potatoes (I usually add 4 tablespoons boiling water). Set aside.

6. Heat a large skillet over medium heat. Add the pepper and toast, stirring, for 1 minute. Add the butter and ¾ cup of the pasta water. Stir to melt the butter.

7. Add the pici to the boiling water. Cook until they float to the surface, 2 to 3 minutes. (They will finish cooking in the sauce.)

8. Using a spider strainer, transfer the pici to the skillet with the butter-pepper mixture. Cook, stirring and adding more pasta water as needed, until the pasta is al dente, about 3 minutes. Remove the skillet from the heat and add the pecorino mixture. Mix vigorously until the cheese melts into the sauce and coats the pasta, adding more pasta water as needed to loosen the sauce so it coats the pici evenly.

9. Divide the pasta among three plates and serve with a sprinkle of pepper and more pecorino on top. Enjoy!

Sheet Pan Diavola Pizza *with the Crispiest Crust*

SERVES 6 (MAKES 2 QUARTER-SHEET PIZZAS)
◆ PREP TIME: 15 MINUTES ◆ TOTAL TIME: 1 HOUR 30 MINUTES, PLUS 1 HOUR 30 MINUTES FOR RESTING

When developing this recipe, I had one goal: the crispiest edges. The secret is a generous amount of olive oil and baking the pizza on the lower rack. This gives you a tender, focaccia-like crumb with an insanely crispy, golden crust on the bottom. When my dad saw a photo of this pizza, he immediately asked my mom to make it for him, and now it's a staple in their dinner rotation.

For toppings, I went with one of my favorite combinations, inspired by spicy diavola—the pizza Doug and I always order when we eat out. That said, you're more than welcome to customize with your preferred toppings, especially if you're not obsessed with spicy foods like we are! My one recommendation is to use fresh mozzarella, as the preshredded kind tends to burn in the hot oven.

PIZZA DOUGH

1½ cups (360 grams) warm water (100° to 110°F; check the temperature with an instant-read thermometer)

2 teaspoons active dry yeast

2 teaspoons sugar

4 cups (480 grams) bread flour, plus more if needed

2 teaspoons kosher salt

Extra-virgin olive oil, for drizzling

PIZZA SAUCE

2 tablespoons extra-virgin olive oil

5 garlic cloves, finely chopped

1 (28-ounce) can whole peeled San Marzano tomatoes

1 teaspoon Italian seasoning

1 teaspoon kosher salt

1 teaspoon sugar

½ teaspoon crushed red pepper flakes

1. **Make the pizza dough:** Pour the warm water into the bowl of a stand mixer fitted with the dough hook (or a large bowl, if making the dough by hand). Sprinkle in the yeast and sugar and mix to combine. Let stand until frothy, 5 to 10 minutes. Stir in the flour and salt.
2. Knead the dough on medium speed until smooth and elastic (it will still be very sticky), 5 to 6 minutes. (If making the dough by hand, turn it out onto a floured work surface and knead, flouring your hands and the surface as needed, until smooth and elastic, about 8 minutes.) Grease a large bowl and flexible bench scraper with olive oil. Use the bench scraper (or your hand) to scrape the dough into the greased bowl. Cover with plastic wrap and set aside at room temperature until doubled in size, 1 to 1½ hours. (If you don't want to make the pizza right away, you can refrigerate the dough for at least 24 hours and up to 48 hours before using.)
3. **Make the pizza sauce:** In a medium pot, heat the olive oil over medium heat. Add the garlic and cook, stirring, until fragrant, about 1 minute. Using your hands, crush the whole tomatoes to break them up as you drop them into the pot, then pour in the juices from the can. Add the Italian seasoning, salt, sugar, and red pepper flakes. Bring to a simmer over high heat, then reduce the heat to low, cover, and simmer until the tomatoes break down,

(recipe and ingredients continue)

PIZZA AND TOPPINGS

½ cup extra-virgin olive oil, divided, plus more for drizzling

12 ounces fresh mozzarella balls or logs, sliced into thin rounds

Dried oregano

6 to 8 ounces spicy salami, such as calabrese, or pepperoni

2 tablespoons crushed Calabrian chili peppers in oil (optional, or add more if you like lots of heat!)

Fresh basil leaves

Freshly grated Parmesan cheese

TIP

You will have extra pizza sauce—refrigerate or freeze it for your next pizza! Or make the Crustless Supreme Pizza Skillet on page 59.

about 20 minutes. Set aside to cool. (The pizza sauce can be stored in an airtight container in the refrigerator for up to 4 days or in the freezer for up to 3 months.)

4. **Shape the pizzas:** Drizzle two quarter-sheet (9 by 13-inch) pans with 3 tablespoons of the olive oil each and tilt the pans to evenly coat. Using an oiled bench scraper, divide the dough into two equal pieces (you can use a kitchen scale to ensure the weight is equal) and place one on each sheet pan. Gently press the dough into an even layer, encouraging it to fill the pan. Use your fingertips to dimple the dough. Drizzle 1 tablespoon of the olive oil over each portion of dough. Cover the sheet pans with plastic wrap and set aside in a warm place until the dough is puffed up, 30 to 45 minutes. (If the pizza dough was refrigerated, let it come to room temperature for about 1 hour, then press it into the sheet pans and spread it as far as it'll go. Cover with plastic wrap and set aside for 30 minutes. Press again to fill the pans—it will have relaxed. Dimple the dough with your fingers, then cover again and set aside for 10 minutes more.)
5. Position a rack in the lower third of the oven and preheat to 450°F.
6. **Top the pizzas:** Spread ½ cup of the pizza sauce evenly over each pizza, leaving the edge of the crust bare (see Tip). Distribute the mozzarella evenly over the pizza. Sprinkle the cheese with a little oregano. Arrange the spicy salami on top, followed by the crushed Calabrian chilies (if using), ensuring that everything is evenly distributed. Drizzle with a little olive oil.
7. Bake the pizzas side by side on the lower rack until the crust is golden brown, 25 to 30 minutes. Remove the pizza from the oven and let cool for a few minutes.
8. Top the pizzas with basil and freshly grated Parmesan. Slice into squares and enjoy! Leftover pizza can be refrigerated in an airtight container for up to 3 days. To reheat, place the pizza slices in a skillet over medium heat, cover, and cook until the bottom is crispy and the cheese has melted, 2 to 3 minutes.

Grandma's Wontons

SERVES 8 TO 10 (MAKES ABOUT 100 WONTONS)
◆ PREP TIME: 20 MINUTES ◆ TOTAL TIME: 1 HOUR 45 MINUTES

FILLING

4 small dried shiitake mushrooms (or fresh shiitakes)

Boiling water, for soaking

1 pound ground pork or 93/7 ground chicken

1 (8-ounce) can water chestnuts, drained and coarsely chopped

2 tablespoons finely chopped fresh ginger

3 scallions, thinly sliced

1 large egg

1 tablespoon soy sauce

1 tablespoon toasted sesame oil

1 teaspoon kosher salt

½ teaspoon freshly ground black pepper

½ teaspoon sugar

¼ cup water

2 tablespoons cornstarch

SAUCE

3 tablespoons soy sauce

2 tablespoons rice vinegar

2 tablespoons toasted sesame oil

½ teaspoon sugar

1 teaspoon toasted sesame seeds

1 tablespoon chili oil or chili garlic sauce (optional)

If I had to pick one signature dish, this would be it. I have so many memories of standing at the kitchen island with my mom and grandma, folding dozens of wontons.

When Doug and I started dating, I won him over with these wontons at a potluck, where I taught him and our friends how to fold them. To this day, it remains one of my most cherished family recipes. My mom makes these whenever she's hosting or when we visit for the holidays, and they always bring back the best memories.

If you've never folded a wonton before, it might seem tricky at first, but don't be intimidated! I've included an illustrated guide on page 194 to walk you through each step. If a little filling sticks out, it's no big deal, just try to wrap the meat as best you can. Once they're cooked and tossed in the sauce, they'll taste fantastic no matter what.

1. **Make the filling:** Place the dried shiitakes in a heatproof bowl and cover with boiling water. Set aside until rehydrated, about 20 minutes. Drain and cut into small dice, then transfer to a medium bowl.
2. Add the ground pork, water chestnuts, ginger, scallions, egg, soy sauce, sesame oil, salt, pepper, and sugar to the bowl with the mushrooms. Mix with a large spoon or your hand until all the ingredients are evenly distributed.
3. In a separate small bowl, mix together the water and cornstarch until dissolved. Add to the filling and mix to combine.
4. **Make the sauce:** In a small bowl, mix together the soy sauce, vinegar, sesame oil, sugar, sesame seeds, and chili oil, if using; set aside.
5. Bring a large pot of water to a boil.
6. **Meanwhile, fold the wontons:** Fill a small bowl with water. Orient a wonton skin in your palm in a diamond shape and place 1 heaping teaspoon of the filling on the bottom corner of the skin, closest to you. Roll from the bottom corner up until the filling is fully covered, then wet the skin to the right of the filling. Hold the wonton with your hands on either side of the filling. Pinch the skin on both sides of the filling to seal (like a candy in a wrapper), then bring both sides in to meet, folding the wet (right) side under the dry (left) side and pinching to seal. (The water will act as an adhesive.) See page 194 for a step-by-step illustrated guide.

HOW TO FOLD A WONTON

my signature dish

FOR FOLDING AND SERVING

2 (12-ounce) packages wonton skins

Toasted sesame oil

Thinly sliced scallions

Finely chopped fresh ginger (optional)

7. Working in batches of 15 to 20 wontons (so as not to overcrowd the pot), add the wontons to the boiling water and cook until they float to the surface and the internal temperature registers 165°F on an instant-read thermometer, 2 to 3 minutes. Using a spider strainer, remove the wontons from the pot, allowing the excess water to drip off, and transfer to a serving bowl.
8. **To serve:** Drizzle the wontons with sesame oil and toss to prevent them from sticking together. Spoon some sauce onto the wontons, saving more to serve on the side. Top with scallions and ginger, if desired, and enjoy!

HOW TO FOLD A *wonton*

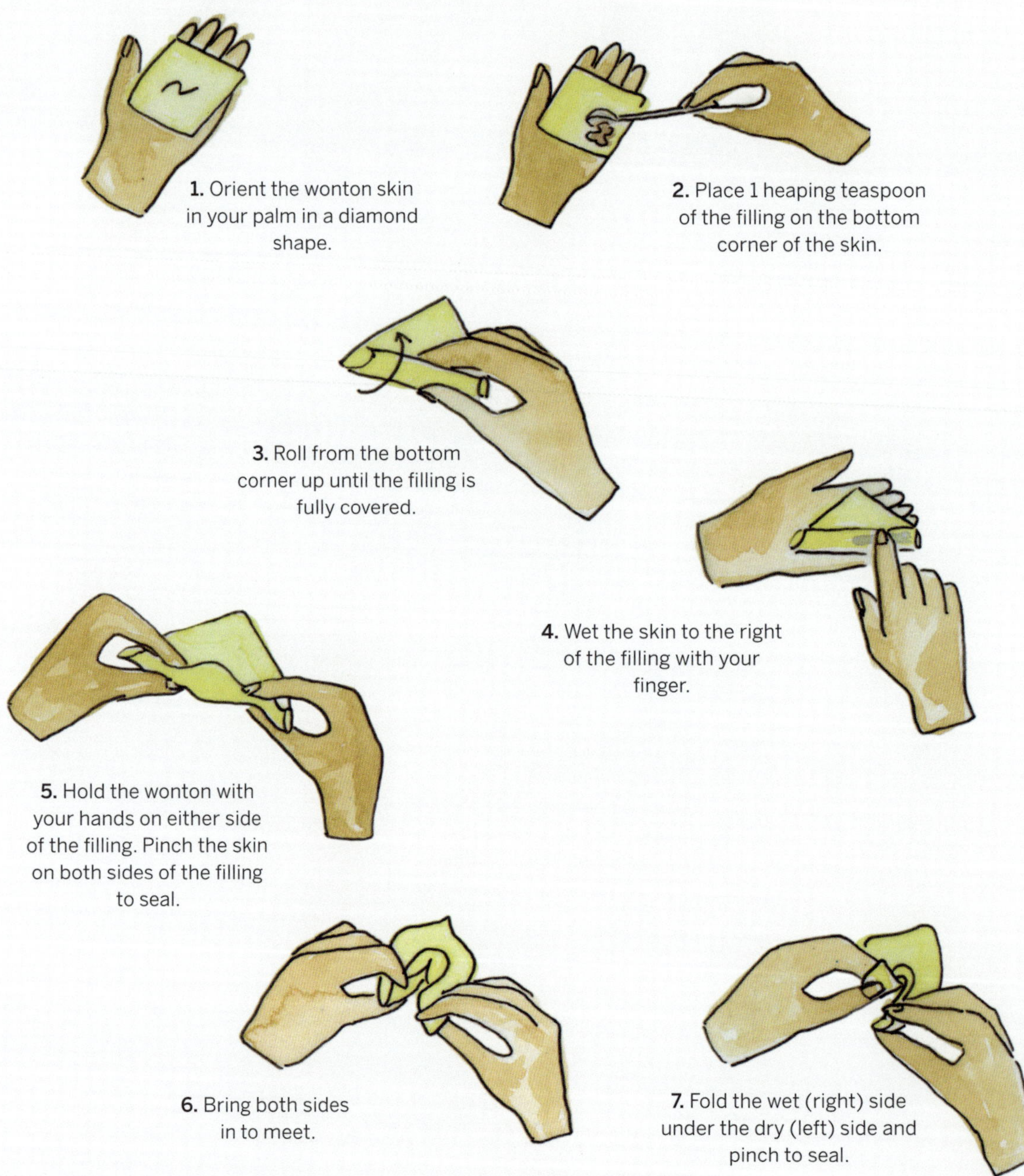

1. Orient the wonton skin in your palm in a diamond shape.

2. Place 1 heaping teaspoon of the filling on the bottom corner of the skin.

3. Roll from the bottom corner up until the filling is fully covered.

4. Wet the skin to the right of the filling with your finger.

5. Hold the wonton with your hands on either side of the filling. Pinch the skin on both sides of the filling to seal.

6. Bring both sides in to meet.

7. Fold the wet (right) side under the dry (left) side and pinch to seal.

Sunday

let's brunch

Perfect Recipes for Rest and Relaxation

This chapter is all about brunch and cozy Sundays at home. Some recipes, such as the savory oats on page 207 (my latest obsession), are perfect for two, while others are ideal for feeding a crowd. You'll also find the sweet treats here, like moist and flavorful Mom's Blueberry Zucchini Bread (page 204) and warm, comforting Chai-Spiced French Toast (page 216). And whatever you do, don't miss my mom's pancakes (page 208)! They're unbelievably fluffy, and everyone who tries them immediately asks for the recipe. Plus, I've got your egg cravings covered, including a step-by-step illustrated guide to poaching eggs with confidence (see page 222).

Jammy Eggs *with Lemon-Garlic Yogurt and Chili Oil*

SERVES 2 ◆ PREP TIME: 15 MINUTES ◆ TOTAL TIME: 25 MINUTES

LEMON-GARLIC YOGURT

1 cup plain full-fat or 2% Greek yogurt

1 garlic clove, grated

1 tablespoon extra-virgin olive oil

Zest of 1 lemon

1 tablespoon fresh lemon juice

¼ teaspoon salt

FOR THE EGGS AND SERVING

4 large eggs

Chili crisp or chili oil, for drizzling

Flaky sea salt, such as Maldon, for serving

Fresh dill and/or mint leaves, for garnish

2 pitas

Extra-virgin oil, for brushing

I went to Turkey a few summers ago and still think about the dreamy combination of eggs and yogurt I had for breakfast. I love how the components blend together and complement each other: The jammy eggs rest on a layer of lemon-garlic yogurt, and as you break into them with a fork or spoon, the yolks mix with the yogurt, creating a creamy dip. There's a kick from the chili crisp and freshness from the herbs, plus plenty of toasted pita for scooping it all up.

1. Bring a medium pot of water to a boil.
2. **Make the lemon-garlic yogurt:** In a medium bowl, mix together the yogurt, garlic, olive oil, lemon zest, lemon juice, and salt. Set aside.
3. **Make the eggs:** When the water is boiling, using a mesh skimmer (or slotted spoon), carefully lower the eggs into the water. Reduce the heat to maintain a gentle boil and cook the eggs for 6 minutes 30 seconds for a runny yolk. While the eggs are cooking, fill a medium bowl with cold water and ice. Transfer the cooked eggs to the ice water and set aside for 2 minutes to cool.
4. Peel the eggs by gently cracking them all over and removing the shell. Cut the eggs in half.
5. **To serve:** Divide the lemon-garlic yogurt between two plates or shallow bowls. Using the back of a spoon, spread the yogurt in a circular motion. Place the eggs on the yogurt, cut-side up. Drizzle with some chili crisp, sprinkle with some flaky salt, and garnish with dill and/or mint.
6. Heat a medium skillet over medium-high heat. Brush both sides of the pitas with some olive oil. Working in batches, toast the pita until golden brown, 1 to 2 minutes per side.
7. Cut the pitas into 6 to 8 wedges and serve alongside the yogurt and eggs. Enjoy!

Egg White Frittata *with Oyster Mushrooms and Goat Cheese*

SERVES 1 TO 2 ◆ PREP TIME: 10 MINUTES ◆ TOTAL TIME: 35 MINUTES

1 tablespoon unsalted butter

3½ ounces oyster mushrooms, separated into individual mushrooms (large mushrooms sliced in half)

Kosher salt and freshly ground black pepper

8 asparagus spears (4 ounces), fibrous ends snapped off, cut into ¼-inch rounds

1 teaspoon balsamic vinegar

¼ cup chopped fresh chives (½-inch pieces)

6 large egg whites (¾ cup; see Tip)

FOR SERVING

Extra-virgin olive oil, preferably a high-quality finishing oil

Crumbled goat cheese

Fresh chives

Crushed Calabrian chili peppers in oil (optional)

TIP

Use the egg yolks for the Miso Carbonara Udon on page 130.

While I love whole eggs, sometimes I'm in the mood for a protein-packed egg white frittata. This one was inspired by a delicious breakfast I had over the holidays at the Ojai Valley Inn. Oyster mushrooms are the star and anchor here, bringing a nice texture and shape. I chop the asparagus into small pieces so it blends seamlessly with the chives, and add a splash of balsamic vinegar for just the right hint of tart sweetness. The goat cheese crumbles on top are a must, as their creaminess ties everything together. And if you like a little heat, serve the frittata with crushed Calabrian chili peppers on the side, adding a bit to each bite for just the right amount of spice.

1. Preheat the oven to 350°F.
2. In a small (8-inch) ovenproof nonstick skillet, melt the butter over medium heat. Add the mushrooms, season with salt and pepper, and cook, stirring occasionally, until golden and starting to become tender, 2 to 3 minutes.
3. Add the asparagus and cook until bright green and starting to become tender, about 2 minutes.
4. Stir in the vinegar and chives and cook until the chives wilt slightly, about 30 seconds. Add the egg whites. Cook for 1 minute, using a silicone spatula to gently scramble the egg whites and stir to combine with the mushrooms and asparagus.
5. Remove from the heat, spread everything into an even layer in the skillet, and scrape down the sides of the skillet. Transfer to the oven and bake until the egg whites are set and no longer jiggle in the center, 6 to 8 minutes. Run the spatula around the edges of the frittata to release it from the skillet and slide the frittata onto a plate.
6. **To serve:** Drizzle the frittata with a little olive oil, sprinkle with some goat cheese, and garnish with chives. Serve with Calabrian chili peppers on the side for heat, if desired, and enjoy!

House&Home

Jambon-Fromage Egg Canoe

SERVES 2 TO 4, DEPENDING ON YOUR APPETITE ◆ PREP TIME: 5 MINUTES ◆ TOTAL TIME: 30 MINUTES

1 French baguette (about 10 ounces)

2 tablespoons salted butter, at room temperature

6 slices deli ham (about 5 ounces)

6 slices Swiss cheese (about 6½ ounces)

4 large eggs

Flaky sea salt, such as Maldon

Freshly ground black pepper

Doug and I love France so much that we even chose to get married there. We especially love Paris, and my first order of business when we land is finding a ham and cheese baguette sandwich (aka jambon-fromage). It's so simple—just butter, cheese, ham, and a crusty baguette—but truly the best.

This recipe combines that classic sandwich with a nostalgic breakfast my dad used to make on weekends—a bull's eye (a slice of bread with a hole cut out, cooked in a skillet with an egg cracked into the center). The egg canoe takes those elements and transforms them into a more elevated yet equally comforting meal. I especially love the way the cheese drapes over the sides of the baguette and melts onto the bread, creating an irresistible, cheesy crust.

1. Preheat the oven to 400°F. Line a sheet pan with parchment paper.
2. Cut the baguette in half crosswise to create two equal pieces, like two smaller baguettes. Slice each half horizontally as you would to create a sandwich, making sure the top piece is thicker than the bottom piece. Set aside the bottom pieces.
3. Using a paring knife, cut out two ovals of about 3 by 2 inches in each top piece. Remove the bread to create holes. (Save the bread to make croutons or simply snack on it!) You will have a total of four ovals. Spread the butter over the cut sides of the bottom pieces of bread. Place the pieces on the prepared sheet pan, cut-side up.
4. Top with the ham, folding each slice so it fits on the bread, then add the Swiss cheese, keeping each slice whole so that it drapes over the bread (it will melt onto the bread and sheet pan into crispy pieces). Cover with the top pieces of baguette. Carefully crack an egg into each hole in the top pieces. A little egg white may seep out between the slices of bread—don't worry if this happens! Sprinkle the eggs with some flaky salt and pepper.
5. Bake until the egg white is opaque and no longer jiggles and the yolks are jammy (slightly runny), 18 to 20 minutes. The outside of the bread will be golden brown and toasted, and the cheese melted.
6. Remove from the oven and let cool for 5 minutes. Cut the bread between the eggs into four sections and serve on plates. (I like to eat mine with my hands like a sandwich!) Enjoy!

Mom's Blueberry Zucchini Bread

MAKES ONE 9 BY 5-INCH LOAF ◆ PREP TIME: 20 MINUTES ◆ TOTAL TIME: 1 HOUR 30 MINUTES

1½ cups (190 grams) coarsely grated zucchini (1 small zucchini)

2 large eggs

½ cup extra-virgin olive oil

2 teaspoons vanilla extract

½ cup (67 grams) granulated sugar

⅓ cup packed (73 grams) light brown sugar

1⅓ cups (160 grams) all-purpose flour

1¼ teaspoons baking soda

½ teaspoon ground cinnamon

½ teaspoon kosher salt

1 cup fresh blueberries

⅔ cup coarsely chopped pecans

FOR TOPPING

¼ cup coarsely chopped pecans

1 tablespoon light brown sugar

Flaky sea salt, such as Maldon

For me to get excited about baking, the recipe needs to be a total winner—and this blueberry zucchini bread is just that! In all honesty, when my mom did her normal routine of hounding me to make her latest creation, I was skeptical. We always brainstorm ideas together and, trust me, not all of them come to fruition. But after a few weeks of her persistence, I finally caved in, and I'm so glad I did! The zucchini and blueberries keep the bread super moist, and it's perfect for breakfast or an afternoon snack (don't forget to sprinkle some flaky sea salt on top to add a little zing!). Nutritious ingredients and not too sweet—yes, please. Fair warning: It's so good that once you start eating, it'll be hard to stop. As with most things in life, Mom was right.

1. Preheat the oven to 350°F. Line a 9 by 5-inch loaf pan with parchment paper.
2. In a large bowl, mix together the zucchini, eggs, olive oil, and vanilla. Add the granulated sugar and brown sugar and mix to combine.
3. In a medium bowl, whisk together the flour, baking soda, cinnamon, and salt.
4. Add the flour mixture to the zucchini mixture and mix until just combined. Fold in the blueberries and ⅔ cup of the pecans. Pour the batter into the prepared loaf pan.
5. **Top the loaf:** Sprinkle the pecans and brown sugar over the batter. Lightly sprinkle with flaky salt.
6. Bake until the top is golden brown and a toothpick inserted into the center comes out clean, about 1 hour 10 minutes. Let the bread cool in the pan for about 15 minutes, then transfer to a wire rack to cool completely before slicing. Enjoy!

Everyone who tries this is obsessed!

ENGLISH BREAKFAST TEA
THÉ NOIR

Savory Oatmeal *with Parmesan Crisps and Chives*

SERVES 4 ◆ PREP TIME: 5 MINUTES ◆ TOTAL TIME: 20 MINUTES

¾ cup (3 ounces) grated Parmesan cheese

2 tablespoons unsalted butter

2 garlic cloves, finely chopped

2 cups chicken stock or water

1½ cups whole milk

¼ teaspoon kosher salt

½ teaspoon freshly ground black pepper

2 cups rolled oats

¼ cup chopped fresh chives

Most people think of oatmeal as being sweet, but I'd argue it's even better savory. It's so soothing and quick to make. This one has the warm, creamy feel of risotto but is lighter and more nourishing thanks to the rolled oats.

The one thing savory oatmeal lacks, in my opinion, is texture. So I added Parmesan crisps—they're super easy to make and always look elegant with those lacy golden edges. Shatter them with your spoon for a bit of crunch and some sharp, salty goodness in every bite. And don't skip the fresh chives, as their mild onion flavor adds just the right brightness to balance the richness.

1. Preheat the oven to 400°F. Line a sheet pan with parchment paper.
2. Make four 1-tablespoon piles of the Parmesan on the prepared sheet pan (leave some space between the piles, as the cheese will expand as it melts). Flatten the piles into roughly 2½-inch rounds. Bake until melted, golden brown, and crisp, 7 to 9 minutes. Set aside and let cool.
3. In a small pot, melt the butter over medium heat. Add the garlic and cook, stirring, until fragrant and starting to turn golden brown, about 1 minute. Add the stock, milk, salt, and pepper. Bring to a simmer over medium-high heat.
4. Stir in the oats and reduce the heat to low. Simmer until most of the liquid has been absorbed and the oats are tender, 5 to 7 minutes. Remove from the heat and stir in the remaining ½ cup Parmesan.
5. Divide the oatmeal among four bowls and top each generously with the chives. Place a Parmesan crisp in each bowl and enjoy! Leftover oatmeal can be stored in an airtight container in the refrigerator for up to 3 days. Just add a little water or milk to loosen it when you reheat it.

Mom's Fluffy Pancakes

SERVES 4 (MAKES 9 PANCAKES) ◆ PREP TIME: 10 MINUTES ◆ TOTAL TIME: 45 MINUTES

2 cups (240 grams) all-purpose flour

2 tablespoons sugar

2 teaspoons baking powder

1 teaspoon baking soda

1 teaspoon kosher salt

2 cups buttermilk

2 large eggs

2 tablespoons unsalted butter, melted

Avocado oil or other neutral oil, such as grapeseed, for cooking (see Tip)

FOR SERVING

Salted butter, at room temperature

Warm maple syrup

My mom makes the fluffiest pancakes with melt-in-your-mouth centers. She always starts by cooking bacon on the griddle, then uses a little of the bacon grease for the pancakes. Her secret to keeping them super moist? Don't overcook them! She takes the pancakes off the griddle just when they're done, leaning ever so slightly toward undercooked. The result is a golden pancake with crisp edges and a subtle tang from the buttermilk. Doug loves them, so whenever we visit my childhood home, she makes sure to stock up on pancake ingredients. We're convinced these are the best pancakes ever, and I can't wait for you to try them and see for yourself!

1. In a large bowl, whisk together the flour, sugar, baking powder, baking soda, and salt.
2. In a medium bowl, whisk together the buttermilk and eggs.
3. Pour the buttermilk-egg mixture into the flour mixture. Using a flexible spatula or a wooden spoon, stir until the batter just comes together. Do not overmix! You want to have some clumps in the batter, which will make the pancakes fluffy. Fold in the melted butter.
4. In a large nonstick skillet or a griddle, heat a thin coating of avocado oil over medium heat. When the skillet is hot, add about ⅓ cup of the batter. (If you are making more than one pancake at a time, leave some space between the pancakes.) Cook until little bubbles form on the surface and pop and the bottom of the pancake is golden brown (lift the edge of the pancake with your spatula to check), about 2 minutes. Flip and cook until golden brown on the second side and just cooked through, about 1 minute 30 seconds. (I usually pierce the middle of the pancake with my spatula to ensure it's cooked through.) Transfer the pancake(s) to a plate and repeat with the remaining batter.
5. **To serve:** Plate the pancakes hot and fresh off the stove with salted butter and warm maple syrup. Enjoy!

TIP

If you made bacon to serve with the pancakes, you can cook them in the bacon grease left in the skillet instead of using avocado oil.

you need to try these! ↗

Spicy Shakshuka *with Feta and Herbs*

SERVES 4 ◆ PREP TIME: 10 MINUTES ◆ TOTAL TIME: 50 MINUTES

2 tablespoons extra-virgin olive oil

1 medium yellow onion (10 ounces), cut into small dice

1 red bell pepper (6 ounces), cut into small dice

3 garlic cloves, finely chopped

1½ teaspoons kosher salt, plus more for the eggs

1½ teaspoons ground cumin

1½ teaspoons smoked paprika

1 teaspoon ground coriander

1 (28-ounce) can whole peeled San Marzano tomatoes

1 tablespoon harissa, plus more if needed

½ teaspoon sugar

6 large eggs

⅓ cup crumbled feta cheese

FOR SERVING

Handful of fresh parsley and/or cilantro, coarsely chopped

Crumbled feta cheese

Olives, optional

Toasted crusty bread or pita

Doug and I went to Morocco last year and instantly fell in love with harissa—not surprising, since we're both big fans of spicy condiments. This North African chili paste adds depth to the shakshuka, bringing both heat and aroma. (Be sure to taste your harissa first, as the spice level can vary!)

Shakshuka can sometimes feel like just eggs in tomato sauce, which is exactly what I wanted to avoid. So, I layered in plenty of spices (cumin, paprika, coriander), a touch of sugar to bring out the tomatoes' natural sweetness, and a shower of fresh herbs at the end. The feta melts into the sauce, creating little pockets of creamy, salty goodness.

This dish is perfect for a family-style brunch. Just set the skillet in the center of the table and serve with plenty of toasted bread or pita for scooping up every last bite.

1. In a large skillet (with a lid), heat the olive oil over medium heat. Add the onion and bell pepper and cook, stirring, until tender, 7 to 9 minutes. Add the garlic, salt, cumin, smoked paprika, and coriander. Cook, stirring, for 1 minute.
2. Using your hands, crush the whole tomatoes to break them up as you drop them into the pot, then pour in the juices from the can. Add the harissa and sugar and mix to combine. Reduce the heat to low and simmer, stirring occasionally, until the tomatoes break down and the flavors meld, about 10 minutes.
3. With the back of a spoon or a ladle, make 6 wells in the sauce for the eggs. Crack one egg into each well. Lightly season each egg with salt. Sprinkle the feta over the top.
4. Increase the heat to medium-low and bring to a simmer. Reduce the heat to low, cover, and cook until the whites are set but the yolks are still runny, 5 to 10 minutes. (This timing varies depending on your stove; check every few minutes for your desired doneness!)
5. **To serve:** Top with a generous sprinkle of parsley and/or cilantro, some feta, and olives, if desired. Serve with toasted bread or pita and enjoy!

Crispy Scrambled Huevos Rancheros

SERVES 4 ◆ PREP TIME: 10 MINUTES ◆ TOTAL TIME: 35 MINUTES

Los Angeles has an unbelievable Mexican food scene, and Doug and I grab Mexican food at least once a week. We love tacos, but when it comes to breakfast, huevos rancheros always feels like a treat. This recipe is my take and is almost like a deconstructed tostada. It starts with crispy tortillas on the bottom (using my go-to oven method instead of frying), layered with refried beans (I'm a bean girl, so I'm all in), soft-scrambled eggs, and plenty of flavorful toppings. The toppings are what really make this dish special, so don't hold back!

TOSTADAS

1 tablespoon avocado oil or other neutral oil, such as grapeseed

4 corn tortillas

Kosher salt

½ cup refried black beans or regular refried beans

¼ cup (1 ounce) shredded Mexican-style cheese blend

SCRAMBLED EGGS

8 large eggs

½ teaspoon kosher salt, plus more if needed

¼ teaspoon freshly ground black pepper, plus more if needed

1 tablespoon avocado oil or other neutral oil, such as grapeseed

½ medium yellow onion (5 ounces), cut into small dice

1 small jalapeño, half of the seeds removed, cut into small dice (see Tip)

FOR SERVING

Medium or hot red salsa

Light sour cream

Sliced avocado

Chopped fresh cilantro

Flaky sea salt, such as Maldon

1. Preheat the oven to 400°F on convection mode (or 425°F on regular bake).
2. **Make the tostadas:** Coat a sheet pan with the avocado oil. Place the tortillas on the sheet pan and rub both sides with the oil. Season one side of each tortilla with salt and bake for 6 minutes. Flip and spread 2 tablespoons of the beans on each tortilla, then sprinkle 1 tablespoon of the cheese on each. Bake until the cheese has melted and the tortillas are crispy and deep golden brown around the edges, 3 to 5 minutes.
3. **While the tostadas are in the oven, make the scrambled eggs:** In a medium bowl, beat the eggs with the salt and pepper.
4. In a large nonstick skillet, heat the avocado oil over medium heat. Add the onion and jalapeño and season with salt and pepper. Cook, stirring, until the onion is translucent and tender, 4 to 6 minutes. Reduce the heat to medium-low and add the eggs. Cook, stirring to scramble the eggs, until cooked to your liking, 2 to 3 minutes.
5. **To serve:** Divide the tostadas among four plates. Spoon the eggs onto the plates, dividing them evenly and slightly covering the tostadas. Drizzle salsa over everything and top with a dollop of sour cream, sliced avocado, and cilantro. Sprinkle with some flaky salt (especially on the avocado) and enjoy!

TIP

For less heat, remove all the seeds from the jalapeño.

Ricotta, Egg, and Spinach Panini *(No Panini Press Needed!)*

SERVES 1 ◆ PREP TIME: 10 MINUTES ◆ TOTAL TIME: 20 MINUTES

1 tablespoon salted butter, at room temperature

2 slices sourdough sandwich bread or your favorite bread

2 tablespoons whole-milk ricotta cheese (see Tip)

¾ cup packed baby spinach, divided

Kosher salt and freshly ground black pepper

1 teaspoon extra-virgin olive oil

1 large egg

¼ avocado, sliced

1 lemon wedge

TIP

Use the rest of the ricotta in the container to make the Creamy Lemon Spinach and Ricotta Stuffed Shells on page 177.

The filling for this panini is inspired by a crepe I used to get at UC Berkeley from a spot called Crepes-A-Go-Go. I'd customize mine with ricotta, avocado, and an over-easy egg—a delicious and balanced combo I've loved ever since!

While you could definitely have this panini for lunch, I've always thought of it as more of a breakfast or brunch item. My mom used to make paninis for my brothers and me before school, even while juggling a million things as a full-time real estate agent. (We were so spoiled!) She'd whip them up with bacon, spinach, and egg on the George Foreman, always getting those perfect grill marks. I've developed a stovetop method that gives you the same panini-like effect—a satisfyingly crisp exterior and a soft, warm filling.

1. Butter one side of both slices of bread and place them on a cutting board, buttered-side down.
2. Spread the ricotta on the unbuttered side of one slice of bread. Top with ½ cup of the spinach and sprinkle with some salt and pepper. Place the second slice of bread on top to close the sandwich, buttered-side up.
3. Heat a grill pan or medium skillet over medium heat. Add the sandwich, place a piece of parchment paper on top, then place a heavy skillet on top to gently press down on the sandwich. Cook until golden brown on the bottom, about 3 minutes. Remove the heavy skillet and parchment, flip the sandwich, and return the parchment and skillet to the top. Cook until golden brown on the second side, 1 to 2 minutes. (Check by lifting a corner. Careful, as it can burn quickly on the second side!)
4. In a small nonstick skillet, heat the olive oil over medium heat. Add the egg and cook until the white is almost set, about 2 minutes. Remove from the heat, flip the egg, and cook for about 1 minute more for an over-medium yolk. I recommend cooking the egg until the yolk is a little more set than runny so it doesn't spill when you cut the sandwich in half.
5. Transfer the sandwich to the cutting board and open it up. Place the remaining ¼ cup spinach on the ricotta, followed by the egg and avocado. Sprinkle the avocado with some salt and squeeze a little lemon juice over. Close the sandwich, cut it in half on the diagonal, and enjoy!

Chai-Spiced French Toast

SERVES 4 TO 6 ◆ PREP TIME: 10 MINUTES ◆ TOTAL TIME: 35 MINUTES

1 cup whole milk

1 tablespoon pure maple syrup, plus warm syrup for serving

1 teaspoon vanilla extract

1 teaspoon ground cinnamon, plus more for serving

½ teaspoon ground cardamom

¼ teaspoon ground ginger

¼ teaspoon kosher salt

Pinch of ground allspice

Pinch of ground nutmeg

Dash of ground cloves

4 large eggs

6 (¾-inch-thick) slices challah

2 tablespoons unsalted butter, plus more if needed

Salted butter, for serving

I've always been a chai girlie. Back in high school, my friends and I would hang out at a local cafe called Si Si, where we'd order these blended chai drinks—almost like a chai-flavored slushie or Frappuccino. When I was brainstorming ideas for French toast, those warm spices immediately came to mind, and I decided to infuse the custard with them. The result is pure magic. Thick slices of challah soak up the spiced mixture, turning soft and custardy inside, while the outside develops a perfect golden crust in the skillet.

1. In a 9-inch square baking dish (or a large shallow bowl), whisk together the milk, maple syrup, vanilla, cinnamon, cardamom, ginger, salt, allspice, nutmeg, and cloves. Add the eggs and whisk until smooth and combined.
2. Add 3 slices of challah (or however many will fit in a single layer) to the egg mixture. Soak for 2 minutes. Using tongs, gently flip and soak on the other side for 2 minutes.
3. In a large skillet, melt 1 tablespoon of the butter over medium heat. Using tongs, lift the challah pieces from the egg mixture, allowing the excess to drip off, and place in the skillet. You should be able to fit the slices in a single layer. Cook until golden brown, 2 to 3 minutes per side. Transfer to a plate and cover with foil to keep warm (or serve immediately). Repeat with the remaining butter and challah. (You can soak the remaining challah slices while the first batch cooks.)
4. Top each piece of French toast with a pat of butter and a sprinkle of cinnamon. Drizzle with warm maple syrup and enjoy!

Mom's Southwestern Frittata

SERVES 6 ◆ PREP TIME: 10 MINUTES ◆ TOTAL TIME: 45 MINUTES

Unsalted butter, for greasing

10 large eggs

1¼ teaspoons kosher salt

½ teaspoon freshly ground black pepper

5 ounces (1 cup) fresh or frozen corn kernels (from 1 ear; see Tip)

1½ cups 4% (whole milk) cottage cheese

2 (4-ounce) cans diced mild green chilies

2 cups (3.3 ounces) baby spinach, coarsely chopped

1 cup (4 ounces) shredded sharp cheddar cheese, divided

Sour cream, for serving

Fresh cilantro leaves, for garnish

TIP

We love using fresh corn when we can!

Isn't she beautiful? I love her so much! ♡

This frittata checks every box: easy to make, big enough for a crowd, and absolutely delicious. Green chilies add a subtle kick, while sweet corn kernels and pockets of melted cheddar create a perfect balance of flavors and textures. The cottage cheese is a quiet hero here, lightening up the eggs without taking center stage. This recipe started with my mom's classic version, but I added my own twist—a dollop of sour cream and a sprinkle of fresh cilantro on top—and now even Mom says that's the way it should be eaten!

1. Preheat the oven to 425°F. Grease a 9 by 13-inch baking dish with some butter.
2. In a large bowl, whisk together the eggs, salt, and pepper until the yolks and whites are combined. Add the corn, cottage cheese, green chilies (with their juices), spinach, and ½ cup of the cheddar. Mix to combine.
3. Pour the mixture into the prepared baking dish and sprinkle the top with the remaining ½ cup cheddar.
4. Bake until the eggs are set and the top is golden brown, about 25 minutes.
5. Let rest for 5 minutes, then cut into squares and serve topped with a dollop of sour cream and some cilantro leaves. Enjoy!

Blueberry-Coconut-Almond Overnight Oats

SERVES 1 (BUT CAN BE EASILY SCALED UP) ◆ PREP TIME: 5 MINUTES ◆ TOTAL TIME: 5 MINUTES, PLUS OVERNIGHT FOR RESTING

½ cup rolled oats

½ cup unsweetened milk of your choice (I like almond milk)

2 tablespoons sliced almonds, divided

1 tablespoon plus 1 teaspoon unsweetened shredded coconut, divided

2 teaspoons maple syrup (see Tip)

¼ teaspoon ground cinnamon

¼ teaspoon vanilla extract

Small pinch of kosher salt

¼ cup fresh blueberries

I always try to accommodate special requests whenever we have houseguests—I want people to feel right at home, and food is a big part of that! Our good friend Cody was coming to visit, and I learned he has a breakfast routine that he swears by: overnight oats. Trying to be low-maintenance, he at first insisted he'd make them himself, but obviously, the host in me wasn't going to let him fend for himself *in my house!*

So, I came up with this overnight oats recipe based on what I had available in my pantry and fridge. Cody loved my spin, and then of course Doug wanted some, too, when he heard the good reviews. We enjoyed them so much that they've now become a household staple. They're also the perfect breakfast to make in advance—you can prep everything in individual portions on a Sunday afternoon and enjoy the oats throughout the week.

1. In a small jar or container with a lid, mix together the oats, milk, 1 tablespoon of the almonds, 1 tablespoon of the coconut, the maple syrup, cinnamon, vanilla, and salt.
2. Top with the blueberries, remaining 1 tablespoon almonds, and remaining 1 teaspoon coconut. Close the jar with the lid and refrigerate overnight or for up to 5 days. Enjoy!

TIP

If you prefer a sweeter breakfast, go up to 1 tablespoon of maple syrup, or taste and adjust to your liking!

HOW TO MAKE THE PERFECT *poached egg*

1. Fill a medium pot with 2 inches of water and bring to a boil over high heat.

2. Place a small fine-mesh sieve over a small bowl. Carefully crack one egg into the sieve and let it drain, gently moving the sieve up and down or tapping it against the bowl. This allows the thinner egg white to drain into the bowl.

3. Transfer the egg in the sieve to another small bowl.

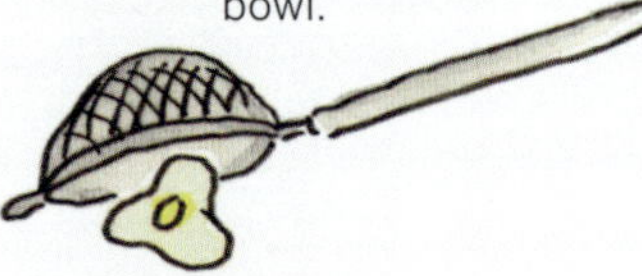

4. When the water is boiling, stir in 1 tablespoon distilled white vinegar and a generous pinch of salt. Reduce the heat to maintain a very gentle simmer (no big bubbles!).

5. Using a large spoon, stir the water to create a gentle vortex.

6. Gently slide the egg into the middle of the vortex. (You can poach up to four eggs at a time. Add them one at a time, waiting a few seconds between each one.)

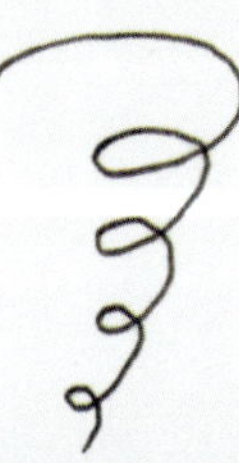

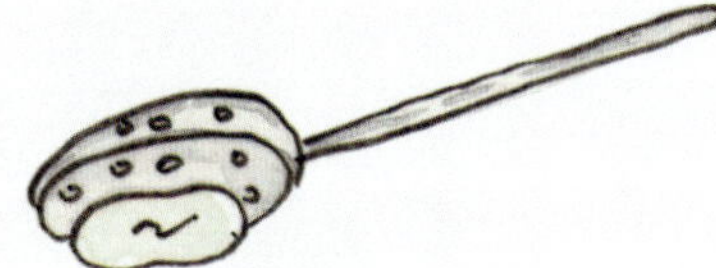

7. Cook until the white is set but the yolk is still runny, about 4 minutes. Using a slotted spoon, transfer the egg to a plate.

Poached Eggs over Rice *with Soy-Scallion Butter*

SERVES 2 FOR LUNCH OR 4 FOR A LIGHT BREAKFAST
◆ PREP TIME: 10 MINUTES ◆ TOTAL TIME: 45 MINUTES

4 tablespoons (½ stick) unsalted butter

2 scallions, thinly sliced

1 teaspoon soy sauce, plus more for serving

Jasmine Rice (page 231)

4 poached eggs (see opposite)

Black sesame seeds, for serving

You won't believe how rich and luxurious this dish tastes. The egg yolk oozes into the hot rice and mixes with the scallion butter, making each bite dreamy and decadent. You get a delicious umami base from the soy sauce and little pops of texture from the sesame seeds. If you're intimidated by poaching an egg at home, don't be! It's not at all difficult, and the result always feels restaurant-grade fancy. Although I typically think of eggs and rice as a breakfast or brunch combo, you could easily make this recipe into a simple dinner by adding a few easy sides (think kimchi, a simple green salad, some toasted seaweed . . . yum).

1. In a small skillet, melt the butter over medium heat. Reserve 2 tablespoons of the scallion greens for garnish, then add the rest to the skillet. Cook, stirring, until slightly softened but still bright green, 30 seconds to 1 minute. Remove from the heat and stir in the soy sauce.
2. Serve the rice in two to four bowls, then top each with one or two poached eggs. Spoon the soy-scallion butter onto the eggs and rice. Top with sesame seeds and the reserved scallion greens. Serve with more soy sauce on the side for sprinkling on top, if desired.

Simple Sides

for every day of the week

Salads, Veggies, Grains, and Starches

My book features recipes from a variety of cuisines—Chinese, Korean, Italian, French, Vietnamese, Thai . . . the list goes on! In this chapter, you'll find an assortment of sides to mix and match as you please. Consider this your go-to for a wide range of dishes, like a bold and flavorful Korean salad (page 236), garlic bread (page 240) that pairs beautifully with Mom's Spaghetti and Meatballs (page 184), and the easiest creamy mashed potatoes (page 232). Most of these recipes are low effort and super quick, like my favorite method for making broccoli (page 243—hint: it's steamed in the microwave!).

Buttery Lemon Rice *with Herbs*

SERVES 4 ◆ PREP TIME: 10 MINUTES ◆ TOTAL TIME: 40 MINUTES

1 cup long-grain rice

1½ cups chicken stock

1 garlic clove, finely chopped

Kosher salt and freshly ground black pepper

3 tablespoons chopped fresh herbs, such as dill, chives, or parsley, plus more for garnish

2 tablespoons unsalted butter, cut into small pieces

1 teaspoon lemon zest

1 to 2 tablespoons fresh lemon juice

This is an elegant side for a simple protein, like fish or chicken. It's perfectly balanced with bright lemon, buttery richness, and fragrant herbs. Feel free to swap in whatever herbs you have on hand—but if you're pairing it with fish, dill is my favorite choice!

1. Place the rice in a medium bowl and cover with water. Gently swish with one hand, then drain the water. Repeat with fresh water, swishing and draining, until the water is no longer opaque (this is to remove excess starch from the rice). Drain the rice in a fine-mesh sieve and transfer to a medium pot with a tight-fitting lid.
2. Add the stock, garlic, ½ teaspoon salt, and ¼ teaspoon pepper to the pot. Bring to a boil over high heat, then reduce the heat to low, cover, and simmer until the liquid has been absorbed, about 15 minutes.
3. Remove the pot from the heat and let rest, covered, for 10 minutes. Uncover and stir in the herbs, butter, lemon zest, and 1 tablespoon of the lemon juice. Taste and season with more lemon juice, salt, and/or pepper, if desired. Serve with more fresh herbs on top and enjoy!

Sesame Quinoa and Kale

SERVES 4 ◆ PREP TIME: 2 MINUTES ◆ TOTAL TIME: 25 MINUTES

1⅔ cups water

1 cup white quinoa or quinoa of your choice, rinsed and drained

8 ounces frozen chopped kale or spinach (2 cups)

1 teaspoon kosher salt

2 tablespoons toasted sesame seeds

1 tablespoon distilled white vinegar or rice vinegar

1 tablespoon toasted sesame oil

1 tablespoon soy sauce

I used to make a recipe similar to this one when I'd just graduated from college and was living with a roommate. Back then, I would serve the quinoa with a fried egg and a little sriracha for a quick dinner. Over time, it's become a staple side dish for just about everything (proteins and saucy mains), and since I always have a bag of frozen kale in the freezer, it feels like a pantry recipe that I can whip up on even the busiest weeknight. You throw the greens and grains into one pot and cook everything together. The seasonings give the quinoa depth and dimension without overpowering it, and the sesame seeds add a little crunch. Leftovers keep for days in the fridge, so top them with a fried egg, and you've got yourself an easy and satisfying five-minute lunch.

1. In a medium pot, combine the water, quinoa, kale, and salt. Bring to a boil over high heat. Cover, reduce the heat to low, and simmer until the water has been absorbed and the quinoa is tender, 18 to 25 minutes. (The cooking time varies depending on the quinoa, so don't hesitate to check and give it a stir to see if there's water at the bottom of the pot. When the quinoa is done, it should be fluffy, and the germ will be visible.)
2. Uncover and stir in the sesame seeds, vinegar, sesame oil, and soy sauce. Taste and adjust the seasonings, if desired, and enjoy! The quinoa can be stored in an airtight container in the refrigerator for up to 4 days.

Add a fried egg to make it a full meal ↗

Jasmine Rice

SERVES 2 TO 4, DEPENDING ON YOUR APPETITE AND SIDES (MAKES ABOUT 3 CUPS COOKED RICE)
◆ PREP TIME: 2 MINUTES ◆ TOTAL TIME: 35 MINUTES

1 cup jasmine rice

1¼ cups water

I almost always make jasmine rice in my 5½-cup Zojirushi rice cooker—that's how my mom does it, too. If you're using a rice cooker, I recommend following the manufacturer's instructions. But if you don't have one or you're traveling without your usual setup, knowing how to make rice on the stovetop is such a useful skill. The trick is allowing the rice to steam (off the heat and without lifting the lid!) for 10 minutes—this helps the grains finish cooking gently. This rice is the perfect base for soaking up all the flavors from the saucy Asian recipes in this book.

1. Place the rice in a medium bowl and cover with water. Gently swish with one hand, then drain the water. Repeat with fresh water, swishing and draining, until the water is no longer opaque (this is to remove excess starch from the rice). Drain the rice in a fine-mesh sieve and transfer to a small pot.
2. Add the water and bring to a boil over medium-high heat. Cover, reduce the heat to low, and cook for 15 minutes (but don't uncover it yet!). Remove from the heat and let stand, covered, for 10 minutes. Fluff with a fork or spoon. If the rice isn't as soft as you'd like it to be, cover again and let stand for 10 minutes more. Keep the pot covered until you're ready to serve the rice (it should stay hot for at least 30 minutes in the covered pot!). Leftover rice can be stored in an airtight container in the refrigerator for up to 3 days or in the freezer for up to 3 months.

TIPS

Choose a heavy pot with a tight-fitting lid so the water doesn't evaporate too much. If you're cooking a bigger quantity of uncooked rice (like 2 cups), make sure your pot is at least 2½ quarts in capacity (rice expands as it cooks!).

You can double this recipe, just make sure to follow the ratio of rice to water: 2½ cups water to 2 cups uncooked rice.

Creamy Mashed Potatoes *with Chives*

SERVES 4 ◆ PREP TIME: 10 MINUTES ◆ TOTAL TIME: 40 MINUTES

2 pounds Yukon Gold potatoes, peeled and cut into 1 by 2-inch chunks

½ cup whole milk

¼ cup sour cream

2 tablespoons unsalted butter, cut into small pieces

1 teaspoon kosher salt, plus more if needed

½ teaspoon freshly ground black pepper, plus more if needed

1 tablespoon finely chopped fresh chives, plus more for serving

This method for mashed potatoes takes inspiration from Michelin-starred chef Thomas Keller. A few years ago, I stumbled upon his recipe while searching for the gold standard for mashed potatoes. I've simplified it into a lighter version that's perfect for weeknights. I love using Yukon Gold potatoes; they have a natural creaminess and buttery flavor that's hard to beat. While the potatoes boil, you measure out the mix-ins so they're ready to go. Once the potatoes are drained, you immediately pour the mix-ins into the pot and let the butter melt in the residual heat (this keeps everything warm).

1. Place the potatoes in a medium pot and add water to cover by about 1½ inches. Bring to a boil over high heat, then reduce the heat to medium-low. Simmer until the potatoes can be easily pierced with a fork, 20 to 25 minutes.
2. Meanwhile, in a small glass measuring cup or bowl, combine the milk, sour cream, butter, salt, and pepper. Set aside.
3. Drain the potatoes in a colander. Immediately pour the milk mixture into the hot pot and stir until the butter has melted and all the ingredients are combined. Return the potatoes to the pot and mash with a potato masher until smooth and combined. Taste and season with more salt and/or pepper, if desired, then stir in the chives.
4. Transfer to a serving bowl and top with more chives. Enjoy!

For an extra silky finish, use a potato ricer

Mom and Dad's Spinach Salad *with Eggs and Mushrooms*

SERVES 4 ◆ PREP TIME: 10 MINUTES ◆ TOTAL TIME: 20 MINUTES

2 large eggs

DRESSING

1 tablespoon plus 1 teaspoon balsamic vinegar

1 teaspoon Dijon mustard

1 small garlic clove, grated (see Tips)

¼ teaspoon kosher salt

¼ teaspoon freshly ground black pepper

2 tablespoons extra-virgin olive oil

SALAD

5 ounces baby spinach

4 white or cremini mushrooms, thinly sliced

¼ cup (1 ounce) thinly sliced red onion

2 slices bacon, cooked until crispy and coarsely chopped (optional; see Tips)

Kosher salt and freshly ground black pepper (optional)

This salad has been a staple in my family for years—my parents make it all the time! It's simple enough to throw together on a busy weeknight, but it also scales up beautifully for special occasions. I even made it on Christmas Eve when I was hosting Doug's family, and everyone loved it.

What makes it so good is how the egg yolk gently coats the spinach when tossed, giving it a delicate richness. The sweetness and crunch from the onion balance things out, and if you're in the mood to jazz it up, crispy bacon bits take it over the top. Want to keep things even easier? Swap the dressing for a drizzle of balsamic vinegar and olive oil, then season with salt and pepper. So simple and so good!

1. Bring a small pot of water to a boil. Reduce the heat to medium to maintain a gentle boil and, using a large spoon, lower the eggs into the water. Cook for 9 minutes. Meanwhile, fill a medium bowl with ice and water. Transfer the eggs to the ice water and set aside to cool for 2 minutes. Peel the eggs and slice into thin rounds.
2. **Make the dressing:** In a small glass measuring cup or bowl, whisk together the vinegar, mustard, garlic, salt, and pepper. Slowly drizzle in the olive oil while whisking until the dressing emulsifies and thickens.
3. **Assemble the salad:** In a large bowl, toss together the spinach, sliced eggs, mushrooms, onion, and bacon (if using). Pour on the dressing and toss to combine. Taste and season with salt and/or pepper, if needed. Enjoy!

TIPS

To cook the bacon, line a plate with paper towels. Place the bacon in a single layer in a cold large skillet, set the skillet over medium heat, and cook, flipping once halfway through, until the fat has rendered and the bacon is crispy, 8 to 12 minutes. Transfer to the paper towel–lined plate to drain the excess fat.

Use a Microplane to grate the garlic.

Simple Korean Salad

SERVES 4 ◆ PREP TIME: 10 MINUTES ◆ TOTAL TIME: 10 MINUTES

DRESSING

1 garlic clove, finely chopped

2 tablespoons soy sauce

2 tablespoons rice vinegar

1 tablespoon toasted sesame oil

1 tablespoon toasted sesame seeds

1 teaspoon sugar

¼ teaspoon freshly ground black pepper

SALAD

1 head green- or red-leaf lettuce (10 ounces), washed well and torn into bite-size pieces

2 scallions, halved lengthwise, then cut crosswise into 2-inch pieces

¼ cup (1 ounce) thinly sliced sweet yellow onion

This salad is inspired by the ones you'll find at Korean restaurants, usually served with banchan—that spread of colorful little side dishes like kimchi and pickled veggies. The sweet and salty dressing gets massaged into the lettuce leaves, wilting them slightly—but in the most delicious way. You still get a nice crunch from the onion and thicker lettuce ribs, which keep the salad fresh and balanced.

1. **Make the dressing:** In a small glass measuring cup or bowl, mix together the garlic, soy sauce, vinegar, sesame oil, sesame seeds, sugar, and pepper until the sugar has dissolved.
2. **Assemble the salad:** In a large bowl, combine the lettuce, scallions, and onion. Drizzle with as much dressing as you like and massage with your hands or toss to coat (for a less wilted version). Enjoy!

Lemony Caesar Salad

SERVES 4 ◆ PREP TIME: 10 MINUTES ◆ TOTAL TIME: 35 MINUTES

I've made several versions of Caesar dressing, and this recipe is one of my favorites—it's light and refreshing, and lets the lemon shine.

That said, the croutons might just be the best part. Infused with grated garlic and coated in Parmesan cheese, they crisp up in the oven, almost frying in olive oil until they become irresistibly crunchy. They add a welcome richness to balance the crisp, refreshing romaine, and become even more delicious as they soak up the lemony dressing.

This is also a great make-ahead recipe. Prep everything in advance (bake the croutons, whisk the dressing, chop the romaine), and when it's time to eat, just toss and serve!

CROUTONS

¼ cup extra-virgin olive oil

2 large garlic cloves, grated

3 tablespoons grated Parmesan cheese

Large pinch of kosher salt

½ French baguette (about 5 ounces), cut into 1-inch pieces (about 3 cups)

DRESSING

1 large egg yolk

2 tablespoons fresh lemon juice

1 teaspoon Dijon mustard

¼ cup extra-virgin olive oil

1 garlic clove, grated

2 tablespoons grated Parmesan cheese

½ teaspoon kosher salt

½ teaspoon freshly ground black pepper

SALAD

1 large head romaine lettuce (14 ounces), chopped into 2-inch pieces

½ cup (2 ounces) shaved Parmesan cheese

Kosher salt and freshly ground black pepper (optional)

1. Preheat the oven to 375°F.
2. **Make the croutons:** In a large bowl, mix together the olive oil, garlic, Parmesan, and salt. Add the bread and toss to evenly coat in the mixture. Spread the bread over a sheet pan in one layer, leaving a little space between the pieces. Bake until golden brown and crispy, 12 to 15 minutes. Set aside to cool.
3. **Make the dressing:** In a small bowl, whisk together the egg yolk, lemon juice, and mustard until combined. While whisking, slowly drizzle in the olive oil and whisk until the dressing emulsifies and thickens. Whisk in the garlic, Parmesan, salt, and pepper.
4. **Assemble the salad:** Place the lettuce in a large serving bowl. Add most of the croutons and shaved Parmesan, saving some to serve on top. Pour the dressing over the salad and toss until evenly coated. Taste and season with more salt and/or pepper, if desired. Top the salad with the remaining croutons and shaved Parmesan and enjoy!

For a richer dressing, add 2 extra Tbsp parm and a few chopped anchovies

The Best Garlic Bread

SERVES 6 TO 8 (MAKES 16 PIECES) ◆ PREP TIME: 10 MINUTES ◆ TOTAL TIME: 40 MINUTES

½ cup (1 stick) salted butter, at room temperature (see Tip)

5 garlic cloves, finely chopped

2 tablespoons finely chopped fresh parsley

1 French baguette (about 10 ounces)

4 tablespoons extra-virgin olive oil

½ cup (2 ounces) grated Parmesan cheese

TIP

I like to use Kerrygold salted butter for this recipe. If you're using unsalted butter, just add a pinch of salt in step 2!

This is one of my favorite sides for a full Italian meal, alongside my Mom's Red and White Lasagna (page 167) or Spaghetti and Meatballs (page 184) and Lemony Caesar Salad (page 239). I've kept the flavors classic with garlic and butter but added parsley for a fresh touch and because those flecks of green are so pretty.

I love how the Parmesan creates a cheesy golden top while the olive oil seeps through the crumb, crisping up the bottom of the baguette. You can prep this recipe ahead of time and bake it just as your guests arrive. It's best served warm, fresh out of the oven!

1. Preheat the oven to 425°F.
2. In a medium bowl, combine the butter, garlic, and parsley. Using a fork or spoon, mix together until smooth and combined.
3. Using a bread knife, halve the baguette horizontally as you would for a sandwich and place on a sheet pan, cut-side up. (If your baguette is too long to fit on the sheet pan, you can cut the pieces in half crosswise to fit.) Drizzle 2 tablespoons of the olive oil over each baguette half, then spread with the garlic butter. Evenly sprinkle ¼ cup of the Parmesan over each baguette half.
4. Bake until the edges and bottom are golden brown and crisp, and the cheese is golden brown, 10 to 12 minutes.
5. Remove from the oven and transfer the garlic bread to a cutting board. Cut into individual pieces and enjoy!

Roasted Parmesan Asparagus

SERVES 4 ◆ PREP TIME: 5 MINUTES ◆ TOTAL TIME: 15 MINUTES

1 bunch asparagus (about 1 pound)

Extra-virgin olive oil, for drizzling

Kosher salt and freshly ground black pepper

¼ cup (1 ounce) grated Parmesan cheese

Zest of 1 lemon

Something truly magical happens when you sprinkle Parmesan on asparagus and roast it in the oven. The Parmesan melts into tiny cheese crisps, while the asparagus becomes tender but with a nice bite. You can also turn this into the simplest fifteen-minute light dinner for one by topping the asparagus with a fried egg.

1. Preheat the oven to 400°F. Line a sheet pan with parchment paper.
2. Hold the tough, woody end of the asparagus (opposite to the tip) and find the spot where it meets the tender part of the stalk. Bend until the tough end snaps off, then discard the ends. (If the stalks are very tough, use a vegetable peeler to peel the ends and make them easier to snap.)
3. Arrange the asparagus in one layer on the prepared sheet pan. Lightly drizzle with the olive oil (1 to 2 tablespoons), toss to coat evenly, and lightly season with salt and pepper. Sprinkle the asparagus all over with the Parmesan. (You want some of the cheese to fall in the cracks between the asparagus stalks, as it will melt and crisp up in the oven.)
4. Roast until the Parmesan is golden brown and the asparagus is bright green and browning at the tips, 8 to 12 minutes. (Keep an eye on the cheese, as it can brown quickly!)
5. Sprinkle the lemon zest over the asparagus. Serve the asparagus with the crispy Parmesan bits and enjoy!

The Simplest Broccoli

SERVES 4 ◆ PREP TIME: 5 MINUTES ◆ TOTAL TIME: 10 MINUTES

1 pound broccoli

3 tablespoons water

1 tablespoon unsalted butter

Kosher salt and freshly ground black pepper

1 lemon, halved

FOR SERVING (OPTIONAL)

Freshly grated Parmesan cheese

Crushed red pepper flakes

Flaky sea salt, such as Maldon

Okay, this might sound weird, but I think broccoli stems are completely underrated. Most people don't know that you can peel off the fibrous outer layer and cook the stems along with the florets. I even munch on them raw—they're like a savory apple with a delicious earthiness and mellow sweetness. This recipe for the simplest microwaved (or blanched) broccoli utilizes the whole head, stems included. It's my go-to vegetable side when I've had a long, busy day and barely have time to cook, let alone make multiple dishes. The trick is to microwave or boil the broccoli until it softens slightly, turns bright green, and is just al dente—but no more than a few minutes; otherwise, you'll be eating mush! Sometimes I'll eat it plain, seasoned with a sprinkle of salt and pepper, though I also love to coat it with melted butter for the perfect rich contrast (if you want to add an extra tablespoon, I won't judge!).

my go-to for busy nights

1. Separate the broccoli crowns and stems. Using a vegetable peeler, peel the thick, fibrous outer layer from the stems, then slice the stems at an angle into ¼-inch-thick ovals. Cut the crowns into florets.
2. Place the broccoli stems in a large microwave-safe bowl. Place the florets on top. Drizzle with the water, cover the bowl with a microwave-safe plate, and microwave until the broccoli is bright green and slightly tender, 4 to 5 minutes. (If you don't have a microwave, see Tip.) Drain the water from the bowl.
3. Add the butter to the broccoli and toss until melted. Season with salt and pepper. You can serve the broccoli in this bowl or transfer it to a serving bowl, if you prefer.
4. Squeeze a little lemon juice onto the broccoli and toss to combine. Taste and adjust the seasoning as needed, adding more lemon juice, salt, and/or pepper.
5. **To serve:** Top with Parmesan, red pepper flakes, and flaky salt, if desired. Enjoy!

TIP

If you don't have a microwave, bring a medium pot of salted water to a boil. Add the broccoli to the boiling water. Allow the water to return to a boil, then cook until the broccoli is bright green and slightly tender, about 1 minute. Drain well and return to the pot, then proceed with step 3.

PERFECT PAIRINGS FOR *effortless entertaining*

DUMPLING PARTY

Honey-Soy Glazed Edamame (page 146)

Mom's Benihana Chicken Fried Rice (page 133)

Grandma's Wontons (page 192)
or
Mom's Golden Crispy Chicken Potstickers (page 172)

ITALIAN FEAST

Mom's Garlic-Butter Shrimp Scampi (page 154)

Lemony Caesar Salad (page 239)

The Best Garlic Bread (page 240)

Mom's Spaghetti and Meatballs (page 184) or Mom's Red and White Lasagna (page 167)

KOREAN COMFORTS

Grandpa's Korean Vegetable Pancakes (page 157)

Simple Korean Salad (page 236)

Korean Braised Short Ribs with Daikon (page 171)

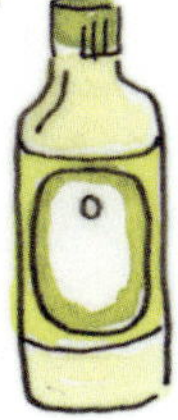

MEDITERRANEAN SPREAD

Spicy Whipped Feta Dip with Toasted Pita (page 150)

Crispy Zucchini Coins with Creamy Lemon-Dill Sauce (page 158)

Lamb Chops with Herb Salsa and Lemon-Garlic Yogurt (page 121)
or
Sheet Pan Mediterranean Chicken Plate with Chickpeas and Tzatziki (page 64)

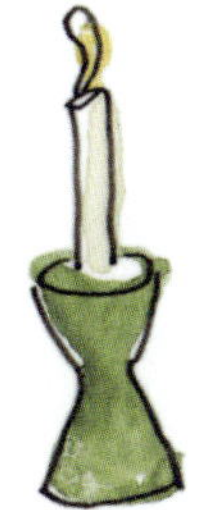

VEGETARIAN TAPAS

Veggie Ceviche Tostadas (page 102)

Grandpa's Korean Vegetable Pancakes (page 157)

Potato Samosa Bites with Raita (page 142)

SWEET AND SAVORY BRUNCH

Mom's Blueberry Zucchini Bread (page 204)

Mom's Fluffy Pancakes (page 208)
or
Chai-Spiced French Toast (page 216)

Mom's Southwestern Frittata (page 219)
or
Spicy Shakshuka with Feta and Herbs (page 211)

A simple showstopping dessert for all (minus brunch!): Vanilla ice cream (Häagen-Dazs is my favorite), drizzled with a high-quality extra-virgin olive oil and sprinkled generously with flaky sea salt, such as Maldon!

grandpa
1959

a love letter

grandpa & grandma
1959

always best friends!
1994

dad, poppy, nana & uncle Alan
1964

Jackson, Michael, Mom & me ♡
1996

ACKNOWLEDGMENTS

This book came together thanks to the incredible people who shared their talents and supported me every step of the way. I appreciate you all so much!

Sanaë Lemoine: Where do I even begin?! Thank you for pouring your heart into this book and for being such an amazing partner. From shaping the narrative so beautifully, to testing every single recipe with precision and care, you went above and beyond at every turn. You are one of the most reliable, thoughtful people I've ever worked with. I love your perfectionist tendencies (lol!), and I feel like I grew into a real professional recipe developer thanks to your support. Thank you for everything, Sanaë!

Amy Neunsinger: Thank you for being the best photographer I could have ever asked for! No one could have brought this book to life like you did. You are an artist in every sense of the word, and it was such an honor working on this project with you. The storytelling came through better than I could have ever imagined, and I loved the props you chose and all the little details that made each scene feel so lived-in and real. I had so much fun shooting this book with you. The ultimate effortless cool girl ;)!

Frances Boswell: You have this amazing way of making food look real and unfussy, yet still absolutely gorgeous and delicious. Thank you for making every recipe in this book shine, and for project managing the cooking of every dish during the shoot like a total pro! I picked up so many little tips and tricks from you that I'll always carry with me. :)

Devon Guio, Hector Prida, Luca Quinn, Kelsey Hellenbrand, and Kennedy Nicks: Thank you for being the best photo shoot fam and for making my very first cookbook shoot such a special experience. You all brought the best vibes, and I had so much fun getting to know each and every one of you!

Bailee Wolfson and Nikki Providence: Thank you for making me feel beautiful during my lifestyle shoot! Because of you both, I started the day with great energy and felt completely at ease.

Elizabeth Hart: Thank you for making this book feel so vibrant and alive with your gorgeous artwork! From day one, your professionalism and dedication meant so much, and I absolutely love how every single illustration turned out.

Jenn Sit: From the first time we spoke, I could feel how deeply you understood me and my mission, and I hoped we'd end up working on a book together. Thank you for being a dream editor and for helping shape this project into what it is today. I'm so grateful for your guidance every step of the way, and for believing in both me and this book. It's been such a joy working with you!

Stephanie Huntwork: Thank you for leading the charge on the creative direction of this book. Our tastes were aligned, which made it such a joy to collaborate with you on the design. It turned out better than I could have ever imagined!

Stephanie Davis, Jina Stanfill, and Jana Branson: Thank you for helping bring *Maxi's Kitchen* into the world with such enthusiasm! It was so fun working with you both.

The larger Clarkson Potter team: Elaine Hennig in editorial, copy editor Ivy McFadden, production editors Patricia Shaw and Joyce Wong, and production manager Jessica Heim.

Sarah Passick and Mia Vitale: The type A East Coast girlies of my dreams. I'm so glad I trusted my gut and chose to work with you. I truly couldn't have asked for better partners in this wild process. You two absolutely crushed it.

Charlotte Collie: Wow, what an exciting ride it's been! I appreciate you so much. You helped me find my way in an industry that was completely new to me, and we've built something really special together. Thank you for being such a big part of my journey and for helping me get to where I am today.

Amy Davila: Thank you for being a dream assistant and for helping me juggle everything while writing this book (and always). I appreciate you so much!

Nicole Scharf, Lexie Sparrow, Dani Haskins, and Hannah Tarro: Thank you to you and the Mona Creative team for your genuine excitement and dedication in sharing *Maxi's Kitchen* with the world.

Mom: Thank you for being my best friend and the reason I love cooking so much. I'll always associate cooking with comfort and love because of you. Thank you for helping me in ways big and small. I know without a doubt I wouldn't be where I am today without you. From brainstorming and testing recipes to flying to LA for our content sprints, you always have a way of bringing fresh energy and joy into my work, especially when I'm in a rut. You're the funniest, most vibrant person I know, and I love you so much!

Dad: Thank you for being the best dad. You're

the highest-character person I know, and I wouldn't be who I am today without you. I'll never forget your words: "Do the right thing, even when no one is looking." Thank you for always being the first to notice when I hit a new milestone, and for your endless support. I love you!

Doug Schuessler: You believed in me before I believed in myself. Even back when I was working in tech, you used to say, "It's Maxi's Kitchen! That's what you're meant to be doing." Your confidence in me gave me the push I needed to take a big risk, dive into the unknown, and chase this dream. You inspire me every day, and I love you to infinity!

Kimchi: For being the cutest sous chef and always bringing the pawsitive vibes. And for snuggling Mommy when she's having a sad day.

Michael Sharf: I'll never forget the year before I graduated college, when you sat me down and pushed me to get serious about my plan for life after graduation. Even though I cried at the time, I can now see that it was one of those life-defining moments. Because of you, I landed a great job right out of college, and from there, everything started to fall into place. Who knows where I'd be now without you.

Jackson Sharf: Thank you for always giving your honest reviews of the new recipes (lol!), sharing ideas for what I should cook next, and making sure I'm using AI to its full potential. Also, thank you for keeping me up to date on UFOs . . . because the aliens are definitely coming, and I need to be ready with snacks to feed them!!

Grandma: I definitely got my love of food from you :). Thank you for always being such a calm, kind, and loving presence in my life, and for passing down some of my favorite recipes, including my signature dish—wontons! I feel so lucky we've been able to share so much time together.

Grandpa: You were an incredible cook with the most discerning palate, and a true perfectionist in the kitchen. I can only hope I inherited a little bit of that from you. Some of my most cherished family recipes are yours, like the Korean vegetable pancakes and jjigae, and every time I cook them, I feel close to you again. I miss you so much!

Nana: The most fashionable lady there ever was. I miss you and cherish all the fun memories we shared, shopping together or sitting at home drawing pictures side by side. Your broccoli and Swiss cheese–stuffed chicken is still one of my favorite recipes, and I'm so happy that so many people will get to make it now, too.

Aunt Susan: I learned so much from you when we were cooking together during quarantine! You taught me how to stir-fry like a pro, always mixing the sauce in a glass measuring cup ahead of time, and I love how you coat chicken or fish in flour before pan-searing. So many of the skills I picked up from you show up in this book and have shaped the way I cook.

Aunt Jennifer: Thank you for all your cooking tips and tricks over the years, like the magic of homemade stock. You're such a fantastic cook, and I learn something new every time we're in the kitchen together.

Abby Hollender: Thank you for sparking the idea of the day-of-the-week theme for this book, and for being the best blogging co-pilot during quarantine.

Andrea and Doug Schuessler Sr.: Thank you for your constant love and support, and for always cheering me on with such enthusiasm. I feel so lucky to have such wonderful in-laws.

Nadine Jane: Part of me wonders where I'd be if I hadn't picked up *Magic Days* on December 7, the day I got laid off, and read that passage telling me to "be bold and be brave." It gave me the nudge I needed to dive into the unknown and chase my dream. I couldn't have asked for a better bestie in this life!

Alex Lasnik: Thank you for being the most thoughtful and supportive friend, and my favorite person to cook for (besides Doug). :) Familia forever.

TO THE MAXI'S KITCHEN COMMUNITY:

This book truly wouldn't exist without you. Your constant support, encouragement, and excitement have meant more to me than you'll ever know. Thank you for showing up, for cooking my recipes, for sending the sweetest messages, and for reminding me that what I share matters, even on days I doubted myself. I feel endlessly grateful to be able to do this work, and it's because of you.

Note: Page references in *italics* indicate photographs.

Q

R

S

Clarkson Potter/Publishers
An imprint of the Crown Publishing Group
A division of Penguin Random House LLC
1745 Broadway
New York, NY 10019
clarksonpotter.com
penguinrandomhouse.com

Library of Congress Cataloging-in-Publication Data has been applied for.

ISBN 978-0-593-80039-3
Ebook ISBN 978-0-593-80040-9

Editor: Jennifer Sit | Editorial assistant: Elaine Hennig
Illustrator: Elizabeth Hart
Art direction and design: Stephanie Huntwork
Production designer: Christina Self
Production editors: Patricia Shaw and Joyce Wong
Production: Jessica Heim
Compositors: Merri Ann Morrell and Hannah Hunt
Food stylist: Frances Boswell
Food stylist assistant: Luca Quinn
Prop stylist: Amy Neunsinger
Prop stylist assistants: Kelsey Hellenbrand and Kennedy Esso Nicks
Photo assistant: Hector Prida | Digital Tech: Devon Guio
Copy editor: Ivy McFadden | Proofreaders: Hope Clark, Sigi Nacson, Erica Rose | Indexer: Elizabeth Parson
Publicists: Jina Stanfill and Jana Branson
Marketer: Stephanie Davis

Manufactured in China

10 9 8 7 6 5 4 3 2 1

First Edition

The authorized representative in the EU for product safety and compliance is Penguin Random House Ireland, Morrison Chambers, 32 Nassau Street, Dublin D02 YH68, Ireland, https://eu-contact.penguin.ie.

Let’s stay in touch :)
For more recipes, visit maxiskitchen.com.

MAXINE SHARF is a culinary creator and recipe developer who is passionate about bringing comfort, confidence, and community to cooking. She takes inspiration from her diverse background as Korean, Chinese, Romanian, Russian, and Polish with a California upbringing. She recently left her ten-year career in tech to pursue her mission to help others feel less intimidated in the kitchen by providing approachable meals, tips, and practices that empower a wider audience. She lives in Los Angeles with her husband, Doug, and their pup, Kimchi.

CLARKSON POTTER/PUBLISHERS
NEW YORK
CLARKSONPOTTER.COM

COVER DESIGN: STEPHANIE HUNTWORK
COVER PHOTOGRAPHS: AMY NEUNSINGER
ILLUSTRATIONS: ELIZABETH HART

BROTH
BROTH